Integrated Test Design and Automation

Using the TestFrame Method

**Hans Buwalda, Dennis Janssen and Iris Pinkster
with Paul Watters**

Addison-Wesley

An imprint of **Pearson Education**

Boston · San Francisco · New York · Toronto · Montreal
London · Munich · Paris · Madrid · Cape Town · Sydney
Tokyo · Singapore · Mexico City

PEARSON EDUCATION LIMITED

Head Office: London Office:
Edinburgh Gate   128 Long Acre, London WC2E 9AN
Harlow CM20 2JE   Tel: +44 (0)20 7447 2000
Tel: +44 (0)1279 623623   Fax: +44 (0)20 7240 5771
Fax: +44 (0)1279 431059   Website: www.aw.com/cseng

First published in Great Britain 2002

© Pearson Education Limited 2002

The rights of Hans Buwalda, Dennis Janssen and Iris Pinkster to be identified as Authors of this Work have been asserted by them in accordance with the Copyright, Designs and Patents Act 1988.

ISBN 0-201-73725-6

British Library Cataloguing in Publication Data
A catalogue record for this book is available from the British Library

Library of Congress Cataloging in Publication Data
Applied for.

The programs in this book have been included for their instructional value. The publisher does not offer any warranties or representations in respect of their fitness for a particular purpose, nor does the publisher accept any liability for any loss or damage (other than for personal injury or death) arising from their use.

Many of the designations used by manufacturers and sellers to distinguish their products are claimed as trademarks. Pearson Education Limited has made every attempt to supply trademark information about manufacturers and their products mentioned in this book.

10 9 8 7 6 5 4 3 2 1

Typeset by Pantek Arts Ltd, Maidstone, Kent
Printed and bound by Biddles Ltd, Guildford and King's Lynn.

The Publishers' policy is to use paper manufactured from sustainable forests.

Contents

3   Analysis   83

5   Execution   193

Foreword

No company can function without IT. Without computer programs and information systems, products cannot be made at all or remain unsold, invoices are not sent, and communications grind to a standstill. IT has developed from being a precondition into being one of a company's primary operations.

This means that heavy demands are made on the system's operation. Quality-to-market is of crucial importance. Double entries in address files may be annoying, but critical incidents can occur if modern technology lets you down during company operations. Poor quality results in loss of clients and damages the company's reputation. In short, a system's failure can have dramatic consequences for the core business of a company or institution.

Elaborate manual testing, to safeguard a high quality-to-market, is a time-consuming process – time that is not usually available because the time-to-market span is becoming increasingly short. Further deregulation and globalization of markets has intensified competitive pressures. Products and services must be launched as rapidly as possible. In practice, however, the development of IT systems often takes more time than expected, while the completion date is always on your tail.

This is the dilemma you face. Elaborate testing takes too much time and any drastic shortening of the test path paves the way for production faults. Just consider the costs of rectifying production faults if they only surface after the development process.

The authors describe a testing method that offers a solution to this dilemma. TestFrame® provides a structured approach to testing thus enabling your organization to perform tests rapidly, as well as thoroughly. The structured testing approach is represented in the TestFrame temple metaphor, and TestFrame phasing. This book discusses ways of putting the TestFrame model and phasing into practice. It does not aspire to be a comprehensive theoretical discussion about testing. However, it does provide a basis for performing tests in a practical way, and contains many examples that clarify key testing principles.

Roadmap

Testing is a complex matter. There is much to say about testing, and this book covers many different aspects. Different stakeholders, such as IT managers, test managers, test analysts, test navigators, project managers, developers, and QA officers, are interested in testing. Not every part of this book is relevant to everyone. The chapter outlining the principles behind the TestFrame method (Chapter 1) is a 'must read' for everyone and is the basis for the other chapters. For specialized groups of readers, the following is recommended:

- IT managers will be interested in the place of testing in an organization, and an outline of the TestFrame approach. This information can be found in Chapters 1 and 2;

- it is recommended that test managers read the chapters concerning preparation of a test project (risk analysis, test strategy, writing a test plan), the chapter concerning test execution (planning of execution, error management) and, of course, the chapter specifically about test management (Chapter 6);

- test analysts should read the chapter Analysis (Chapter 3) where a method is presented that leads to a structured, maintainable test set. Special attention is given to selecting the right testing techniques for the job at hand. Since test analysts are greatly influenced by choices that are made during the preparation, this chapter is particularly relevant;

- test navigators are the testers who are concerned with automating the test. Navigation (Chapter 4) discusses test automation within TestFrame, and is a 'must read' for them. Since these activities are directly related to some tasks that are performed during the test analysis, Chapter 3 is also recommended;

- project managers and developers will mainly be interested in the interfaces between development and testing. These are described in the preparation, execution and test management chapters (Chapters 2, 5 and 6);

- QA officers focus on the test process seeking to answer questions such as 'is it measurable, traceable and provable?' TestFrame provides a means of achieving a structured, controlled test process with tangible products. This information is found throughout the book. However, a QA officer could begin with Chapter 1 and read other chapters when the need occurs.

Acknowledgements

The TestFrame Research Center supported the writing of this book. The Research Center is part of CMG. Its aim is to carry on developing the TestFrame method and testing as a field of expertise within CMG.

This is also an appropriate place to thank several people for the enormous amount of work they have carried out. First and foremost, the authors want to thank all the people who have contributed to the book – Elvira Beekman, Bob van de Burgt, Rolf Daalder, Dirk van Dael, Erik Jansen, Maartje Kasdorp, André Kok, Marc Koper, Bob Mohr, Peter den Ouden, Jan Paulusse and team Rotterdam, Henk Sanders, Chris Schotanus, Anita Vocht and Michiel Vroon.

No less important are the reviewers who have gone through all the material and provided useful comments. Thank you Martijn Brouns, Erik Brouwer, Steven Frisart, Edwin Hubers, Gerrit de Koning, Rik Marselis, Frank Stolker, Jon van der Strate, Kie Liang Tan, Bob Verhoeff, Jeroen Voorn, Michel Wemmenhove, Menno Wieringa and Leon Wolters. In addition, several anonymous reviewers' contributions improve the book.

Finally, we would, of course, like to thank our customers – they gave us the opportunity to apply and improve TestFrame* in challenging test projects.

*TestFrame is a registered trademark of CMG.

1 Introduction

1.1 What is testing?

Most books that cover the subject of testing start out with a definition which is 'written in stone'. However, in keeping with the practical focus of this book, we would like to demonstrate what testing involves by considering a simple example. In his classic work 'The Art of Software Testing' [Myer 79] Glenford J. Myers begins with a self-assessment test designed to illustrate the need for structured testing.

Myers uses the example of testing whether a triangle is scalene, isosceles or equilateral, using integer values. An effective and efficient test set that covers this problem consists of 13 test cases, plus the required expected outcome associated with the test cases, making it possible to score 14 points (one point for each test case and one for the expected outcomes). For the complete solution, we refer to [Myer 79]. When we look at effectiveness, research has shown that even highly trained software developers only score an average of 7.5 points out of the possible 14. This means that if these senior developers are involved in testing information systems, an average 45% of potential bugs are not being detected. Remember this figure the next time your subway train is late because the scheduling computer has a bug, or your bank balance is reported as –$10,000 because an insufficient number of test cases were applied in testing a production system.

Using this example, you can also look at the efficiency of the test set that was created. If there were several test cases that covered the same point, then those extra test cases didn't have a lot of added value (no extra risks were covered). Much effort is required to develop individual test cases, and long-term time commitments are required to maintain them. A test set should be developed in such a way that maximal coverage is achieved with a minimal amount of test cases.

If you do Myers' test in a five-minute time span, you'll get a feeling for developing test cases in the kind of time span which most testers have to cope with. Testers must analyze complex information systems, often with a minimum of time allocated to the task.

As you can see, even from this simple example, testing is a complex discipline that requires rigor and the strict application of logic to test all possible outcomes. Our role as testers is to develop test cases and analyze expected outputs, to verify that a system under test reacts as predicted. Testing should be undertaken in a highly structured manner, so that a predefined coverage can be achieved in a given timeframe. Testing methods and testware should always be developed so that they can be reused in the next project. Therefore, the definition of testing that we will use in this book is *the organized process of proving deviations between the actual and the expected functioning of an information system.*

1.1.1 Why do we test?

Without testing, we have no way of establishing the quality of an information system. This means that the product we are developing could have faults that may damage our business when we implement it. Some faults can cause minor disruptions (the back office can only use their keyboard to approve a transaction, a mouse click does not work), but others can be potentially life threatening (the dispatch center of a hospital gives wrong information to the drivers of the ambulances). Therefore, we need to establish which faults are nested in an information system before it is released.

Some developers believe that the goal of testing is to ensure that an information system does what it is supposed to do. While this is certainly an important part of testing, it is not a complete requirement. When we test an information system, we want to add value to it – testing costs money, so there must be a cost benefit in performing tests. This means adding quality through the identification of issues, and reporting them to the development team responsible for fixing them. Therefore, the assumption that we should start with is not that an information system works correctly, but rather that it contains faults which must be identified. Testing should aim to identify as many faults as possible. Looking at testing in this light can give you a very different mindset – you will be looking for faults and failures instead of monitoring if the information system performs as described. Our test cases will be more focused on the thing testers really want, finding those bugs!

The bottom line is that testing gives information about the quality of an information system. Not all encountered failures have to be solved before an information system can be taken into production – instead of 'unknown bugs', they become 'known errors' and can be scheduled for debugging by a developer. Testers provide this information to the decision makers in an organization so that a well-founded risk assessment can be undertaken prior to an implementation decision being made.

1.1.2 Facts of life in testing

Now that we have examined the rationale for testing, we will review the general conditions that influence software testing. Testers can influence some of these conditions, others are 'facts of life' which must be dealt with practically. It is always good to know which conditions testers cannot influence so that expectations about testing outcomes can be managed effectively. Some 'facts of life' are:

- testing is always risk based – where there are no risks, we should not put any effort into testing an information system;

- you cannot test everything – some risks will always remain, even in a fully tested system. Take a calculator, for example – it is impractical to test every calculation which can conceivably be performed;

- you can demonstrate that there are faults in an information system, but you cannot say with certainty that there are no faults;

- Hans Schaeffer, a testing expert from Norway, says that bugs are social creatures – if you find errors in one area, you would expect to find more errors in that specific area. Thus, the testing effort can be redirected to that area;

- testing is a job that is very distinct from development, requiring special skills, even if it is not always looked upon that way.

1.1.3   Testing and development

In previous years, testing was considered to be just another phase in the cycle of system development – testing followed coding as night follows day. This implied that a precondition to testing was that coding was largely finished, and that any code changes identified by testing would be minimal. Testing was always on a critical path, and every delay that the development team suffered meant less time for testing. Faults in an information system were identified in the testing phase only by the obvious method of executing the code.

Since those times, the whole conception of testing has changed. Firstly, it has been recognized that faults cannot be found only by executing the code – potential defects can be identified much earlier in the development cycle. For example, every product developed during a project can be tested (in terms of requirements, designs, etc.) by using techniques such as reviews, structured walkthroughs, and inspections. Identifying faults earlier means that the costs of rectifying any fault are much lower. There are two reasons for this.

- There is less recoding to be undertaken because the fault does not migrate from early to late cycles. When a fault is discovered during the requirements phase, only the requirement in question has to be rewritten. In contrast, when a failure that originated during the requirements phase is discovered during user-acceptance testing, the requirement, functional and technical design, and the codebase all have to be fixed. Worse still, all of the tests for each of these phases must be repeated.

- When a failure occurs after the system has already shipped, or is already in production, there are both technical and financial consequences. The technical consequences involve recoding and retesting, which can be done given the appropriate time and resources. The financial consequences of fixing a bug in a shipped product are more serious – loss of revenue, loss of customers, and loss of faith in the product can all result from bugs which cause an information system to shutdown (until a bug fix can be provided). The worst case scenario is that an information system operates for some years giving incorrect data before a bug is discovered.

The cost of fixing faults increases exponentially with time. A bug found and fixed during the early stages of a project, when the specification is being written, can cost next to nothing, while the same bug found after the product is shipped might costs thousands of dollars. [Boeh 79] has modeled this phenomenon, with the relationship between cost and the time taken to identify a bug shown in Figure 1.1.

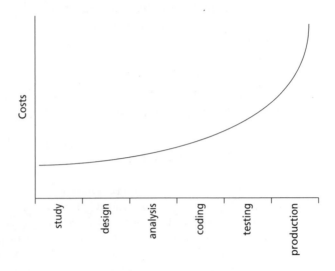

Figure 1.1   Relation between when a bug is identified and costs

The relationship between cost and the time taken to identify bugs implies that testing should start as early as possible in a project. Apart from financial considerations, there is a second key reason why testing should start as early as possible – the total time available for testing is maximized when testing begins during the study and design phases, rather than after the coding phase. Even during analysis, the specification of test conditions can make best use of the time available, even if those cases are not evaluated until after coding has been completed. The

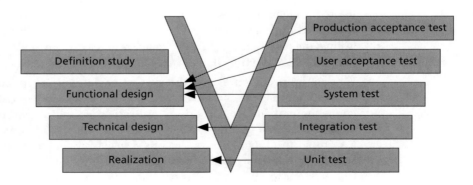

Figure 1.2   The V-model

TestFrame approach can be tuned to ensure that testing begins as early as possible, since it makes use of the widely accepted V-model, in which every phase of development is linked to a phase in testing, as shown in Figure 1.2.

The left side of the V-model comprises the development phases in a 'standard' system development project. The right side comprises the recommended phases in testing. Every phase in development is linked to one or more phases in testing. The phases in testing represent the execution of tests, preparations, analysis, and automation of a test phase, starting at the same time as the related phase in development.

1.1.4 Quality of testing

As we have already stated, the goal of testing is the measurement of quality in an information system. But how do we establish the quality of a test which itself measures quality in an information system? If we find zero faults in a program, does that mean that the software does not contain any? It may well indicate that the set of test cases was insufficient to detect any nested faults. If we create a test set that reveals many faults during a project, but is created in such a way that we have to create a new test set when the next version of the information system is developed, is that an acceptable outcome from a quality assurance perspective?

To establish the quality of the test process, we need to evaluate the test process itself against several properties of a quality standard. Each characteristic views the testing process from a different perspective.

- *Effectiveness*. Given the amount of time and money available for testing, we have to prioritize the allocation of our testing effort. In the test strategy, the risks of the system under test are well defined – the amount of time and money available for testing, prioritized and translated into test conditions and test cases using the right test techniques. By matching these test conditions to the requirements, the completeness of the test set is enhanced, and the importance of specific test results becomes apparent.

- *Efficiency*. We want to test as much as possible in as short a time as possible. To do this, we must create a test set that realizes the coverage we need with a minimal number of test cases. Thus, we want to eliminate test cases that overlap, since they have no added value. Instead, our goal is to ensure that every test case focuses on a unique aspect, or a set of related aspects. As with effectiveness, test techniques are very helpful tools in developing efficient testware.

- *Measurability*. To determine if a test has been successful, the test results must be measurable. This means that test cases and test scenarios should be made in such a manner that the result is quantifiable according to binary logic. The result of the execution of a test case should be 'passed' or 'not passed' – never a 'maybe'.

- *Divisibility*. There are many different aspects of an information system that could be tested. Not all aspects are equally important, especially not to different kinds of stakeholders. For example, end users are generally not concerned about software maintainability – their focus is on time-to-market. On the other hand developers may be primarily interested in maintenance as it defines their future workload. This means that there are different kinds of tests (white-box and black-box) which are undertaken by different stakeholders. It is important that the division of responsibilities concerning testing is made clear to all stakeholders before testing commences, otherwise completeness may not be achieved.

● *Maintainability*. One of the main problems with testware is maintenance. After the initial project, the test set should be maintained so that it can be used for the next release of the information system being tested. Maintenance should be made as easy as possible, otherwise the test set will be neglected. Thus, the structure of the test set should be as simple as possible, and formally registered – thus if a specification changes, the affected test cases should also be noted. This not only means adding new test cases, but also that those which are no longer needed should be removed. Maintainability has a big impact on reproducibility.

● *Reproducibility*. Since we try to avoid developing 'throw away software', we should also not develop 'throw away testware'. A lot of time and money is wasted when a test is not easily reproducible, since new tests must be created. Since we want to ensure that our tests are replicable with the same test cases, a well-developed test set makes it possible to retest and regression test with a minimum of effort. These tests are particularly well suited to automation since a computer can, if required, repeat test cases again and again.

1.2   An introduction to TestFrame

High demands are made on the operation of Information and Communication Technology (ICT) systems. Quite simply, many systems need to operate perfectly. Poor quality would result in loss of clients and damage to a company's or organization's reputation. Testing is an important prerequisite to delivering quality systems. However, elaborate testing methods and manual techniques are very time consuming, even though time is the one commodity that development usually has very little of – after all, time is money! On the other hand, shortening the testing process to be able to market a product more quickly is not really an option in terms of quality. Even if tests are actually carried out, are they sufficiently reliable to allow ICT systems to be confidently put into operation? Only a reliable test can reliably answer the following question – will the information system or computer application still work after installation? A thorough test process can guarantee this. A well thought out strategy and test plan makes a fast and reliable testing process possible, thus enabling an organization to achieve both a short time-to-market, and a high quality-to-market.

A number of recurring problems can be observed within test processes. These issues include:

- too little attention paid to testing;
- the testing process is difficult to manage;
- a lack of clarity about the results of the test process;
- a lack of clarity about the time that the test process will take to be completed;
- a lack of clarity about the costs of the test process.

TestFrame provides a structured approach to testing rapidly and thoroughly. The TestFrame model and TestFrame phasing are the cornerstones of this process. This chapter gives a brief description of both, and the links to the products that result from both.

1.3   The TestFrame model

A good software development model consists of a number of well-defined parts, each with its own methods. The principles underlying this approach are analogous with the structure of a Greek temple, as shown in Figure 1.3. Firm foundations and strong pillars combine their individual strengths to support the roof.

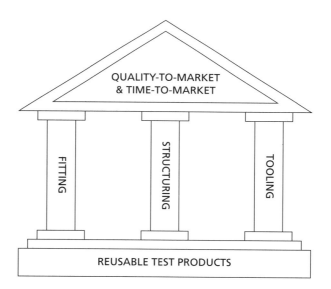

Figure 1.3   The TestFrame model

In this model, the roof symbolizes an organization's business objectives – a high quality-to-market, combined with a short time-to-market. Achieving these often contradictory objectives requires a strong base, which is provided by reusable test products that are easy to maintain. Without testing products that exhibit these properties, it is very difficult to support the objectives of high quality at low cost in a short time.

The three pillars are the three factors which ensure that the business objectives are achieved – fitting, structuring and tooling. When provided with the appropriate tools, which are customized for a specific organization, success is highly likely. TestFrame as a whole makes it possible to perform the best and the most appropriate tests concurrently. The Greek temple model provides an important starting point for developing and implementing a test strategy in the context of an established test policy.

1.3.1   Reusable test products

Test products often receive poor treatment from project stakeholders. In everyday practice, many organizations must set up complete tests from scratch, even just for minor adaptations, since existing tests have been lost or can no longer be used. To achieve a short time-to-market, tests need to be both easy to maintain and reusable. Quality-to-market requires that the various test phases result in a proper risk assessment of the product in question.

1.3.2   Fitting

In the preparation phase, it is important that sufficient attention is paid to tailoring the testing method so that it is easy for an organization to manage. The right means, and a thorough approach, yield little success if the tests are ultimately not used. Test processes designed using TestFrame are embedded in organizational structures, and forge links with the development and management processes of the information system to be tested.

Some examples of test process fitting include:

- the process for developing a unit test deviates from a user acceptance test. The unit test is a so-called 'white-box' test, which requires a great deal of knowledge about the contents of the software. In contrast, a 'black-box' test is typically selected for a user acceptance test, since it requires more expertise with the actual material;

- test processes that link different development processes according to a sequential approach differ from test processes that link development processes carried out via an iterative, dynamic variant;

- if an organization already has a structured test and wishes to automate it, the emphasis should not be on the degree of comprehensiveness during the process – that should already have been defined. The process will primarily focus on translating the current test into a format that can be automated.

This flexibility enables the various testing activities to be adapted to:

- the various phases of the development and management process;
- the type of test process being carried out;
- the test organization.

This method of structuring the test is typical of the 'fitting' characteristic of the TestFrame model.

1.3.3 Structuring

A TestFrame process yields tangible deliverables. These products (such as a test strategy, a test plan, clusters, test conditions, test cases, and navigation scripts) can be very easily subdivided and categorized into small, manageable modules. Thus, the introduction of TestFrame renders test procedures more transparent and uniform. The organization develops test standards which can be reused in the next test. The test itself, and the various test tasks involved, is therefore more clearly defined. The costs of the test are known in advance and it is clear what has been tested to a specific level of detail. In addition, insight into the approach and the status of the test process can be gained at all times, ensuring that the test project can be adjusted in a timely manner if necessary. This method enhances the quality of both the test process and the test products, resulting in higher quality for the tested system.

1.3.4 Tooling

Automated testing can reduce the problems briefly described in the Introduction. The use of test tools, or software developed outside these tools, in languages such as C, C++, Java, or Visual Basic, enable the tests to be carried out more rapidly, unambiguously, and consistently. TestFrame makes optimum use of modern and widely-used tools. Close attention is paid to the maintenance of auxiliary programs since spending more time on controlling these programs than on manual testing, would not produce a cost–time benefit. Using automated test programs is not an ideological requirement for good testing, but usually results in the lowest overall cost. In practical terms, if a manual tester can carry out the work faster (or more efficiently), then that tester should be used in preference to an automated system.

TestFrame is based on the following ethos – if a well-maintainable test is set up correctly the first time around, only a small number of adaptations to the test material will be required in the future. The time saved becomes apparent when only 5 or 10 percent of the system is modified due to an update. The original test material can be reused to test the 95 or 90 percent of retained code. This speeds up and facilitates the testing of regularly updated versions of systems. For example, salary processing systems which use social insurance data are updated annually.

In addition to developing testing tools, appropriate project management tools must also be acquired for test planning and structuring version maintenance. Since test products can be reused during every revision cycle, the investment in developing good test tools is recovered after only a few revisions. In addition, the TestFrame method is not ICT system specific – if a particular system is replaced by another, the testing method can still be successfully applied.

1.4 Phasing with TestFrame

The time allocated for setting up and carrying out tests is all too often ad hoc. Thus, it is not surprising that chance plays a major role in the reliability of the ICT system concerned. To avoid this reliance on random factors, testing has to be recognized, by the organization, as a key characteristic of a successful system. This implies that a thorough risk analysis needs to be performed, and that an adequate budget is allocated with sufficient access to appropriate resources. Taking testing as seriously as development may seem expensive and time consuming, however, as we have pointed out, this investment is recovered rapidly. Conversely, consider the costs of a fault discovered after all the branch offices in an organization had already installed some new software – the help desk and support teams would be kept occupied for days, and the programs have to be recalled and amended.

The set up and implementation of TestFrame in an organization consist of four phases:

- preparation;
- analysis;
- navigation;
- execution.

TestFrame's phasing describes each part of a test process from the preliminary study (serving as the basis for the assignment) up to and including the final evaluation of the path. The four phases recur in each new test process (except the Navigation phase, which is not specified if the test is carried out manually).

The method does not work according to compulsory steps prescribed in a rigid plan or phasing model. As the arrows in Figure 1.4 indicate, the phases can be completed in different sequences. However, many projects logically begin with the Preparation phase.

- In the Preparation phase, the scope of the test processes, as well as the test strategy to be followed, is defined.
- Subsequently, the test cases are created in the Analysis phase.
- If the test is automated, the navigation scripts are developed in the Navigation phase.
- Finally, the test is carried out and the testware is managed in the Execution phase.

The Analysis and Navigation phases can be carried out simultaneously if the system is available. This necessitates precise coordination between these phases. Part of the Execution phase can also be carried out at the same time as analysis and navigation. This also requires the system to be available. In the Execution phase, the test is actually carried out (manually or by the computer) and the project's test products are given to the organization to be managed. Whenever necessary, a particular phase can be repeated, or previous ones can be referred to, depending on the test results.

Let's examine some examples of how this interplay between phases works in practice.

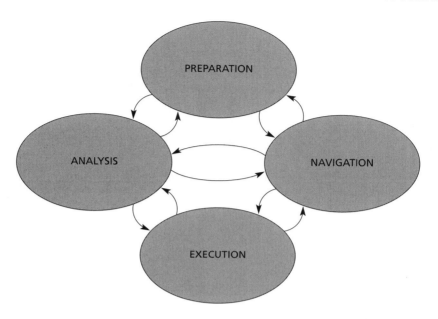

Figure 1.4   TestFrame phasing

- A test tool used during the Navigation phase to realize the automated execution of the test appears not to operate properly. This is despite the fact that a technical test has been carried out, prior to the use of the tool, to check whether the test tool was technically able to work with the system being tested. In such an example, in the TestFrame phasing it is possible to go back from the Navigation phase to the Preparation phase to assess whether another test tool should be selected or if the test needs to be carried out manually.

- During the Analysis phase, it is apparent that the documentation provided is not sufficient to construct a comprehensive test set, although this was one of the prerequisites specified in the test plan. In this case, a jump back to the Preparation phase can be made to amend the planning (and possibly the strategy), and to consider alternatives. For example, experts may be consulted in preference to the poor documentation provided.

- An analyst has developed test cases that provide insufficient detail to be processed by the computer. For example, there may be a lack of clarity concerning the data to be entered. Interaction occurs between the Navigation and Analysis phases to amend the analysis enabling the test to still be carried out by the computer.

1.4.1   TestFrame products

Each phase of a TestFrame process produces concrete, reusable products. Figure 1.5 shows which products are typically produced during a TestFrame process in each phase. These phases, with the accompanying products, are discussed in further detail in the Preparation, Analysis, Navigation and Execution chapters.

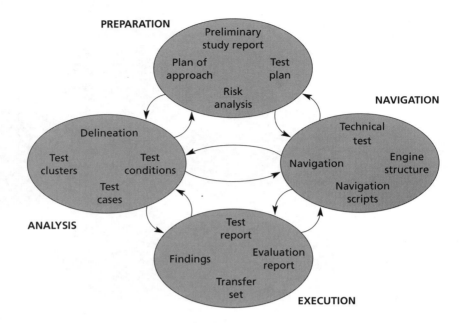

Figure 1.5 Test products, linked to TestFrame phasing

The following sections provide a brief description of the various steps involved in TestFrame phasing.

1.5 Preparation

The Preparation phase is essential if a test process is to be structured according to the TestFrame method. With clear positioning, this initial phase can be kept as short as possible. This approach recognizes that the longer the delay between planning and development, the less motivated developers will become. Only a reliable test can answer the question, 'will the information system or the application still work after installation or adaptation?' A thorough test process guarantees this, to the limits defined by the test designer. A well thought out preparation phase makes it possible for the organization to devise a fast and reliable test process, enabling it to achieve both a short time-to-market and a high quality-to-market.

The following activities are carried out in the Preparation phase:

- preliminary study of the assignment, including execution of a risk analysis of the system being tested;
- examining the current and required test environment;
- examining the current and required test organization;
- drawing up the test plan, including a description of the test strategy (based on the risk analysis of the system being tested) and test planning;
- structuring the test environment;

- structuring the test organization by allocating clear tasks and responsibilities;
- setting up error management to provide feedback about the findings to the development group;
- training employees;
- defining priorities and making decisions;
- selecting the test techniques and methods to be used;
- setting up an infrastructure to enable the test analyst to record information, and the test navigator to install programs, develop scripts, and perform the actual test on the system.

Most of the products created in the Preparation phase can be reused (such as the test strategy) based on the risk analysis of the system being tested. The emphasis of the strategy will no doubt shift with new versions of the target test object, but the greater part of the test strategy will remain the same. This is also true for the test environment overview. The existing overview can be used as the basis for future test projects, to avoid having to make a full and new inventory of the test environment.

A number of important products created in the Preparation phase are described briefly below.

1.5.1 Risk analysis

The first step in the Preparation phase is undertaking a risk analysis in order to identify possible problems. These problems can occur in both the system to be tested and the organization concerned. For example, there may be an existing system that must be replaced by a new system. Preparing for the new system introduces a set of problems and risks. Within an organization there needs to be a person (or team) with the authority (and experience) to determine whether the test results meet the defined standards. If the test results cannot be authorized, this will lead to a lack of clarity which can obstruct the test process's success. Checklists for undertaking risk analysis are available within TestFrame. Based on the 'score per feature', the main risks in a project can be determined, and suggestions made for managing these risks.

1.5.2 Test strategy

The test strategy describes key factors which are important during the preparation and execution of the test. In cooperation with the stakeholders, it is decided which factors are to be tested in each test type and by whom. The test strategy contains:

- organization structure;
- test type;
- cluster matrix;
- cluster cards.

Details will be discussed in the next chapter.

1.5.3   Test plan

Ultimately, the test plan is the guideline for the test team during the execution of its activities. The test plan comprises the following items:

- organizational elements;
- characteristics of the test's content (test strategy, acceptance criteria, and the thoroughness of the test);
- test activities;
- a list of products which need to be created, and who is responsible for creating them.

1.5.4   Test planning

Drawing up a realistic plan always proves to be harder than first appears. What makes it difficult to develop a time schedule for the test is its dependence on the system's development path – a delay in the build process always leads to delays in the execution of the test process. An explicit linkage between the planning schedules of the build and the test processes can make test planning more manageable.

The Preparation phase is often concluded with a pilot. If necessary, a second pilot can be executed with an additional objective, until the method has been fully tuned to the organization.

1.6   Analysis

The test products that result from the Analysis phase (such as clusters and action words) can be reused in the following test processes. In regression tests, for example, the analysis of functionality or parts of the system that have not been modified can be fully reused. Analysis often needs to be adapted for new or modified functionality, or for other parts of the system. It is possible to reuse certain action words in the tests for different test objects. This typically concerns action words for the test object's user interface.

The following activities can be carried out in the Analysis phase:

- analyzing the application;
- defining the clusters;
- defining the test conditions;
- defining the test cases and their action words.

1.6.1   Clusters

In order to enhance the reliability of the test, TestFrame divides it into units called clusters. These clusters give the tests a logical structure which makes it easier to survey the products, and simplifies the process of retesting.

1.6.2 Test conditions

Subsequently, the test conditions within a cluster are defined. Test conditions are the translations of the system specifications into verifiable requirements. They are further specified in concrete test cases that constitute the transition to actual testing.

Figure 1.6 shows an example of the correct presentation of a new client. This is a test condition (named CLTC1) that has been defined within the cluster Client (CLT). This structure is built up according to the second column (structuring) of the Greek temple, which is crucial for a short time-to-market and high quality-to-market. The transparency of the test's structure achieved by this method enhances the possibility of maintaining and reusing test products.

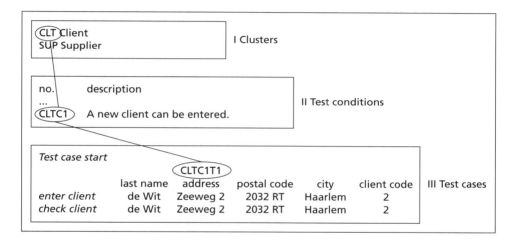

Figure 1.6 Test cluster structure

1.6.3 Action words

Test cases are detailed using action words. Examples of action words in Figure 1.6 are 'enter client' and 'check client'. An action word is always linked to test data (including the input data and expected output data). General arguments are created to obtain this specific information. The arguments of the action word 'enter client' are 'last name', 'address', 'postal code', 'city' and 'client code'. The data that is actually entered in these fields is the test data.

Within the TestFrame method, the action words act as the control mechanism for the test to be performed. The action words are reproduced directly in the reports.

Test products created in the Analysis phase can also be reused in the following test processes. In regression tests, the analysis of non-modified functionality or non-modified system parts can be fully reused. Analysis needs to be added or adapted for new and modified functionality or system parts.

1.7 Navigation

Test products developed in the Navigation phase (such as test tools and navigation scripts) can be reused in follow-up projects as well. Regression tests are particularly suitable for this purpose – navigation products for non-modified functionality or system parts can be fully reused. Only the navigation products for new and modified functionality or system parts need to be added or adapted.

The following activities can be executed in the Navigation phase:

- a technical analysis of the target system being tested, including the execution of a technical test;
- drawing up the navigation design;
- creating navigation scripts and implementing action words;
- 'debugging' the navigation scripts.

1.7.1 Test tools

Tooling is the third column of the Greek temple that symbolizes how TestFrame supports the business objectives of high quality-to-market and short time-to-market. Test tools can speed up and greatly simplify the test process. In an automated TestFrame process, actions (keystrokes, mouse movements and visual control) executed by a tester for a manual test are adopted by a navigation script in a test tool environment.

1.7.2 Navigation script

The required actions are recorded in a navigation script that acts as a control program. The script can be further adapted. The main advantage of using test tools is that navigation scripts that have been recorded once can very easily be repeated without the tester's intervention. In this way, a large number of tests can be executed unattended. Automating routine and often boring test activities has the additional advantage that it makes tests more reliable by eliminating error due to human intervention. Automation prevents the possibility of a tester repeating an error, or forgetting the actions that resulted in the error.

1.7.3 Separating analysis and navigation

The separation between analysis and navigation is characteristic of TestFrame's approach – drawing up the system's functionality to be tested is separated from the actual execution of the test. It should be noted that navigation is only required for an automated execution of the test.

The knowledge required for the analysis are an insight into the business processes, and the risks that threaten these processes. The test analyst defines the test's priorities on the basis of knowledge about the information system and the test criteria – what has to be tested, what can be tested, and how thorough does the test need to be? The test analyst does so in collaboration with end users and experts in the field.

Navigation requires more technical experience. The navigator uses test tools and writes navigation scripts, which are automated test programs that control the test's execution.

Separation of tasks also implies separation of data – that is, a distinction between test data (the test analyst's data) and the navigation scripts (the navigator's programs). As a result, the testware (test products developed in both the Analysis and the Navigation phases) are easier to maintain – duplications or redundancies are prevented, and modifications are necessary in one place only.

When constructing a new system, the test analyst can build up the collection of test cases at the same time. While the system is being constructed, the navigator can begin developing the navigation scripts. This form of parallelism saves a considerable amount of time.

1.8 Execution

In the Execution phase the test is carried out on the basis of the analysis and, if the test is automated, the navigation scripts. It is important that the test is carried out unambiguously and consistently. If test cases that have been defined beforehand (as recorded in the Analysis phase) are not adhered to, the results will lose some of their explanatory value. For example, if some test cases are not carried out, the interpretation of the overall test results will be ambiguous. Having the computer conduct the test ensures clarity and consistency.

The following activities are usually carried out in the Execution phase:

- test execution (the initial test as well as the retest);
- test results review;
- registration of the findings;
- transfer of the test products and test results;
- handing over test products for management and maintenance;
- evaluation of the test project.

A proper execution of the test requires an overview of the test results, any irregularities found, and insight into the various versions of the information system. Inaccuracies in this part of the process can undermine the quality-to-market value. Test management consists of four parts:

- structuring and maintaining a test report;
- error management;

- version control;
- transfer of the testware and the information system to be tested to the management or production environment.

The main products resulting from the Execution phase are the test report, and the results of error management.

1.8.1   Test report

During a test run, either the tester or the test tool should record the successful completion and the failure of individual tests, resulting in a formal test report. Any deviations observed during the test should be reported. Even minor deviations, such as an incorrect screen text, could have serious consequences during production and must be reported. The test report may also identify more serious errors, such as the peak capacity of a system to cope with a predefined number of transactions.

Not everyone in the organization needs the same level of detail about the test results. Thus, several versions of the test report are usually drawn up. All the reports include at least the following items:

- the identification (including version number) of the application and of the test;
- the total number of errors found;
- the number of successful tests as a percentage of the total number of tests;
- the errors found.

Figure 1.7 shows a simple example of a report created by the computer. The figure does not show the full test report. The first section shows the initial part of the report, which includes the time the cluster was created, and by whom. It also shows the first action words that were executed. The second section contains the summary – the percentage of the test that was successful and the percentage that failed.

The example shows the action words used as steps that comprise the actual test. Products are presented twice, stating 'product code', 'name', 'color', 'type' and 'weight'. The testware subsequently checks the system's messages. In the second phase, the system checks whether the products have been presented successfully, and whether a particular color code has been retained. This is where an error is detected (result: failed).

1.8.2   Error management

If an error has been found in the ICT system, which must be corrected, it is important to monitor the correction of the error closely. The purpose of managing the findings is to describe and monitor the errors in the ICT system and the testware. All the parties involved in system's development or maintenance must be informed of the errors or deviations that have been found in the version concerned.

```
System to be tested          : Order system
System version               : 231
main script                  : FAT.AWL, version: 2.00, date: June
test started on              : 23-07 at 09:19:18
─────────────────────────────────────────────────────────────
cluster directory            : h:\test\scripts\
cluster                      : Test cases PRO Product
version                      : 1.1
date                         : 05/01
author                       : Tester
─────────────────────────────────────────────────────────────
TEST CASE PROC1T1     Product codes must be unique

8:                           Product code  product  color  type  weight

9:  product entry            p2           nail     black  AAX   1
      >>Message: Transaction executed correctly.

10:                          Product code  product  color  type  weight

11: product entry            p2           nut      gray   AAX   1
      >>Message: Value in product code field not allowed.
```

```
114: check message           Value in color field not allowed
>>>>>FAILED                  Transaction executed correctly.
─────────────────────────────────────────────────────────────
Test completed at            23-07 09:20:42

Summary

Time elapsed                           : 01:24
Number of test lines                   : 61
Number of test cases passed            : 13 (87%)
Number of test cases failed            : 2
Failures at line                       : 23   114
```

Figure 1.7 Example test report

Deviations or faults can be divided into various categories, depending on the seriousness of the problem. The most important category of errors are those that render the system's implementation impossible. The second category consists of problems that cause important parts of the ICT system to fail. The third category comprises cosmetic problems, such as a language error in the help text, or an incorrect error message.

This division into categories is useful for the management since it provides insight into the specific nature of the problems observed. Generating such overviews regularly makes it possible to closely monitor the development of the system's quality, as shown in Table 1.1.

Table 1.1 Example of findings overview

Category	1st run	2nd run	3rd run	Total
Program errors				
cat. 1	1	0	0	1
cat. 2	7	5	1	13
cat. 3	2	1	1	4
Total program errors	10	6	2	18
Errors in test environment	3	2	0	5
Errors in specifications	2	1	0	3
Total	15	9	2	26

Repeating tests may be necessary if errors that must be corrected have been found in the ICT system. For this purpose, the desired phase of the test model is referred to (e.g. Preparation, Analysis, Navigation, or Execution).

The various phases can be run as often as necessary to make the information system operate properly. Once the tests achieve the desired result, the subsequent phases can be executed.

The Preparation, Analysis, Navigation and Execution phases discussed in this chapter will be described in further detail in the following chapters.

1.9 Summary

This chapter has briefly described the TestFrame model by using the Greek temple metaphor. The temple symbolizes the idea that a thorough and well thought out structure guarantees long-term stability in software development, in the same way that Greek buildings have survived for many centuries. Poorly designed operating systems lead to negative responses from developers and the organization as a whole. Properly functioning systems lead to positive responses, and give the organization a good reputation.

TestFrame phasing provides a guideline for structuring a test process, both for the initial execution and for testing a new release. The model describes each part of a test process from the preliminary study to the evaluation. It is not a fixed phase plan, but instead provides a flexible framework within which a customized solution can be provided for each test process. If necessary, certain phases can be executed several times.

Tangible products are created in each phase. This clarifies which products need to be generated during and at the end of the process. The clear description of the activities required to achieve these test products leads to a better insight into the test process's status. The process is therefore easier to control.

Tooling supports the various phases. Tooling varies from the use of project management tools for drawing up the test planning, to using test tools that enable the automated execution of the test.

Besides the test project itself, TestFrame phasing emphasizes the transfer after the project has been completed. Procedures are developed that ensure that the test products are maintained in their entirety and are kept up-to-date.

The synthesis of these processes results in a highly controlled environment that creates clearly defined, reusable test products. This ensures that the system's pre-determined quality level will be achieved, and that the completion time of the test process is kept to a minimum, guaranteeing a high quality-to-market and a short time-to-market.

2 Preparation

2.1 Introduction

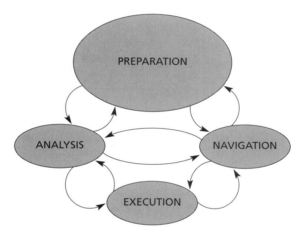

As Chapter 1 has shown, thorough preparation is crucial for completing an effective and efficient test process. The main preconditions and risks that exist are reviewed in the Preparation phase. The most important issues are laid down in the test plan. Before starting a test process using TestFrame, a preliminary study and a risk analysis must be undertaken. The study and analysis results are used as the basis for deciding whether TestFrame will be used for the test process concerned. The test strategy is also important as it states the test objective to be achieved, and how to measure whether that objective has been achieved. This makes it possible to assess the system's quality.

Agreements must be made about the test environment and the way in which it will be structured. A test cannot be initiated without an appropriate test environment. Furthermore, the structure and updating of a project file must be addressed. These subjects are discussed in more detail in this chapter.

A number of risks can be identified when testing a system, because the test could prove to be a bottleneck to the timely implementation of a system. TestFrame defines two checks to chart the risks and, where possible, to control them – the preliminary study and the risk analysis. The objectives of the preliminary study are to determine the scope of the test process and to identify any risks at an early stage (see [Hetz 88]). The risk analysis takes place at a later stage and specifies the same subjects in more detail, thereby creating a clear image of the possible risks and suggesting possible risk reduction measures. Individual areas requiring attention are described in general terms, and a number of questions are asked, providing insight into the activities, products, and the test process.

2.2 Preliminary study

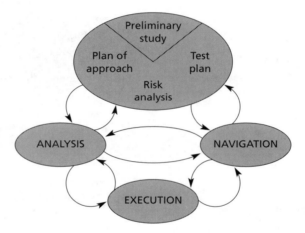

The preliminary study is conducted through an interview between the test specialist and the client, the person responsible for the introduction of the new or changed system. If specialized knowledge of the system to be tested is required, other stakeholders may be involved in this discussion. The status of the system to be tested is determined in general terms in relation to the environment using a checklist as a guide. The principal issues involved in the test process are described in a discussion report.

The preliminary study is divided into a number of principal issues:

● general;
● organization;
● test effort;
● physical test environment;
● documentation/experts.

2.2.1   General

Important issues concerning the structure of the system to be tested are identified in this part of the preliminary study. For example, is the system newly built? has it been rebuilt? Based on these general characteristics, decisions can be made about how to use TestFrame and which criteria apply to the desired result. An inventory should also be created noting the availability of tools such as documentation and prototypes.

A selection of questions that can be asked follows.

Is the system company critical, i.e. does the system support the primary business process?

The quality of the test, its depth, and scope often depend on the importance of the system to be tested. The higher the importance, the more is invested in testing to guarantee perfect performance.

Who developed the system? Was it developed in-house or is it a package implementation?

If it has been developed in-house, a great deal of attention must be paid to the unit test, the integration test, and the system test. Subsequently, the user acceptance test and the product acceptance test must be carried out. A decision can be made to use TestFrame for all the test types. However, it is also possible to use TestFrame for only one type of test.

If the system is a package implementation, the supplier typically has tested it to ensure that it meets the functional and technical specifications, on the basis of which it was purchased. However, a functional acceptance test still needs to be undertaken to check whether the functionality of the delivered system meets user expectations, and to test the correct implementation and parameter settings.

Is the system newly built or does an existing system need retesting?

For an existing system there are a number of sources of knowledge which can be used to create a new test set including available documentation, current system version, experienced users and, possibly, an existing test set. If the application's user interface is not greatly modified, the old version of the system to be tested and its existing tests can also be used as a basis for the navigation required, if automated test execution is chosen.

If a new system needs to be built, the future users, together with the already defined specifications, will serve as sources to create a test set. In such a situation, another question is also important – is a prototype available? If not, problems can arise when the clusters are translated into test cases via test conditions, because the way in which the data will be presented to the system is still unknown.

Therefore, navigation scripts that may be required cannot be created. It is critical to know just when a prototype or system part will be available for testing.

Even if a prototype is not available, a TestFrame implementation can still be initialized. To this end, the quality and depth of the documentation needs to be assessed. Another prerequisite, in this case, is the availability of an expert in the field during the test process.

The implementation of TestFrame can initially be limited to detailing the analysis (clusters, test conditions, and test cases) until a prototype or an operative system becomes available. Then the navigation scripts may be created if an automated test solution is chosen.

Which test types are used?

In practice, a large number of test types can be defined, including:

- unit test;
- integration test;
- system test;
- functional acceptance test;
- user acceptance test;
- production acceptance test.

The implementation of TestFrame can be different for each type of test. The implementation of the tests is customized using TestFrame based on the underlying test type(s).

What is the system's expected life span?

It is reasonable to expect that a system implemented as an interim solution justifies less test effort than one that will support business processes for many years. The extent to which each application to be tested is company-critical should always be taken into account. The frequency of testing is also related to this issue and may also depend on whether or not automated execution is selected.

2.2.2 Organization

A test organization is allocated the tasks of test preparation, test execution, test control, and test management, using a planned and often project-based approach. Several issues should be considered when structuring a test organization.

Does the company already have a test organization?

If there is no test organization, creating it can be incorporated into the TestFrame project. If there is a test organization, its structure needs to be reviewed and maybe changed. For example, the test organization may change because of the introduction of automated testing. There needs to be a navigator who draws up navigation scripts, for instance, and the management of test deliverables will be changed accordingly. However, the fitting column of the temple metaphor has to be taken into account, in the sense that the revised test organization structure must suit the existing organization.

What is the relationship between the test organization and the project organization?

The test organization can operate in partnership with the project organization, or it can be part of the project organization. Depending on the test type, test and project organization may have to be separated.

Which development method is used?

For the structuring of the test process it is important to know which development method is applied. Sequential 'waterfall', iterative, and component-based are common methods which have wide differences. The basic principles of a test set for a new built system must be consistent with the development method used (filling).

2.2.3 Test effort

A number of issues must be taken into account to determine the total effort required for testing.

Automated or manual testing?

Test cases developed conforming to the TestFrame method are suitable for both manual and automated test execution. Whether the test will actually be carried out by computer can be decided at a later stage. However, it is best to determine the options for automation of the test as early as possible, because of the implications for planning the test process. For instance, the set-up of an automated execution of the test will require more planning time. Additional products and specialized knowledge may also be required to enable the test to be carried out. This extra effort must be offset against the time gained during the automated test run. This time gain increases as the test is run more frequently. For that reason, the frequency with which the system needs to be tested is also reviewed in this phase.

Repeated testing of the system

The key reason for repeating the test is the issue of different releases. In many cases, only a minor part of the system needs to be adapted for a new release. Automated execution of the test greatly reduces the effort required for testing parts that have not been modified. These parts are also tested to ensure that the modification does not affect unmodified code in an unexpected way.

Content and nature of the modifications

The content and nature of the modifications for each release are critical. For example, a wide distribution of modifications throughout the system requires greater effort in modifying existing test assets. It is important to distinguish between the different types and effort of activities required for maintaining the test assets. These activities can be divided over the TestFrame phases: Preparation, Analysis, Navigation and Execution.

The following questions are relevant for both the development process, and the maintenance and management of information systems.

How many releases are issued in each period / for each project?

The number of releases issued can be one of the factors that determine the test effort required, and the justified investment.

How many times (on average) will the test be repeated for each release (due to errors or adaptations)?

In other words, what is the average quality of the resulting software? The need to repeat the test several times affects the completion time of the test to be executed. If many repetitions are necessary, using automated tools should be considered.

What percentage of the part of the system to be tested is modified for each release?

If only a small percentage is modified, the additional test effort is relatively small. However, minor modifications can sometimes unexpectedly affect other parts of a system. Thus, minor modifications require both testing and also running regression tests on other parts of the system.

In the case of functional modifications, the nature of the modification has to be reviewed, as well as the affected functionality. It may therefore be necessary to modify parts of the existing test set as well.

If the test is automated using navigation scripts, the modifications in the appearance of the system take on a new significance. Table 2.1 indicates the risk of system modifications.

Table 2.1 System modifications and risk indication

Change	Risk
Many functional changes, but small coverage over the system	Low
Many functional changes, large coverage over the system, low impact on input and output functions	Moderate
Many functional changes, high impact on input and output functions	High

What is the average amount of test data that needs to be adapted after a software modification?

The term 'test data' means the data that must be available in the test object's database in order to be able to carry out a useful test. If the amount of data that has to be adapted is large, the nature of the adaptations, and the affected functionality, must be reviewed. If only a limited part of the test data must be adapted each time, an automatic update should be considered.

It is also possible to periodically use test data derived from the current production data. This approach can be problematic if it is not clear which data is available when the test takes place. To avoid unexpected situations, the test data has to be examined first and this will require extra time. Exploring options for keeping the data static by, for example, always executing the test on the same data offers many advantages.

The quantity of test data used is also important. If the test is conducted with large amounts of production data, replacing backups will generally take more time. This can affect the test's completion time if the original data is required by a cluster. However, for certain tests the volume is crucial (for example, during a performance test). Another option is to set up test data using an initial database, which will then be used as the basis for each test.

Table 2.2 indicates the risk created by adaptations of test data.

Table 2.2 Adaptations of test data and risk indication

Change	Risk
Many changes in test data, small coverage over systems functions	Low
Many changes in test data, possibility for static test data	Low
Many changes in test data, large coverage over systems functions and or test data	Moderate

On average, how much time is spent on testing a new release?

When answering this question, a distinction needs to be made between the time required to complete the various phases of the test process (Preparation, Analysis, Navigation and Execution).

What percentage of system development time is used for testing a new release?

The answer to this question indicates the willingness to invest in tests. Many organizations seriously underestimate the total time required for testing.

2.2.4 Physical test environment

When testing systems, it is important to know how the test environment is organized in a physical sense. Is a separate environment available for testing? or is the environment shared with, for instance, the development department? The latter case may create organizational problems when the test needs to be run or developed. Which platform is used? which interfaces are available? and do they also need to be tested?

For an automated test run, it is also important which on-screen user interface is used. Is it a character user interface (CUI), as in the commonly used mainframe and UNIX applications? Or is a graphical user interface (GUI) used, as Microsoft Windows? This level of description determines if, and in which way, a test tool can be used. It may be necessary to decide which test tool is most suitable on the basis of a technical test, in the form of a pilot.

To determine the scope of the test project, it is also necessary to know the scope of the application to be tested, such as the number of screens and interfaces. The questions below may be useful in determining the parameters of a physical test environment.

On which platforms does the system to be tested operate?

As described above, it is important to know on which platforms the system operates, in view of the tools that may be used.

Can the selected or desired tool be used on the platforms concerned?

If the answer to this question is unknown, an expert can determine which user interfaces can be tested with test tools available on the market. If a test tool cannot be used, the option of using a different test tool needs to be examined. It is always wise to run a technical test first.

If there are interfaces that cannot be tested directly with test tools, the option of testing the user interface through another system, which can be accessed using a test tool, should be examined. Creating auxiliary programs requires extra time, and recovering the investment may well be difficult. However, you should never compulsively automate a test – situations may occur in which it is better to opt for manual test execution.

How many interfaces, including the GUI/CUI, are there and how many require testing?

These questions are important, as they reveal the technical scope of the system to be tested early on.

Is there a test environment where the system, including the interfaces to be tested, is available?

If there is no independent test environment for the testers, or if the test environment is not solely allocated to the test organization, organizing an independent test environment should be considered. A shared test environment presents the following risks: adjustment problems; the environment may not be representative; tests fail because data has been modified in the meantime; locking problems; and availability.

Is the maintenance of the test environment arranged clearly?

Matters that need to be considered include: hardware maintenance; promotion of new software; creating backups; and executing restores.

Is the test organization able to maintain the test data itself?

If the test organization is dependent on production data, for example, the following problems may occur: test runs may be delayed due to dependency on third parties; data in the database may change, and therefore the output cannot be predicted exactly; production data can be privacy-sensitive; and a large database takes a long time to restore.

Can other users adapt the test data?

It is possible that data might be modified, or even disappear unintentionally, during testing if appropriate access controls are not enforced.

Is there any data dependency?

If there is, it can be reduced by adding special features to the clusters, thereby simplifying the test run. However, creating additional features takes time, making the test process more expensive. One example of such a feature is selecting test data from the database which can subsequently be used in the clusters. Data dependency exists if the execution of a test cannot be predicted unambiguously. This can, for example, be caused by the periodic update of the test database by the production department, or because the predicted output changes over time (i.e. a time dependency). It is preferable to have a fixed subset of data, and a set test run date for the tests. In all other cases, additional functionality needs to be built into the clusters. This requires additional activities, and is therefore more expensive in terms of cluster development. Savings can be achieved if the tests are run several times.

2.2.5   Documentation/experts

Testing requires knowledge of the system concerned and the field generally. The simplest way to obtain this knowledge is to consult the available documentation. If there is none, or it is incomplete or incorrect, all the required information will have to be collected in another way. One possibility is consulting systems experts, and experts in the field concerned. However, such experts are often unavailable before or during the test process since they have other tasks to fulfil. Alternatively, analysts can draw up documentation based on an existing operative system. A prerequisite for this approach is that the current system operates correctly.

Documentation is also drawn up during the test process and after the test's completion – it must also be maintained after the test process has been completed.

The following questions provide insight into the availability of knowledge.

What documentation on the system is available?

An inventory needs to be made of the available documentation. This may consist of functional or technical designs, system documentation or user manuals.

What is the documentation's status?

If there is insufficient documentation, or if it is not updated, the use of experts is necessary. Undertaking an analysis of an operative version of the system can be very helpful.

Are there any experts in the field available?

Is the organization prepared to dedicate experts in the field to the test process?

2.3 Risk analysis

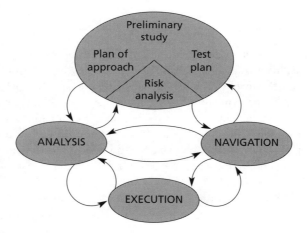

Risk analysis is a tool used for the detailed analysis of test process risks. It is a further elaboration of the questions asked during the preliminary study. The tool is based on evaluations of several critical TestFrame projects.

This risk analysis is meant to chart the risks, in detail, for a specific TestFrame project. It identifies the possible problems which may arise during the project, and acts as a stimulus for taking measurements as early as possible.

There are several points to consider when using risk analysis. For every point of concern, other questions are asked, and a choice can be made based on the given answers. The aim is to identify the risks, and not just to fill in the 'right' (or most desirable) answers. The questionnaire should not be considered to be complete since every specific situation has a number of unknown risk factors. It contains several columns that are used to identify risks and describe the data:

● the 'risk factor' column shows the weighting of factors which have been predefined;

- the 'selected factor' column contains the factor that applies to the situation for which the risk analysis is being performed;
- the 'weight' column indicates the weight of the subrisk that is reflected in the total risk. This weight is a fixed value, and is set on the basis of past experience in other TestFrame projects;
- the product of the selected factor and the weight results in the 'risk value';
- the 'max' column represents the maximum risk. The individual responsible for completing the risk analysis determines which answers apply, and therefore which risk values need to be calculated. If an item is not applicable, the value zero is selected.

In risk analysis, the subjects are divided into the following groups:

- the system under test;
- the test;
- the project;
- the project team;
- the relationship of the client to the project;
- the organization and culture of the client;
- the techniques employed;
- the automated test execution.

The totals of the risk value (the current risk) and the maximum possible risk are shown for each group of questions within the risk analysis. To maintain and keep track of the stated risks, specific measures can be defined.

Table 2.3 shows the TestFrame risk analysis.

Table 2.3 TestFrame risk analysis

SYSTEM UNDER TEST

No.	Description of the system under test	Choice	Risk factor	Selected factor	Weight	Risk value	Max risk
1.1	The development and test activities of a system that supports the core processes of an organization will get more priority and a greater budget than a secondary system. The system is a …	primary system	0	–	4	–	20
		subsystem of a primary system	2	–		–	
		secondary system	5	–		–	
1.2	Systems that support the core processes of an organization are often more complex and therefore more effort is required for test activities. The system is a …	secondary system	0	–	4	–	20
		subsystem of a primary system	2	–		–	
		primary system	5	–		–	

Table 2.3 Continued

No.	Description of the system under test	Choice	Risk factor	Selected factor	Weight	Risk value	Max risk
1.3	In some cases the repair of defects (or downtime) of the system in the production environment is very expensive. Other systems are replaced relatively easily, for example by manual procedures. The non-functioning of the system under evaluation is...	relatively easy to cope with	0	–	4	–	20
		very expensive	2	–		–	
		not possible	5	–		–	
1.4	The test process is simplified when the changes that are implemented in the system under evaluation are fewer with respect to the previous release process. The test can also be simplified when a working version of the system is available during the development of the test set. The system is …	stable and available	0	–	5	–	20
		unstable and available	2	–		–	
		new, under construction	4	–		–	
1.5	The impact of defects in the system increases with the the number of concurrent users of the system. The system must support …	up to 5 concurrent users	0	–	2	–	6
		6 to 30 concurrent users	1	–		–	
		over 30 concurrent users	3	–		–	
1.6	How many types of users have to work with the system under evaluation (also bear in mind supporting users such as system administrators, maintenance personnel, etc.)?	up to 3 types of users	0	–	2	–	6
		4 to 6 types of users	1	–		–	
		over 6 types of users	3	–		–	
1.7	Is it easy to use and control the system's functionality or is extra tooling required?	Data input and validation during testing is easy	0	–	3	–	9

Table 2.3 Continued

No.	Description of the system under test	Choice	Risk factor	Selected factor	Weight	Risk value	Max risk
		Data input and validation is difficult (e.g. several screens and files must be processed)	1	–		–	
		Additional tools are required for data input and/or validation	3	–		–	
1.8	Are the system's functions clearly documented and is this documentation available?	Yes	0	–	3	–	9
		Partial	1	–		–	
		No	3			–	
	TOTAL					0	110

THE TEST

No.	Description of the test	Choice	Risk factor	Selected factor	Weight	Risk value	Max risk
2.1	The scope of the test activities is … Examples of definitions are: ● all subsystems will be tested; ● each input field will be tested on its characteristic features; ● only the important subsystems functions will be tested; ● an application, system, integration, functional acceptance, performance, load test or a combination.	defined, clearly stated	0	–	5	–	15
		known globally	1	–		–	
		not defined	3	–		–	
2.2	A TestFrame project can support several goals – for example to prove if the quality of a version of a system is sufficient, or to improve the efficiency of the test process (improved speed over lower cost). Is the goal of the test project the improvement of the test process efficiency?	Yes	0	–	5	–	15
		No	3	–		–	

Table 2.3 Continued

No.	Description of the test	Choice	Risk factor	Selected factor	Weight	Risk value	Max risk
2.3	Is the goal of the TestFrame project the reduction of test personnel?	Yes	0	–	5	–	20
		No	4	–		–	
2.4	Several TestFrame pilots are possible – for example: • concept – to give a good understanding of the TestFrame method; • learning (small subsystem, full scope). To distil a working method for using TestFrame under the given situation; • proving (complex subsystem, full scope). To determine the usability of TestFrame. To determine whether the TestFrame way of testing is useable, or when applicable, automated testing is matching with the development processes used in the organization. Are TestFrame pilots performed?	Yes, several	0	–	3	–	12
		Yes, exactly one	1	–		–	
		No	4	–		–	
2.5	Has the organization got sound expectations with respect to the results of the TestFrame project or pilot?	Yes	0		3	0	12
		No	4			0	
2.6	Is a recent regression test available for testing the target application at the start of the TestFrame project?	Yes	0		3	0	9
		No	3			0	
	TOTAL					0	83

THE PROJECT

No.	Description of the project	Choice	Risk factor	Selected factor	Weight	Risk value	Max risk
3.1	Is the total project executed under fixed price and/or fixed date conditions? (Withfixed price/date projects customers usually demand more functionality than contractually stated.)	No	0	–	4	–	12
		Yes, but with the necessary prerequisites	1	–		–	
		Yes	3	–		–	
3.2	Is a clear test organization defined?	Yes	0	–	4	–	12
		No	3	–		–	
3.3	Are all the necessary test projects starting points such as test environment, tools, etc. defined and approved?	Yes	0	–	4	–	16
		Not yet, but the definition of starting points is part of the project	2	–		–	
		No and the definition of starting points is not in the project's scope	4	–		–	
3.4	The scope of the test project can be the extension of an existing testset or the creation of a new testset. The project's scope is …	maintenance	0	–	4	–	12
		extension of testware	1	–		–	
		development of new testware	3	–		–	
3.5	The estimated length of the test project expressed in days is … (limited to test resources only – a working day is based on the amount of work one	less than 65 days	0	–	3	–	15
		between 65 and 125 days	1	–		–	

Table 2.3 Continued

No.	Description of the project	Choice	Risk factor	Selected factor	Weight	Risk value	Max risk
	person can accomplish per day with six months TestFrame and, if applicable, tool experience)	between 125 and 200 days	2	–		–	
		between 200 and 300 days	3	–		–	
		between 300 and 500 days	4	–		–	
		more than 500 days	5	–		–	
3.6	The estimated timeframe of the test project (expressed in working days) is ...	less than 20 days	0	–	3	–	15
		between 20 and 30 days	1	–		–	
		between 30 and 40 days	2	–		–	
		between 40 and 60 days	3	–		–	
		between 60 and 100 days	4	–		–	
		more than 100 days	5	–		–	
3.7	Can the test project be divided into timeboxes (e.g. RAD) where the system's functions are developed in logical, coherent, and self-contained units? (If the project exists of exactly one timebox: No.)	Yes	0	–	3	–	6
		Most are	1	–		–	
		No	2	–		–	
3.8	Are timeboxes that are executed in parallel autonomous? (If the project exists of exactly one timebox: Yes)	Yes	0	–	4	–	8
		Most are	1	–		–	
		No	2	–		–	

Table 2.3 Continued

No.	Description of the project	Choice	Risk factor	Selected factor	Weight	Risk value	Max risk
3.9	The project exists of how many timeboxes? (The number of independent timeboxes gives the same number of independent components. This implies a consistent development process (for users and developers), integrating components, etc.)	up to 3	0	–	4	–	12
		4 or 5	1	–		–	
		6 to 10	2	–		–	
		over 10	3	–		–	
3.10	Is it clear for the customer that some of the test effort can only be executed after the delivery of the system?	Clearly stated in the project's planning Enough time reserved	0	–	4	–	20
		A small gap is planned between the delivery of the system and the delivery of the test results	2	–		–	
		The delivery of the test results is planned independent of the delivery of the system	5	–		–	
3.11	Is a procedure defined for approving the testware? Is it clear how the test will be approved with analysts, navigators, users and management?	Yes	0	–	4	–	12
		No	3	–		–	
3.12	Are acceptance criteria defined for the configuration and the content of the testware itself?	Yes	0	–	4	–	12
		No	3	–		–	

Table 2.3 Continued

No.	Description of the project	Choice	Risk factor	Selected factor	Weight	Risk value	Max risk
3.13	Is it clear how to deal with changes in starting points, functional specifications, requirements, standards, etc.? Is a change control procedure defined and is this procedure connected to the change control procedure of the system under evaluation.	Yes, is connected to the system's change control procedure	0	–	3	–	15
		No, independent of system	3	–		–	
		No	5	–		–	
3.14	Additional complexity can be introduced when the TestFrame project depends on deliverables of other projects. The test project depends on how many other (running) projects?	No dependencies with other (running) projects	0	–	2	–	4
		1 or 2	1	–		–	
		3 or more	2	–		–	
	TOTAL					0	171

THE PROJECT TEAM

No.	Description of the test team	Choice	Risk factor	Selected factor	Weight	Risk value	Max risk
4.1	Is a project leader assigned to the test project? (Sufficient management experience is necessary.)	Yes, on a full-time basis	0	–	5	–	15
		Yes, on a part-time basis but sufficient	1	–		–	
		Yes, on a part-time basis but insufficient	2	–		–	
		No	3	–		–	

Table 2.3 Continued

No.	Description of the test team	Choice	Risk factor	Selected factor	Weight	Risk value	Max risk
4.2	It is better for the project when the project leader (PL) has experience with TestFrame projects. Does the PL have experience with TestFrame projects?	PL was involved in other TestFrame projects	0	–	3	–	9
		Was involved as PL in non-TestFrame projects and is conceptually strong enough to pick up TestFrame methodology quickly	1	–		–	
		Was involved in TestFrame projects as a team member or has experience as team leader of small projects	2	–		–	
		Doesn't have practical TestFrame or PL experience	3	–		–	
4.3	If TestFrame is new to the organization, does the PL have organizational skills to embed new methods and technology and to manage the project's environment?	Yes	0	–	4	–	16
		No	4	–		–	
4.4	Domain experts are essential on the test project. Especially when the requirements of the application under evaluation are complex, and are poorly or not documented. How do analysts relate to domain experts?	Average 3 analysts on 5 domain experts	0	–	3	–	12
		Average 1 analyst on 4 domain experts	1	–		–	
		No domain experts available	4	–		–	

Table 2.3 Continued

No.	Description of the test team	Choice	Risk factor	Selected factor	Weight	Risk value	Max risk
4.5	Are the analysts and navigators (test team) capable of working in an independent and structured way?	All test team members can work independently	0	–	3	–	9
		Most test team members can work independently	1	–		–	
		No, or a few test team members can work independently	3	–		–	
4.6	Are the test team members capable of demonstrating that they prefer giving structure to their product?	Yes	0	–	3	–	12
		In potential, not demonstrated yet	1	–		–	
		Do not have affinity with	4	–		–	
4.7	Are all analysts capable of clear communications with the project's environments	Yes	0	–	3	–	9
		In potential, not demonstrated yet	1	–		–	
		No	3	–		–	
4.8	When the team increases, the number of communication lines also increases. What is the size of the test team?	1 or 2	0	–	2	–	10
		3 or 4	1	–		–	
		5 or 6	3	–		–	
		Over 6	5	–		–	
4.9	Do all analysts have knowledge of the relevant test methods and techniques?	Yes	0	–	3	–	9
		No	3	–		–	

Table 2.3 Continued

No.	Description of the test team	Choice	Risk factor	Selected factor	Weight	Risk value	Max risk
4.10	Do the analysts have experience with TestFrame?	All were previously involved in TestFrame projects	0	–	3	–	9
		Most were previously involved in TestFrame projects	1	–		–	
		None or a few were previously involved in TestFrame projects	3	–		–	
4.11	Is enough testware review capacity available? (Only applicable when this capacity is not in the project's scope.)	Yes	0	–	5	–	20
		No	4	–		–	
4.12	When the workload of the organization is high, the participation of the domain experts on the project can come under pressure. What is the workload of the domain experts apart from the activities within the project?	Low	0	–	3	–	9
		High	3	–		–	
4.13	Are the project's domain experts in charge to decide what is and is not within the test scope? (Enough quick-wittedness, independence and control of the domain experts are critical factors in the success of the project. This mandate must be given by management and must be supported by all units involved.)	Yes	0	–	4	–	8
		No	2	–		–	

Table 2.3 Continued

No.	Description of the test team	Choice	Risk factor	Selected factor	Weight	Risk value	Max risk
4.14	Are domain experts capable of separating essentials from side issues? Is the user capable of weighting the requirements in terms of being required, desirable or optional?	Yes	0	–	2	–	6
		No	3	–		–	
4.15	Are the test team members motivated to participate on the project?	Yes	0	–	4	–	12
		Rather not	3	–		–	
4.16	In the field of the organization of the customer, the project team members have ...	all the necessary knowledge	0	–	4	–	12
		enough knowledge	1	–		–	
		insufficient knowledge	3	–		–	
4.17	Are the domain experts capable of cooperating with the analysts? (Think about subjects concerning length of communication lines, transparency, frequency and intensity. Physical placing and atmosphere in the workplace play important roles in this matter. In an ideal situation the domain experts are part of the project team.)	Yes	0	–	3	–	12
		Can do when prerequisites are	2	–		–	
		No	4	–		–	
4.18	When the end user organization is made up of several departments/ stakeholders this could mean that potential opposing interests must be overcome. The end user organization exists of ...	1 department	0	–	4	–	16
		2 departments	1	–		–	
		3 departments	3	–		–	
		Over 3 departments	4	–		–	

Table 2.3 Continued

No.	Description of the test team	Choice	Risk factor	Selected factor	Weight	Risk value	Max risk
4.19	The estimated turnover of project personnel (developers and users) is ... (For example, is the replacement of a test team member or a user within a timebox acceptable?)	Nil	0	–	4	–	12
		Restricted	2	–		–	
		High	3	–		–	
	TOTAL					0	217

CLIENT–PROJECT RELATIONSHIP

No.	Description of the relationship	Choice	Risk factor	Selected factor	Weight	Risk value	Max risk
5.1	The choice for adopting the TestFrame methodology is ...	made explicitly by the client	0	–	4	–	12
		made in consultation with the client	1	–		–	
		made implicitly	3	–		–	
5.2	Is the client aware that a short-term investment is required and that this investment will have long-term results where the advantages are difficult to to quantify? (Applicable on the transition to structured and automated testing.)	Yes	0	–	4	–	12
		More or less	2	–		–	
		No	3	–		–	
5.3	Is the client experiencing external pressure for the development of repeatable regression tests? (For example auditors, accountants, mother organization.)	Yes	0	–	4	–	12
		No	3	–		–	

Table 2.3 Continued

No.	Description of the relationship	Choice	Risk factor	Selected factor	Weight	Risk value	Max risk
5.4	Is the project control from the client organization clearly covered and high enough in the organization?	Yes	0	–	3	–	9
		No	3	–		–	
5.5	Is the client organization willing and ready to accept a new test method? (The willingness of the client organization, management and end users, to accept the new and changing properties of the TestFrame method is crucial for a successful realization.)	Yes	0	–	4	–	12
		No	3	–		–	
5.6	Is the client organization capable of implementing a TestFrame test?	Yes in a mature way	0	–	3	–	9
		Hardly – too much innovative enthusiasm or ungrounded conservatism	3	–		–	
5.7	Many changes in the structure of the client organization can delay the project. The organization is …	stable, remains stable	0	–	4	–	20
		unstable, becomes stable, new organization known	1	–		–	
		stable, becomes unstable	4	–		–	
		unstable, remains unstable during the project	5	–		–	
	TOTAL					0	86

CLIENT ORGANIZATION AND CULTURE

No.	Description of client organization and culture	Choice	Risk factor	Selected factor	Weight	Risk value	Max risk
6.1	The culture of the client's organization can be characterized as ...	open with a healthy degree of ambition	0	–	4	–	12
		average	1	–		–	
		closed, non-cooperative, conservative	3	–		–	
6.2	The organization itself can be characterized as ... (Think about the need to keep to rigid standards and procedures applicable within the organization. These could restrict the decisiveness in the project.)	flexible, quick, and strong drive for results	0	–	5	–	15
		not rigid, in a way a drive for results, but existing procedures and approaches are not thrown overboard easily	1	–		–	
		pretty formal, commissions, steering committees and many other communication groups	2	–		–	
		strongly hierarchical, long communication lines, decision making is highly political	3	–		–	

Table 2.3 Continued

No.	Description of client organization and culture	Choice	Risk factor	Selected factor	Weight	Risk value	Max risk
6.3	The change capacity of the client organization is ... (Is the client organization capable of dealing with changes or is it very conservative and putting up resistance?)	high	0	–	3	–	6
		moderate	1	–		–	
		low	2	–		–	
	TOTAL					0	33

THE TECHNIQUES EMPLOYED

No.	Description of the techniques employed	Choice	Risk factor	Selected factor	Weight	Risk value	Max risk
7.1	Is tooling available to bring the testware under version control?	Yes, and had experience with	0	–	3	–	9
		No	3	–		–	
7.2	Is a separate environment available for testing?	Yes	0	–	5	–	20
		No	4	–		–	
7.3	In what way is the test environment linked with the development environment?	Independent, stand alone	0 2	– –	5	– –	20
		Is partly using the system					
		Totally integrated	4	–		–	
7.4	Is the test environment always available for each test?	Yes	0	–	4	–	16
		No	4	–		–	
7.5	Are test runs influencing the production environment?	No	0	–	5	–	20
		In a limited way	2	–		–	
		Yes	4	–		–	

Table 2.3 Continued

No.	Description of the techniques employed	Choice	Risk factor	Selected factor	Weight	Risk value	Max risk
7.6	Are standards and guidelines complete and stable? (Standards and guidelines applicable to name conventions, user interface, coding, documentation standards, templates, etc.)	Yes	0	–	4	–	12
		Not completely	2	–		–	
		No	3	–		–	
7.7	How many technical environments are in the test scope? (The number of hardware/software platforms, e.g. Dos/Windows with PowerBuilder and C++ (= 2 environments); a Sybase Database server and an AS/400 system (= 2 environments); the use of a Sybase database server and an IBM mainframe.)	1	0	–	4	–	12
		2	1	–		–	
		3 or more	3	–		–	
7.8	How many interfaces are there with other systems? (With how many other systems (not in the project scope) must the test communicate?)	0	0	–	4	–	8
		1 or 2	1	–		–	
		3 or more	2	–		–	
7.9	Is the test environment in line with the production environment? (Included are hardware and software; e.g. amount of internal memory, type of display, network, middle ware, servers.)	Completely identical	0	–	4	–	12
		Almost identical	1	–		–	
		Strongly diverse	3	–		–	
7.10	Is the application to be executed on one or several platforms?	1	0	–	3	–	9
		2	1	–		–	
		3 or more	3	–		–	
	TOTAL					0	138

AUTOMATED TEST EXECUTION

No.	Description of the automated testing	Choice	Risk factor	Selected factor	Weight	Risk value	Max risk
8.1	Will automated testing be used on the project? (If not, the rest of the questions are irrelevant, select risk factor 0.)	No	0	–	5	–	15
		Yes	3	–		–	
8.2	Are the navigators (test team members) capable of working independently?	All are	0	–	3	–	9
		Most are	1	–		–	
		None or a few are	3	–		–	
8.3	Are the navigators experienced with automated testing according to TestFrame methodology?	All have TestFrame experience	0	–	3	–	12
		Most have TestFrame experience	1	–		–	
		None or a few have TestFrame experience	4	–		–	
8.4	Do the navigators have knowledge of and experience with the environment of the system under evaluation?	All have	0	–	4	–	16
		Some have	1	–		–	
		None have	4	–		–	
8.5	Are the navigators experienced with the selected test tool? (For example, Winrunner.)	All are	0	–	4	–	16
		Some are	1	–		–	
		One or a few are, but all followed the training course	4	–		–	

Table 2.3 Continued

No.	Description of the automated testing	Choice	Risk factor	Selected factor	Weight	Risk value	Max risk
8.6	The system development team can often supply the test team with useful technical details about the application's environment, platform and other details required for navigation. Is technical support included in the project's budget?	20% or more budget (human resources) available for support	0	–	4	–	12
		5 to 20% budget (human resources) available for support	1	–		–	
		No budget for technical support	3	–		–	
8.7	Is a test development environment available and is it solely available for the project?	Yes, available for the project only	0	–	3	–	12
		Yes, but must be shared with other projects	2	–		–	
		No	4	–		–	
8.8	Are standards and guidelines for navigation scripts complete and stable?	Yes	0	–	4	–	12
		Not completely	2	–		–	
		No	3	–		–	
	TOTAL					0	104

2.4 Test strategy

A test strategy is defined as 'the steps and actions necessary to optimally employ the scarce test capacity'. The purpose of this strategy is to minimize risks when the system goes into production. The majority of testing efforts are directed to those parts of the system where the likelihood of risks is the highest. In this way, the highest possible guarantee of quality can be given with the lowest possible costs. A well defined test strategy makes it possible to enable the right people to perform the appropriate testing efforts on time, and with the least expense. The most important end product of the test strategy is a first clustering, which describes the aim of the test. Each cluster is described individually, with the following parameters:

- the stakeholder ('owner');
- who performs the test;
- when the testing is to be performed;
- the content of the test;
- priorities, means of approach, and environment.

The test strategy should be composed by a testing consultant, or an experienced testing analyst. Clusters are the primary starting points for the rest of the test material.

For every project, a test strategy should be created. Of course, the effort devoted to developing a test strategy should be in proportion to the size of the project. The need for an extensive description of a test strategy also should be in proportion to the extension of the expected test efforts. A large, complex and risky project requires a large allocation of test efforts. However, even small projects work best when a well-planned test strategy has been devised.

The following areas need to be specifically addressed when developing a test strategy:

- organization structure;
- test departments;
- cluster matrix;
- cluster cards;
- verification and evaluation.

2.4.1   Organization structure

The test strategy must begin with the organization itself. Various stakeholders will work with the system in the future, and therefore the system must support the client business processes as specified.

Each part of the organization can consider the system from their own point of view, and will have their own set of responsibilities with respect to the target system. To ensure the greatest commitment from the user community, they must be involved in drawing up the requirements of the system. These will be translated into acceptance criteria for test purposes.

The requirements of the system which stakeholders have are often (but not always) included in the specifications. Some requirements are considered to be self-evident. However, all requirements, both described and self-evident, should be included in the test. Table 2.4 gives an example of the different requirements of different stakeholders. The principal decides who will be involved in determining a test strategy. Each of these parties (hereafter, stakeholders) will be involved in, have an interest in, and have certain requirements of the system. Different stakeholders will often not have the same requirements. Table 2.4 gives one example characteristic per stakeholder. Of course, stakeholders will usually have more characteristics of concern.

Table 2.4 Example stakeholders

Stakeholder	Characteristic
Managers	Cost saving
(End) users	Usability
Functional administrators	Manageability, logical concept
Technical administrators	Manageability, conformance to standards
Operational administrators	Manageability, performance, applicability
Help desk	Traceability
Developers	Flexibility
Audit	Security

To decide just who is the stakeholder for a certain characteristic, one must ask the question, 'Who is responsible (for a certain problem), when something goes wrong?' This rationale is made clear in the following example. One Monday morning, the postman delivers a parcel containing a new costume. The previous Saturday you were attending a party at which you would have liked to have worn this costume. You complain about this to the postman and tell him to take the parcel back since the clothing company shipped the parcel too late. Although you blame the postman, the real culprit is the clothing company, since it is directly responsible for serving its customers.

2.4.2 Quality attributes and their relative importance

Most expressed requirements that exist in the areas of usability and performance are usually explicit. However, implicit requirements are often much harder to elucidate. One way of determining these is to use the quality attributes defined by the International Quality Standard ISO 9126. Within TestFrame, an extended version is used, as developed by the Software Engineering Research Centre (SERC). In Table 2.5, six main quality attributes are listed (in bold), along with a further division into detailed attributes and a short definition. The quality attributes added by SERC are printed in italics.

This list is comprehensive, and in daily practice not all the stakeholders for an attribute are identified. There are also attributes for which multiple stakeholders feel responsible. This is not relevant because the goal is to explicitly identify requirements.

Table 2.5 Quality Attributes Extended Version ISO 9126

Functionality	**The degree to which assumed or described needs are present**
Suitability	The degree to which functions that support the specified tasks are present
Accuracy	The degree of correctness of the system effects (i.e. output)
Interoperability	The degree to which the system can interact with other systems
Compliance	The degree of adherence to domain-related standards and legal requirements
Security	The degree to which unauthorized access, whether deliberate or accidental, is prevented
Traceability	*The degree to which correctness of data processing by the system can be assessed at several points during process execution*
Reliability	**The degree to which the system performs under defined conditions during a defined timeframe**
Maturity	The frequency with which failures occur
Fault tolerance	The degree to which the system maintains a specified level of performance during failures in the system or interfaces
Recoverability	The degree to which the system is able to re-establish its level of performance after a power failure or hardware failure
Availability	*The degree to which the system is available to provide its specified level of performance*
Degradability	*The degree to which the primary system functions are re-established after power failure or hardware failure*
Maintainability	**The effort required to implement changes**
Analyzability	The amount of effort required to diagnose the cause of failure
Changeability	The amount of effort required for modification or fault removal
Stability	The risks of unexpected effects of a modification
Testability	The amount of effort required to validate or test modifications
Manageability	*The amount of effort required to make the system available again for normal use*
Reusability	*The degree to which parts of the system are reusable for other systems*
Usability	**A set of attributes that influences the effort required for use, and on the individual assessment of such use, by a stated or implied set of users**

Table 2.5 Continued

Understandability	Attributes of software that influence the user's effort in recognizing the logical concept and its applicability
Learnability	Attributes of software that influence the user's effort in learning its application (for example, control, input and output)
Operability	Attributes of software that influence the user's effort in operation and operational control
Explicitness	Attributes that influence the clarity of the software product with regard to its status (such as progress displays)
Customizability	*Software attributes that facilitate user customization by reducing the effort required for use, bringing increased user satisfaction*
Attractivity	*Attributes of software that influence the satisfaction of latent user desires and preferences through services, behavior and presentation beyond actual demand*
Clarity	*Attributes of software that influence the processes of making the user aware of the functions it can perform*
Helpfulness	*Attributes of software that influence the availability of instructions for the user on how to interact*
User-friendliness	*Attributes of software that determine the user's satisfaction*
Efficiency	**A set of attributes that determines the relationship between the level of performance of the software and the number of resources used, under stated conditions**
Time behavior	Attributes of software that influence response and processing times, and throughput rates when performing its function
Resource behavior	Attributes of software that influence the number of resources used, and the duration of such use, when performing its function
Portability	**A set of attributes that determines the ability of software to be transferred from one operating environment to another**
Adaptability	Attributes of software that influence the opportunity for its adaptation to different specified environments, without applying other actions or means than those provided for this purpose
Installability	Attributes of software that influence the effort required to install the software in a specified environment
Conformance	Attributes of software that make the software adhere to standards or conventions relating to portability
Replaceability	Attributes of software that influence the opportunity and effort required to use it in place of other software in the same environment

Using these quality attributes, the amount of risk can be determined by using either the main attributes or the detailed attributes. At first, the different stakeholders will assign to each quality attribute a relative importance. These relative importance values indicate whether a quality attribute is more or less important than another. In general, most attention (and test efforts) will be devoted to functionality. For that reason, functionality will often be the only attribute that is tested in practice. It is very possible that certain quality attributes are unimportant for the system because they do not pose strong risks. For example, portability is often not highly valued, since the system may only ever operate at one location on a single operating system.

2.4.3 Test types

After the stakeholders have been assigned responsibility for quality attributes, the attributes must be translated into concrete requirements that can be tested and distributed over different test types.

A definition of a test type is *a test with a certain scope, executed by or for a certain manager, with a certain purpose*. The following test types are recognized:

- UT = unit test – a test of an independent, executable part of the program;
- IT = integration test – a test of the interoperability between the programs (internal) or complete information systems (external);
- ST = system test – a test of a complete (sub)system;
- FAT = functional acceptance test – a test of described and assumed functions (does the system do what it is supposed to do?);
- UAT = user acceptance test – a test whether users can work with the system;
- PAT = production acceptance test – a test whether the system can be taken into maintenance.

To determine the test type for each quality attribute, the following criteria are used:

- which test environment is required;
- who is the owner of the environment;
- attributes that require a similar test environment should be grouped under the same test type;
- cost of finding faults.

Some tests make extensive demands of the test environment. For instance, performance testing requires a copy of the production environment, which can be difficult (and expensive) to set up. At this stage in testing, there should be no elementary faults, removing the need for 'heavy' environments. It is important to determine a suitable test environment to test the system requirements – elementary tests are no less important than more complex tests performed at a later stage.

Quality attributes are shown with the corresponding test types in Table 2.6.

Table 2.6 Quality attributes with test types

	UT	IT	ST	FAT	UAT	PAT
Functionality	X	X	X	X	X	
Reliability	X	X	X	X		X
Maintainability						X
Usability					X	
Efficiency						X
Portability						X

2.4.4   Cluster matrix

In the cluster matrix, it is important to realize that the first clusters designed are not the final ones. The clusters will be further divided according to the standard TestFrame method.

In a cluster, it is decided WHO will test WHAT, and WHEN the testing will be done (i.e. stakeholders, quality attributes and test types). The clusters from the cluster matrix form the basis for further analysis. Defining the scope of the test assignment is thus made possible enabling steering on time, budget and quality. The matrix shows the main line of who is testing what, without delving into detail. It is a valuable tool when allocating tasks and responsibilities.

The test manager is responsible for composing a test team that will conduct the test on behalf of the stakeholders. Further elaboration of the test strategy is continuously tuned in collaboration with the stakeholders, and the team or teams conducting the tests. This is recorded in the cluster matrix, as shown in Table 2.7.

Table 2.7 Cluster matrix

Test type / Stakeholder	UT/IT/ST	FAT/UAT	PAT
Development department	Standardization Fault tolerance Adjustability		
Help desk		Traceability Helpfulness	
Administration department			Fault traceability Stability Accessibility
End user		Suitability Accuracy	
Audit			Security Auto-recovery Ability Stability

In the clusters from the matrix, the test design is started and continuously updated. The matrix is also a useful instrument for planning, since it is input for the test plan, and will be composed at the beginning of a test project. The information per cluster is further elaborated in cluster cards.

2.4.5   Cluster cards

In composing a test, a large amount of information is required. This information is sometimes difficult to obtain, and may be presented in an unstructured fashion. One way of recording the information in a structured way is through the use of cluster cards. Using the information from these, the test project can be monitored. The cards make a proper distribution of test efforts over the different test types possible. Table 2.8 shows which information is gathered for each cluster.

Table 2.8 Cluster cards

Cluster	<Logical cluster name>
System	<System name and version>
Stakeholder	<Who is responsible for defining the system requirements? Who has an interest in this cluster?>
Test type	<To what test type will this cluster belong?>
Test Department	<What test department is responsible for this cluster?>
Accountable	<Who approves this cluster? Who grants permission?> This may be a client or project manager rather than the stakeholder.
Priority	<If this cluster is not accepted, does that mean the roll-out phase can not take place?> <ul><li>What is the relative importance of this cluster? This priority influences the sequence in which the clusters will be planned.</li><li>Priorities are recorded for each cluster (must have, should have, could have, nice to have). During the analysis phase, a priority must be assigned to each test condition.</li></ul>
Timebox	<What are the time constraints?> <ul><li>Has the time at which the system should be taken into production been determined?</li><li>How will the required time be determined (estimate method, 'traditional' method)?</li><li>Perhaps the available time is determined for several clusters at once. Distribute the time over the different clusters (do this keeping the priority in mind).</li></ul>

Table 2.8 Continued

Quality attributes	<Summarize the quality attributes belonging to the test> ● If desired, a description can be given of the way in which each characteristic is to be tested. ● Use characteristics of the scope table to indicate further detailing of the high-level quality attributes.
Specifications	<Only the system requirements as defined by the stakeholder are described here> ● Every system demand must be related to the quality attributes or test characteristics. ● In the test analysis, the system requirements (along with the stakeholder) are translated to test requirements (i.e. test conditions). ● Determine the priority of each separate test condition here or during the test analysis.
Acceptance criteria	<The translated system requirements all have a priority> ● The stakeholder accepts the cluster if all conditions with a priority 'must have' have been approved, or all conditions, with a priority 'must have' and 'should have' have been approved, or every other predefined criteria has been met. ● Make sure that the means of evaluating the acceptance criteria are specifically indicated.
Managing time, budget and quality	<Project managers steer on time, money, functionality and quality> ● Test managers cannot steer on functionality so three steering variables remain. ● Often the system is delivered late. The end date will, however, be maintained. How do you deal with this? ● More funds (extra resources) must be weighed against lesser quality (execute fewer test conditions). ● Since the risks are known, the stakeholder can decide whether he will take the risk that comes with the unexecuted test condition.
Test technique	<How will the system requirements be tested?> ● Static tests: auditing and reviewing? mapping to a style guide? or ● Dynamic tests: decision tables, entity lifecycles, data flow analysis?

Table 2.8 Continued

Test environment	\<Is it known what the requirements are and how these will be tested?\>
	• If so, then this will have consequences for the test environment that is required. The result should be that the test environment must be achievable. If not, then the test technique must be altered. For example, if there is no production-like environment available, the performance can not be measured directly and must be obtained through extrapolation. However, extrapolation is one small step away from a complete guess, and must therefore be used with caution.
	• Which environment is required to execute the described tests? Both the technical environment, necessary resources and time dependencies have to be mentioned here.
	• Is a copy of the production environment necessary, or can a laboratory environment suffice?

These cluster cards are worked out with more detail in the Analysis phase. There will probably be no single moment at which the test strategy is 'finished' since some columns will never be filled in. These unfilled columns will translate into risks to the test project, or action points that will have to be picked up by the test manager as soon as possible.

2.4.6 Tuning

The stakeholders can determine if their interests are sufficiently covered by the cluster cards. It is important to obtain this commitment from the stakeholders. What is expected from other parties, in terms of resources and environments, can be translated into a commitment by these parties. In the further processes of test design and execution, the content of the cluster cards must be verified. To conclude, deviations from the original starting points are determined in order to learn for subsequent trails.

2.5 The test plan

An important part of the preparation is drawing up the test plan. The test plan can be viewed as the guideline for the test team while it executes its activities. It describes the components of the test (such as the scope, thoroughness and strategy) as well as procedures and techniques associated with the test approach. The plan is based on the results of the preliminary study, the TestFrame risk analysis,

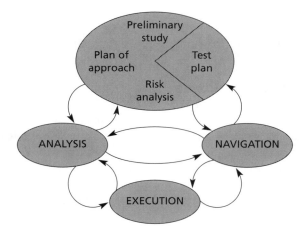

and the structure and the importance of the quality properties laid down in the test strategy. Eventually, the plan has to be submitted to the client for approval. More information on test preparation can be found in [Blac 99].

This section discusses drawing up a test plan and provides tips for formulating the plan clearly and practically. The various parts of the plan are addressed here. The organizational characteristics and test content are also addressed, in addition to the possible products resulting from the test project. The test manager is responsible for writing the test plan. Other specific topics with regard to test management are discussed in Chapter 6.

2.5.1 Test plan versus plan of approach

Developing a test, in the context of a test process, can be regarded as a project in itself. This means that a test project is made up of preparation, development, and execution. A plan of approach is required to control these phases. Such a plan describes the wishes and requirements, responsibilities, conditions of the project, and other project-related criteria.

Besides the plan of approach, the test project also has a test plan. The test plan specifies the test strategy, the approach, and the responsibility and control of the test project in more detail. In the test plan, the planning and the costs are divided into parts within the test project and resources are linked with test project roles.

Thus, a test plan can be seen as a subplan that forms part of the overall plan of approach. However, thanks to the greater degree of detail it provides, the test plan has immediate added value.

One difference between a plan of approach and a test plan is reusability – after a project has been completed a plan of approach is filed, whereas parts of a test plan can be reused. A plan of approach only describes issues that are relevant for the project concerned, whereas the strategy described in the test plan can be reused for testing new versions of the test object. This means that a test plan needs to be properly managed, and not just filed.

As soon as the testing is an independent project, unrelated to the development of the test object, the plan of approach can be combined with the test plan. All means, resources, time, etc. are then allocated to the testing.

2.5.2   Test plan structure

A test plan also forms part of the category of project documentation, and must therefore meet the same conditions as the other products in this category. That is why the same composition (management summary, introduction, conclusion, etc.) is used for the plan as for the other documentation, and the same layout applies.

Besides these standard parts, the test-specific issues also need to be addressed. The principal issues and parts pertaining to a test plan are as follows:

- description of the assignment;
- defining the scope of the assignment;
- filling in the TestFrame test model;
- specifying the time schedule;
- defining quality assurance;
- describing the test organization;
- defining standards and procedures.

2.5.2.1   Description of the assignment

Defining the assignment is a key factor for measuring the success of the test process. The assignment needs to be formulated clearly, unambiguously and concretely, so that the assignment's objective is understood by all stakeholders. All the parts are identified explicitly, including parts that will not be tested. To make this identification easier, an assignment can be divided up into a number of sections. The following list contains a number of sections that can be used for this purpose, each accompanied by an explanation.

- *Test products*

Being able to reuse the test products is TestFrame's core principle. Therefore, the test products created during the test process must be defined. The name, objective and minimum content the product has to meet must be described. Examples of test products include general cluster documentation, test conditions, test cases, action word documentation, navigation scripts, and test reports. It follows that some test products can be cancelled if the test is executed manually (such as navigation scripts).

- *Importance*

A test object's importance can serve as a basis for further determining the scope and strategy of the test. A greater test effort is justified for mission-critical business systems.

● *Starting points and prerequisites*

The starting points describe the minimum requirements that have to be met at the beginning of the test process ('what is'). The prerequisites describe the minimum requirements during the test process ('what is required').

The conditions that need to be fulfilled in order to start it, and the requirements to be met during it, must be taken into account during the definition of these two factors.

The starting points and prerequisites described in the plan of approach can be referred to. If, in the test plan writer's opinion, the starting points and prerequisites are incomplete, additional test process-specific starting points and prerequisites can also be included.

An example of a starting point is the availability of all required elements of infrastructure. The availability of sufficient personnel with TestFrame knowledge, a full test database, the availability of documentation or an installed test tool can also serve as starting points. Approval of the test plan can be included as a prerequisite.

● *Assumptions*

Any assumptions made with regard to the test process must be explicitly mentioned here. Assumptions are defined as clear formulations made to create a clear basis for the plan in a world full of uncertainties. Uncertainties typically arise due to a temporary shortage of information or decisions.

It is recommended that all assumptions be identified as soon as possible, and submitted to the client for feedback.

● *Risks*

Identifying risks early in a project increases their controllability, as it is always easier to control a known factor than an unknown factor. If applicable, risks can be copied from the plan of approach and are, among other things, relevant for evaluating the availability of staff and means. However, such general risks need to be complemented by specific risks for undertaking the test process. The TestFrame risk analysis can be consulted for this purpose if necessary – it states a risk reduction measure for each risk, including those responsible for it.

2.5.2.2 *Defining the scope of the assignment*

In addition to the description of the test assignment, it is important to record its scope – what will, and what will not be tested; what is the working method; and what are the system boundaries. This is recorded in the test strategy. There are several key issues with regard to the description of these limits and these are explained below.

● *Scope and thoroughness*

The test object must be described clearly using the version or release number of the test object, making it clear which version is used as a starting point. In addition, the parts of the object which will and will not be tested must be described. The parts which will be tested manually must be identified, as must those which will undergo an automated test.

The parts to be tested must be prioritized in cooperation with the client, making it clear to everyone which parts will be tested, and to what extent. Those parts which will be omitted if the planned time period proves to be insufficient must also be identified – these will be determined by the priorities of the various clusters, described earlier in the test strategy.

The thoroughness of the test is closely related to the testing method. For example, it is possible to test both positively and negatively, depending on the test involved. If only one of these methods is selected, the selection or exclusion must be justified.

● *Test techniques*

The test techniques employed, such as decision tables, must be described along with the scope and thoroughness of the test. Chapter 3 discusses a number of test techniques in more detail. The reasons for selecting one or more techniques should always be justified. The selection of a particular technique usually depends on the time available (i.e. using a known technique or learning a new technique), the objective of the test, and the scope and thoroughness of the test.

● *Dependencies on other systems*

A test object is sometimes dependent on other systems. There can, for example, be direct data links (such as interfaces) but also functional links (such as an external text editor). In practice, external dependencies such as interfaces are often overlooked, leading to a large number of errors in the application. These errors can be prevented by proper allocation of responsibilities. All external dependencies should be described, and the extent to which their presence endangers the test should be clearly detailed. The method for testing interfaces and functional links should be indicated.

2.5.2.3   Filling the TestFrame test model

As mentioned above, the TestFrame model describes each part of a test assignment from consultancy, as the basis of the test assignment, up to and including its evaluation. This description is composed of four different phases, each with its own specific tasks. Within the TestFrame method, it is not necessary to execute these phases and tasks in a fixed order.

If necessary, one particular phase can be repeated several times. Some phases need not be executed at all (for example, if a test is executed manually the Navigation phase is omitted). This flexibility makes it possible to adapt the appropriate test activities to the various phases of the development or management process, and to the existing organization.

Therefore, the test plan must describe how these phases and tasks are substantiated – it must be indicated clearly which phases will be executed and which will not; who is responsible for which phase and how the task fields are implemented.

2.5.2.4 Specifying the time schedule

Just like any planned activity, the test plan must include a schedule. This schedule links the required means, staff, test products, and activities to each other and distributes them over the time allocated. The schedule has to be presented in detail including items such as:

- when to start with the analysis of test cluster 1;
- when to start with the navigation of test cluster 1;
- when is retesting scheduled?

This schedule must be related to the various phases within TestFrame. Of course, this planning has to be linked to the priorities described in the cluster cards in the test strategy. A cluster with a low priority will be allocated a later stage for analysis and execution than a cluster with a higher priority.

2.5.2.5 Defining quality assurance

In addition to time-to-market, TestFrame also emphasizes quality-to-market. One of the guarantees of quality-to-market is the caliber of the test products. This needs to be ensured, for instance, by means of reviews (colleague tests) carried out on the various test products. For example, the functional part (clusters, test conditions, and action words) is usually assessed by a second test analyst. The technical part (navigation scripts) is typically reviewed by a second navigator. This redundancy clearly has an impact on staffing and resource planning. The test plan must describe how quality is assured, which procedures will be followed, and what standards will be applied.

2.5.2.6 Describing the test organization

The test organization must be defined and the roles identified within the test organization fully described. Examples of roles that can be identified include test manager, analyst, navigator, and user. The test plan should indicate which roles would actually be fulfilled within the project concerned. The tasks, responsibilities, and authorizations pertaining to each of these roles must also be indicated.

The requirements that the various reports need to meet (progress, problem reports, etc.) must also be elucidated. For example, what is the reporting frequency? for whom are they intended? and what is the report's primary objective? The consultation structures which exist within the test process should also be indicated.

2.5.2.7   Defining standards and procedures

Norms, standards and procedures need to be defined for testing and they should be included in the test plan. They ensure the following desirable outcomes:

- better assurance of quality within a project;
- transfer and communication between the various stakeholders within the project proceeds more smoothly;
- transfer to the existing organization is improved.

Issues such as how errors are dealt with, how the test environment will be maintained, and when the system will be considered to be approved all have to be described and specified. The following issues must be specifically addressed by the test plan:

Issue management

The test process produces issues because of which the test object may have to be adapted. The procedure to be used for the processing of these issues must be clearly described. Issues that have to be clarified must include:

- Who is the development team contact with regard to issues?
- Who allocates problems, and who supervises the way they are solved?
- Who provides technical support?
- How are the issues recorded?
- What is the processing procedure?
- What is the consultation structure between testers and developers with regard to issues?

For more information about issue management, please see Chapter 5.

Configuration management

The procedure for managing the test object and related testware should be described. The version management of the testware is ultimately the test team's responsibility.

One of the issues that must be addressed in configuration is that modified objects may only be installed in the test environment with the test team's permission, after action has been taken on the basis of the errors. This is to prevent a test from failing when a different version of the object under test is unexpectedly being used. The change management documentation also has to be updated since the documentation is intimately connected to the testware.

In addition, the way in which change requests are dealt with must be indicated. If this results in extra tests being required, a bottleneck could be created in the project. Therefore, the test team must be informed so that any new tests can be included in the test plan.

Acceptance procedure

The products to be created must be described, stating who has the authority to accept what, and when. This is closely related to the defined acceptance criteria.

Maintenance after the test's completion

The maintenance of the testware (test cases, test scripts, test files, test environment, etc.) after the test must be described. In addition, roles and responsibilities associated with the maintenance of the testware should be noted. Also, what will be maintained should be described (the whole test environment or only specific parts). Funds should be reserved and procedures initiated for training the test managers who will be involved at a later stage.

2.5.2.8 Miscellaneous

Other parts of a test plan that must be described include the way in which the project is evaluated, when it should be completed, and who is going to draw it up. At the close of a test process, a final report should be created. It must contain the expected results in comparison to the achieved results. Any differences will need to be explained and/or investigated. The plan should state when the final report is to be completed, and who is going to be responsible for drawing it up.

All the parts described in the sections above intersect in the test plan – the preliminary study report, the risk analysis results and the test strategy.

In the Preparation stage, attention also has to be paid to test environment structuring. This is the subject of the next section.

2.6 Structuring the test environment

The availability of a well-structured test environment is one of the primary critical success factors in executing a test process. In practice, providing an appropriate test environment proves difficult. Often, problems with structuring the environment create delays in the test process' original time schedule.

This section describes the steps to be taken to develop an appropriate test environment with the aim of making it available at the required time, including who exactly should execute just which activities to achieve the desired outcome. It can be used as a scenario for the actions to be performed. Firstly, the structure of the test environment for testing the test object is addressed. Naturally, sufficient attention also needs to be paid to the physical work environment (work area layout). This is described in Section 2.6.10.

A highly systematic approach should be used to structure a test environment. It should specify the following steps.

1. Determine the effect of the test's scope on the test environment.
2. Draw up an inventory of the (future) production environment.
3. Draw up an overview of the required test environment.
4. Describe the differences between the test environment and the (future) production environment.
5. Describe the responsibilities for structuring the test environment.
6. Describe the responsibilities involved in maintaining the environment during the test project.
7. Structure the test environment and maintain it during the project.
8. Describe the responsibilities of test environment maintenance after the test project.
9. Maintaining the test environment after completion of the test project.

This section is based on the structuring of a single specific test environment for a single application. In the event of frequent testing of several applications, it is useful to examine whether it is possible to use the test environments for several projects.

2.6.1   Step 1: Determine the effect of the test's scope on the test environment

The scope of the test assignment influences the structure of the test environment. There is a big difference between the environment required for a program test (a laboratory-like environment), and that designed for a production acceptance test (i.e. an environment that is almost identical to production). Structuring a production-like environment for a program test is usually unnecessary. Conversely, a production acceptance test cannot be executed correctly and completely in a laboratory-like environment. A clear definition of the scope of the test is therefore necessary to be able to chart the required test environment.

Examples of possible test environments are:

- an environment for program testing, and the system test;
- a functional acceptance test environment;
- a user acceptance test environment;
- a shadow environment which is almost identical to production, especially appropriate for performance testing.

The key requirement which determines the structure of a test environment is that the development and the test environments must always be separate to prevent the environments from affecting one another. The consequence of not separating environments could be that the development team could not continue its work while a test was being carried out.

The end product of Step 1 is the determination of the type of test which will be executed.

2.6.2 Step 2: Draw up an inventory of the (future) production environment

When a test environment is set up for acceptance tests, a production environment often serves as a model. If the current production environment deviates from the environment that will prevail when the tested system is implemented, that future production environment must be taken as the starting point. This happens when other applications have to be added to the production environment before the system to be tested now is entered.

Experts from the development, operation and IT departments chart the (future) production environment. If such an overview is not yet available, it needs to be drawn up by order of the test manager and supervised by that person.

The end product of Step 2 is an overview of the (future) production environment. This step can be skipped for a program test, where an inventory of the laboratory-like environment required can be drawn up immediately.

2.6.3 Step 3: Draw up an overview of the required test environment

The overview of the required test environment is developed from the basis of the overview of the (future) production environment. What must be determined is whether it is useful (and indeed possible) to structure the test environment in accordance with the overview of the (future) production environment. Possible reasons for deviations are:

● because of the test type, it may not be necessary to include all the components – as mentioned above, this is less important for a program test than for a production acceptance test;

● the available budget;

● a situation in production that cannot be reproduced in the test environment;

● the complexity of the production situation.

It is possible that a particular real situation cannot be simulated adequately in a test environment. For example, in an integration test, where the link between a stock trade system and the stock exchange's stock transaction system is tested, a test environment of that stock exchange needs to be available. If not, the test transactions will actually be executed!

As mentioned above, the test organization determines the required test environment in collaboration with the development, operations and IT departments. It is important that the overview is explicit and unambiguous. Version numbers of components must be included in the overview for clarity.

Table 2.9 shows examples of what typically needs to be included in the test environment overview.

Table 2.9 Components required for testing grouped by category

Category	Components
Hardware	• PCs • Terminals • Input equipment (e.g. scanners) • Output equipment (e.g. printers) • Servers • Routers • Encrypters • Network maintenance services • Mainframe capacity • Storage capacity (storage space for disks, tape) • Modems • Power, cables
Software	• Application under test • Database software (which databases) • Operating system • Backup/restore functionality • Database management system • Authorization • Logging software • Tracing software • Communication layers • Conversion software • Mainframe tools (e.g. JCL scheduling) • Datum manipulation tools • File manipulation tools • Test tools
Communication	• Interfaces (internal, external) • Data communication lines (e.g. X-25, ISDN) • Public networks (e.g. telephone lines) • Connections to systems outside the organization

For some tests, it is necessary to manipulate the system date and this can have unforeseen consequences. Consider a situation in which data processing over several days is tested – such as transactions that only need to be carried out on the following working day. In order to be able to run the test within one day, it is essential to be able to change the system date. In practice, this single action can have quite a dramatic effect, particularly for multiuser systems. For example, other applications that use the system date cannot be tested in the same environment at that time, and occasionally not even on the same workstation.

Not infrequently, several test environments must be able to carry out the test concerned. These issues need to be addressed when drawing up the required test environment.

The end product of Step 3 is an overview of the required test environment, including component version numbers.

2.6.4 Step 4: Describe the differences between the test environment and the (future) production environment

Once the build-up of the test environment has been determined, the differences between the test environment and the (future) production environment can be identified. This includes a description of the reasons for these differences. Examples of differences between the production and the test environments are:

● testing with a different version of a component (such as the operating system) because the new version is not currently available;

● not including certain components in the test environment because they are not essential to the objective of the test to be run (e.g. not placing encryption systems when running a functional acceptance test);

● the local placement of a data set, whereas in production this data set is accessed via a data communication connection.

After listing the differences, the risks taken due to deviations in the test environment have to be listed and recorded. A test may be run properly on one modern PC, but if other PCs are used in production it is possible that the application will not operate properly. It is appropriate for the test organization to determine the risks in collaboration with the development, operations and IT departments.

After developing the test environment overview, and describing the deviations between the test and the production environments (and associated risks), all documents should be submitted to the client for approval. Alternatively, this documentation can be included in the test plan. Usually, the client must approve the test plan before the test environment is structured. After the client's approval, the required components are allocated and components that are not currently available ordered.

The end products of Step 4 are:

● an overview of the differences between the test environment and the (future) production environment;

● risk analysis of the differences;

● test environment overview (separate or included in the test plan) as approved by the client;

● allocated components and the ordering of other required components.

2.6.5 Step 5: Describe the responsibilities for structuring the test environment

To ensure that the structuring of the test environment runs smoothly, it is essential to record who is responsible for the execution of all tasks which must be performed. The responsibilities to be allocated include taking care of the various components (retrieving, installing, etc.) mentioned in Table 2.9. Responsibilities such as who installs required test tools and who populates the database must be assigned to individuals or groups.

The test organization determines the responsibilities in consultation with the departments involved. It is advisable to go through the products created in the previous steps with them, and to link a responsible person to each relevant part. Subsequently, a concrete scenario for the structuring of the test environment is drawn up describing when all actions are to take place and any dependencies between actions. For example, which actions can be executed simultaneously, and which need to be executed sequentially. To this end, a project management tool should be used.

The end product of Step 5 is an overview of the persons responsible for structuring the test environment, approved by all the parties involved, and subdivided into tasks, with a scenario for structuring the test environment.

2.6.6   Step 6: Describe the responsibilities in maintaining the test environment during the project

During the test project's execution, the test environment needs to be maintained. In order to ensure a systematic and structured execution of test environment maintenance, it is essential to state who is responsible for executing all the required tasks. These tasks include:

● manipulating the test data at the test organization's request;
● restoring the databases;
● creating the backups;
● monitoring the data's integrity;
● remedying faults in the test environment;
● installing new, approved versions of the application to be tested in the test environment;
● coordinating the use of the environment by several projects.

The test organization determines the responsibilities, in consultation with the development, operations and IT departments. All the parties involved should agree on the tasks and responsibilities. The overview can be prepared separately or it can be included in the test plan.

The end product of Step 6 is an overview, approved by all the parties involved, of the maintenance of tasks to be completed in the test environment during the test project.

2.6.7   Step 7: Structure the test environment and maintain it during the project

In this step, the test environment is actually structured in accordance with the test environment overview (see Step 3), and the agreements made with regard to it (see Step 5).

After implementing the test environment, it will be maintained in accordance with the agreements laid down in the approved overview of tasks and responsibilities, with regard to the test environment maintenance during the test project (see Step 6).

For a systematic execution of the structuring and maintenance of the test environment, it is often helpful to include the persons on the test team who actually take care of structuring and maintenance.

The end product of Step 7 is a structured and maintained test environment to be used during the test project.

2.6.8 Step 8: Describe the responsibilities of test environment maintenance after the test project

After the test project has been completed, the test environment also needs to be maintained. To this end, it is important to record which personnel are responsible for executing the maintenance tasks after the test project has been completed. This can entail the transfer of the maintenance of the project organization to the line organization. Examples of responsibilities to be allocated here include filing the test environment, maintaining the components, maintaining the test tools, and making the test environment available when a new test project is initialized. The test organization determines the responsibilities, in mutual consultation with the development, operations and IT departments.

The end product of Step 8 is an overview of responsibilities with regard to the maintenance of the test environment after completion of the test project, approved by all the parties involved and subdivided into discrete tasks.

2.6.9 Step 9: Maintaining the test environment after completion of the test project

After the test project has been completed, the test environment will be maintained in accordance with the agreements laid down in the approved overview of tasks and responsibilities (see Step 8).

The end product of Step 9 is a maintained test environment after completion of the test project (in between two projects).

2.6.10 Work area

In addition to the test environment for testing the information system, the testers' physical work area also constitutes part of the test environment. The test team should be able to carry out its work under suitable conditions. The requirements for a work area include office software (word processor, spreadsheet program, project management tools, etc.), work space, conference rooms (to be used for user sessions and project progress meetings), furniture, a copier, and a coffee machine.

Table 2.10 shows a summary of the nine steps along with the products from each.

Table 2.10 Summary of a phased plan for structuring the test environment

Step	End products
1. Determine the impact of the test scope on the test environment	Answer to the question, 'what kind of tests must be executed?'
2. Analyze the (future) production environment	Overview of the (future) production environment
3. Describe the required test environment	Overview of the required test environment(s), including version numbers
4. Describe the differences between the test environment and the (future) production environment	Overview of different test environments and (future) production environments
	Risk analysis
	Customer approval
	Allocated components
	Ordering of required components
5. Describe the responsibilities for structuring the test environment	Overview of responsibilities for configuring the test environment divided into tasks
	Screenplay test environment configuration
6. Describe the responsibilities for maintaining the test environment during the test project	Overview of responsibilities for test environment maintenance during the test project divided into tasks
7. Structure and maintain the test environment during the test project	A configured and under maintenance test environment during the project
8. Describe the responsibilities of test environment maintenance after the test project	Overview of responsibilities for test environment maintenance after project close out, divided into tasks
9. Test environment maintenance after completion of the test project	Under maintenance test environment after project close out

2.7 Project file

A project file is constructed and maintained to make available all the information that has been recorded electronically and in writing during a TestFrame project. The file provides ways to enable the 'monitoring and control' function in a TestFrame project. The project results which are intended to be reused in future adaptations of the target system are not recorded in the project file.

The test manager is responsible for the layout of the project file. It must contain at least the following sections:

- Planning: test plan, detailed planning of the test project, and products maintenance plan.
- Monitoring and control: list of actions, list of risks, list of agreements and decisions, progress reports, error reports, quality assurance products, correspondence, minutes of meetings, test reports, final report test project, and test project evaluation report.
- Standards and procedures: within the test project.

The test manager is responsible for managing the project file and ensures that it is updated and complete at all times. The project file is dynamic and will be improved, changed, and continuously expanded over the course of the project. When the project has been completed the project file is filed.

2.7.1 Planning

Test plan

The test plan indicates the following:

- what will be tested during the project;
- to what extent these elements will be tested;
- how the test will be conducted;
- who draws up and runs the test.

The test plan section provides a detailed description of the plan. The project file must contain at least an approved and updated version of the test plan. The latest version should describe the adaptations made since the initial version, and the reasons why these adaptations were made. If necessary, the previous versions of the test plan can also be filed.

Detailed planning of the test project

The detailed planning of the test project provides insight into the tasks and activities executed. In addition, it contains the time characteristics such as completion time, and parallel or sequential execution of activities. The project file must contain at least an approved and/or updated version of the detailed planning – known as the baseline. The latest version indicates the adaptations made since the baseline and the reasons why these were made.

Product maintenance plan

The detailed planning should be complemented by an overview that indicates the status of each test product. This overview is called the product maintenance plan and contains the following information about each test product:

- planned completion date;
- planned approval date;

- actual completion date;
- actual approval date;
- approval by;
- current status.

Table 2.11 shows an example of the overview in the context of the products maintenance plan.

Table 2.11 Example products maintenance plan

Product	Plan finished	Plan approved	Realization finished	Realization approved	Approver	Status
Test plan	1-01	8-01	31-12	5-01	K. Johnson	Approved by client
Test environment	1-02	8-02	2-02	7-02	B. Robson	Approved by test organization
Configured test tool	1-02	8-02	2-02	7-02	T. Smith	Approved by navigators
Clustering	1-03	15-03	10-03	15-03	K. Johnson	Approved by client
Test conditions cluster customer	15-04	22-04	15-04	22-04	K. Johnson	Approved by client
Test cases cluster customer	18-04	22-04	18-04	22-04	K. Johnson	Approved by client
Navigation cluster customer	30-04	4-05	2-05	5-05	B. Robson	Approved by test organization
Test conditions cluster account	15-05	22-05	14-05			Review phase started
Test cases cluster account	18-05	22-05				Design phase
Navigation cluster account	30-05	4-06				Not started yet
Test report system test	15-06	22-06				Not started yet
Final report system test	25-06	30-06				Not started yet

2.7.2   Monitoring and control

List of actions

A list of actions is maintained during the test process, showing the actions required for the test project to succeed and which have not been included in the planning. This is necessary for issues that require further examination, or which only surface later in the process. Using the list, the test manager can monitor which actions must be taken and by whom. To maintain appropriate control, the list of actions must be constantly updated. For support, it is useful to state the date of the latest update on the list of actions.

The list of actions provides the following information about each action:

● a description;
● who carried out the action;
● when the action was recorded;
● when the action had to be completed;
● its priority;
● its current status.

An example of a list of actions is shown in Table 2.12.

List of risks

A list of risks shows the risks and bottlenecks that became apparent during the risk analysis, and which need to be monitored. Risks that arise, or are identified during the test project, are also stated on the list. A measure is defined for each action and this is monitored during execution.

The following information is stated on the list of risks for each risk or bottleneck:

● when it was registered;
● the phase of the project during which it was discovered;
● its priority;
● a description and consequences;
● the risk-reducing measure to be taken.

When the risk-reducing measures have been taken the risk still needs to be monitored. Therefore, it must not be removed from the list. Table 2.13 shows a list of risks.

Table 2.12 Example of a list of actions

No.	Action	By	Start	Finish	Priority	Status
1	Create authorizations (user-ID & password) for test team	J. Smiths	30-08-2000	02-09-2000	Urgent	Closed
2	Make presentation for management for new test approach	D. Melsom	05-09-2000	07-09-2000	Medium	Open
3	Set up of project file	P. Adams	05-09-2000	07-09-2000	High	Open

Table 2.13 Example of a list of risks

No.	Date	Project	Project phase	Priority	Risk	Mitigation strategy
1	15-09	PIB 9804	Specification of test conditions	High	Input of users is lacking causing delay in test condition review activities (including approval)	Get in touch with the chief of the user department to explain the consequences and to request additional capacity.
2	20-09	PIB 9804	Setting up test environment	Urgent	Test environment not configured because required PCs are not available, not delivered by supplier	Temporary testing on old equipment so long as there is no impact on system functionality. Also escalating the situation via the customer to the supplier to speed up delivery.

List of agreements and decisions

The list of agreements and decisions contains issues that have been decided prior to the project. Agreements and decisions made during the project are also included. The agreements and decisions outline the framework within which the project is executed.

The list of agreements and decisions must include at least the following:

● description;
● who made the agreement or the decision;
● date on which the agreement or decision was made.

An example is shown in Table 2.14.

Table 2.14 Example of list of agreements and decisions

No.	Agreement or decision	Date	By
1	Progress will not be reported to the project manager but to the line manager	15-06	Steering committee
2	From 1 August the input of system users will be reduced from 3 days to 1 day a week.	1-07	Test manager

Progress reports

The test manager periodically submits progress reports to the client. The interval is determined in consultation between the test manager and the client. In particular, the completion time of the project is addressed in each report, to ensure that there is still sufficient time to undertake any actions that may be required in response to a report. These progress reports should state:

- results which have been achieved over the past period;
- what the current state of affairs is with regard to planning, including reasons for any deviations;
- bottlenecks which have been detected;
- action which is expected from the client (see the list of actions);
- what the expectations are for the next report period.

The progress reports should be filed in the project file.

Quality assurance products

During a TestFrame project various quality assurance measures are taken to enhance the test project's quality. The products resulting from these measures, such as reports from peer-to-peer reviews, reviews by experts in the field, audits, inspections, structured walk-throughs, and code inspections of navigation scripts also need to be filed.

Correspondence

All correspondence relating to the project should be filed. For example, e-mails, letters, memos, discussion reports, and acceptance documents.

For major projects it is recommended that all the correspondence is filed – in particular involving parties outside the project team – in a correspondence log-book. This makes it easy to trace when correspondence was received, or sent and to which party.

Minutes of meetings

Minutes should be kept of all the meetings held during the TestFrame project. They must contain at least the agreements and decisions made. A report of the various views expressed (in summary) should be made when important decision-making meetings are held. Actions, risks, bottlenecks, and agreements or decisions resulting from these meetings are included in the lists concerned and monitored from there.

Test reports

Test reports are created as a result of the test execution in a TestFrame process. These state which test cases have been successfully completed, and which have failed. The form these reports take can vary, depending on whether the test was manual or automated. To be able to substantiate the results of the test execution, the test reports are filed in the project file.

Error reports

Errors resulting from the test execution need to be carefully registered and moni-tored. An error report obviously indicates which errors have been made but also which errors have not been discussed, which are being dealt with by the develop-ment team, and which can be retested. For a more detailed description, see Section 5.7. This issue management also forms part of the project file.

Final report

The final report of a TestFrame project contains a portrayal of the development of the test project and advice with regard to the transfer to the next phase (for exam-ple, from system test to user acceptance test, or from production acceptance test to production). The final report also serves notice as an end-of-responsibility and as a transfer document – it therefore needs to be included in the project file.

Evaluation report

After a TestFrame project has been completed, an evaluation is conducted which focuses on its successes and failures. The evaluation forms the input for the next test project, and is therefore included in the project file.

For long-term projects, interim evaluations should be undertaken. The project can then be adjusted and improved on the basis of the errors.

2.7.3   Standards and procedures within the project

The standards and procedures to be used are defined in the Preparation phase of a TestFrame project. Standards and procedures that must be defined are:

- documentation standards;
- standards with regard to analysis;
- standards with regard to navigation;
- version management procedure;
- backup and recovery procedure;
- issue management procedure;
- acceptance procedure.

2.8   Summary

A number of issues must be examined during the Preparation phase. Firstly, the general part is surveyed: how important is the test object for the organization? Subsequently, the way in which the test is organized is reviewed including test preparation, test development, test execution, control, and management. All the efforts needed to conduct the test should be catalogued, with emphasis on the physical test environment. In addition, it is advisable to find out whether knowledge can be obtained from current documentation, and which experts can be consulted.

Naturally, the risk involved in a test project then needs to be systematically addressed. To this end, a risk analysis can be used. Based on the results of this, measures can be taken to reduce the risk.

These results are included in the test plan. In the Preparation phase, the test strategy is also determined. Structuring a test environment is a key activity in this phase. Using the phased plan, the test environment should be available in time, since a proper test environment ensures the correct execution of the tests.

Finally, maintaining a project file is very important for 'monitoring and control' during the test period, and also in connection with accountability during subsequent audits.

3 Analysis

3.1 Introduction

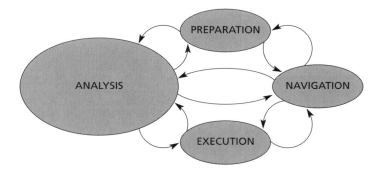

The aim of the Analysis phase is to set up a comprehensive test which can be reused. To achieve this goal, it is imperative to use a systematic working method so that the risk of leaving gaps in the analysis, making the test set incorrect or incomprehensive, is reduced. This phase focuses primarily on the activities executed to ensure that the test set's content is correct and sufficiently comprehensive. Examples of such activities are analyzing the application to be tested, and designing the test documentation (subdivided into clusters, test conditions, test cases, and designing action words). These activities yield a number of products. This chapter discusses these along with test techniques that can be used to create TestFrame products. It concludes with a section on data dependency, which is a prime consideration when designing and executing test sets.

One of TestFrame's key aspects is the test set structure. A test set needs to be structured in such a way that it is accessible and transparent. The more frequently the test is used, the greater the importance of an appropriate structure. Using a logical and systematic approach increases the test material's effective lifespan. The test analyst creates the structure by stating, in lucid terms, what has to be accomplished and subsequently proves that it has been successfully completed. Such a structure shows clearly where the required information can be found at any time.

Most test projects demand that the test can be run once more with the produced material, implying that the test set will almost certainly be reused. It must also be possible to adjust a test set to a system modification easily. Table 3.1 provides insight into the risks involved in the transfer of test material. The risk can be limited if the test set needs little adjustment, and sufficient working knowledge is available. This is usually guaranteed if the staff who worked previously with the existing test set can be redeployed to the current project. The risk is proportionally greater if considerable adjustments have to be made and insufficient knowledge is available to execute the test again. In all other cases, the risk can be considered to be moderate.

Table 3.1 Risk levels of a regression test

Risks for execution regression test	Sufficient knowledge/ same staff	Insufficient knowledge/ new staff
Existing test set	Low	Medium
New test set + enhancements	Medium	High

Table 3.1 shows the importance of a maintainable and transferable test set. Maintainability is a key consideration at the beginning of the process, and moves beyond plain accessibility. Once it has been established that the test set will be used more than once, reusable material needs to be created. To do this, the test analyst puts themselves in the position of those to whom the test set will be transferred.

Someone from the user's department typically adopts the material. In such cases, the test material's quality has to meet additional requirements. It can, for instance, be useful to make test set documentation available through help files, or to put it on the local intranet. The latter is particularly important if several branches of a large organization must become familiar with the contents of the test set. If the test set is only to be used locally, such a time investment is typically unjustifiable.

3.2 Test set structure

The TestFrame method is based on a logical and systematic test set structure. This structure is developed at the start of a test project, within well-defined boundaries. The documentation for every test project comprises analysis documentation, action word documentation, and navigation documentation. The latter is only used in the case of an automated test (see Chapter 4).

Figure 3.1 shows a number of important analysis products resulting from the test process:

- initial database – standard tables and records required to execute the tests;
- division into clusters – the way in which the system has been divided into testable units;
- general cluster documentation – recording of general information per cluster, and important information for the execution of the cluster;
- test conditions – one list of criteria to be tested per cluster;

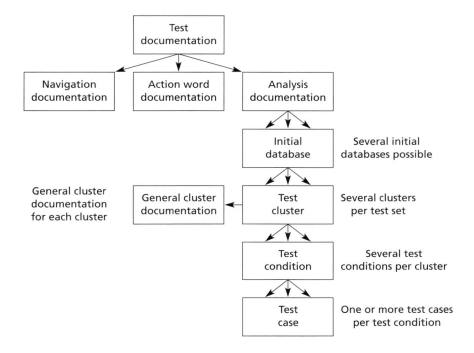

Figure 3.1   Test documentation set up

- test cases – per cluster, more detailed specification per test condition of test conditions as a function of input specifications and output predictions;
- action words documentation – overview of existing action words, their status, and operation.

3.2.1   Initial database

One or several initial databases can be used per test process. Usually, one database is used per cluster, and general cluster documentation is recorded. Several test conditions can be drawn up per cluster, which can subsequently be specified in one or more test cases. In some cases it is also possible for a single test case to cover several test conditions.

3.2.2   Division into clusters

General documentation is laid down about the particulars of a cluster, usually in a separate document (for example, a separate worksheet in a spreadsheet). The contents of the cluster can be described in general terms. For example, it can contain general cluster documentation that indicates the test flow – are a large number of input actions specified first, followed by a series of checks? or are all sorts of input validations tested, in which the test cases are totally independent of one another? This is important information for the person entrusted with cluster maintenance.

3.2.3   General cluster documentation

In addition to a general list of the functionality tested using the cluster, it is also important to list the functionality that will not be tested in the cluster. This forces implicit assumptions to be made to form an explicit test plan. However, it should be indicated in which cluster the functionality concerned would be tested, or the reason why it will not be tested.

The following items are examples of information that can be recorded in the general cluster documentation:

- the number of batches to be run;
- the required number of computers;
- which user-IDs will be used during the test – this is especially important when several tests are to be executed simultaneously. If the same user-IDs are used in two different clusters and these tests are executed simultaneously, authorization problems could arise;
- which product ranges are used in the cluster – if a product is modified in one cluster and the same product is removed from another cluster, this could cause problems if the tests are executed simultaneously;
- the required time period for the automated execution of a test (for planning objectives).

If the names of the screens and files tested in the cluster have been documented, this can support the maintenance activities in the test set.

3.3   Scope

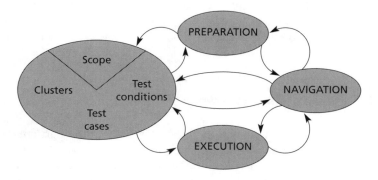

Defining scope consists of two parts. The first is the assessment of the current available documentation, such as functional designs, technical designs, and user manuals or course material – this is known as basic information assessment. The second part involves assessing the degree of coverage of the testing, with questions such as 'what will be tested?' and 'is the test set effective and efficient?' For more information on this particular subject see [Mari 95].

Characteristics such as completeness, timeliness, consistency, and legibility are considered during the assessment of the basic information. This is primarily the test team's task, but experts in the field, or managers and developers can also become involved.

For determining the depth of testing, it is very important that the number of test cases is systematically limited beforehand. This is necessary to prevent an individual tester from straying during the test process. If there are no guidelines, important items can be overlooked. Consultation with authorized senior staff can prevent this from occurring.

3.3.1 Determining the basic information

If complete and updated documentation is not available, it must be created. If it is not desirable or possible to create the documentation, other tools may provide the basic information. For example, an analysis of the system to be tested can be created based on information from experts in the field. However, this requires the experts' involvement in the test project. The required information can also be obtained from an analysis of an information system that is already being used in a production situation. In the TestFrame method, the lack of available documentation does not preclude analysis – a different approach needs to be taken.

3.3.2 Determining the test's depth of testing

The first step in determining the depth of testing is to specify the test areas. This means laying down the parts of the system that you want to test, such as functions, screens, modules, and batches. It is equally important to indicate what you do *not* want to test. This creates a full picture and will prevent areas from being overlooked. The specified test areas indicate what will be tested. For that reason, they are often used directly as a basis for formulating the clusters.

The second step in judging the degree of coverage is to determine thoroughness. The literature on this subject describes a systematic reduction of the number of test cases as 'coverage' – this is the coverage offered by the test set in relation to the number of options the system offers. Previously identified test areas, and the resulting clusters, usually constitute the basis. When the thoroughness has been determined, the aim is to assess the clusters in relation to other clusters. For example, a decision can be made to test areas that constitute part of a system's core functionality in greater depth than other parts. Such defined priorities determine whether a more systematic strategy or a more intuitive approach is chosen. It could be decided that certain areas will not be tested yet, or to assign them a lower priority to indicate that, although they have been identified, a conscious decision has been made not to further specify them. This prevents confusion about what will and what will not be tested. All the system parts to be implicitly tested are made explicit in this way.

Distinctions can also be made within specific aspects that will be tested, such as the layout, validation, or performance of a system. All this depends on the importance granted to a certain test area. Table 3.2 of the test determination for the 'Flying High' test object provides an example of how the thoroughness of a test can be described. The example consists of a template with a list that can be used to define the test's scope. In this example, the template is completed for a system test that primarily focuses on functionality. The template can be adjusted if the situation requires.

It is impossible to draw up a completely comprehensive test set since, theoretically speaking, the number of test conditions and test cases would be finite but very large. In practice, the aim is to limit the number of test conditions and test cases.

3.3.3   Example of defining the scope for a test object

This example of how to determine test thoroughness is based on the testing of the Flying High flight reservation system. This small Windows application is used by tour operators to make reservations for airline tickets. The application contains various input and overview screens, and data can be viewed in the screens.

In order to be able to test the Flying High system thoroughly and systematically, the features that will be tested, and those that will not, must be outlined clearly.

Table 3.2 Defining the scope of the Flying High system

AUTHORIZATION

	Aspect	Test?	Motivation
1.1	Assessment for each user group menu	No	Only one user group
1.2	Physically carry out the transaction for different user groups – check the authorization for each user group by carrying out transactions using one authorized and one unauthorized person	No	See 1.1
1.3	Testing authorization on screen level – some input fields can be used by the user A and not by user B	Yes	Authorization regarding requesting data
1.4	Assessment of authorization tables	No	See 1.1
1.5	Separately assess client and server side authorization	No	See 1.1

PERFORMANCE

	Aspect	Test?	Motivation
2.1	Response times	No	In this stage only system functionality is tested. Performance will be tested in another stage
2.2	Number of transactions per minute	No	See 2.1
2.3	Maximum system load	No	See 2.1
2.4	Impact on resources of critical applications	No	See 2.1
2.5	Stress test	No	See 2.1
2.6	Maximum concurrent users logged on to the system	No	See 2.1
2.7	Synchronization, duration batches	No	See 2.1

CRITICAL FAILURES

	Aspect	Test?	Motivation
3.1	Restart and recovery	No	In this stage of the test functionality will be tested – critical failures will be tested at a later stage
3.2	Cut off system's power supply	Yes	See 3.1
3.3	Recovery procedure – how does the system recover from a critical failure?	Yes	See 3.1

FUNCTIONALITY

	Aspect	Test?	Motivation
4.1	Ergonomy	No	Tested in user acceptance test
4.2	Tab order forwards and back	No	Tested in unit test
4.3	Range checks/value limits (1-100 for value limit on, under, over, far below and far above value limit)	No	See 4.2
4.4	Code values – how many valid values and invalid values are checked?	No	See 4.2

FUNCTIONALITY (*Continued*)

	Aspect	Test?	Motivation
4.5	Field type: integer, decimal, character, etc. – are correct input values accepted and are erroneous values rejected by the system?	Yes	Extensively tested in unit test – minimally a positive test will be executed for each field in system test
4.6	Field width	No	See 4.2
4.7	Precision of values, correct round off	Yes	For calculations – tested during program test
4.8	Fields enabled/disabled	Yes	Tested during unit test – only tested during system test in case of functional dependencies (in some cases disabled and others enabled)
4.9	Fields protected/unprotected	No	Not applicable
4.10	Bold, underlined, italic, blinking	No	Not applicable
4.11	Default values – situation depending on defaults?	Yes	Extensively tested during unit test – only tested during system test in case of functional dependencies
4.12	Correctness of fixed text on screens	No	See 4.1
4.13	Mandatory or optional, depending on situation	Yes	This is tested in the unit test – in the system test this will only be tested if a functional validation depends on it
4.14	Validation of date fields (special date validations)	Yes	See 4.5
4.15	Checks on overview screens	Yes	
4.16	Initial cursor position	No	See 4.1
4.17	Which fields have both input and output functionality and are both functions working?	Yes	(Included button for overriding values calculated by system)
4.18	Paging up and down on overview screens	No	Less impact on functionality
4.19	Correctness of menu structure – screen order	No	See 4.1
4.20	Operation of defined function keys	No	Not applicable

FUNCTIONALITY (*Continued*)

	Aspect	Test?	Motivation
4.21	Are the right help functions implemented and are the help functions implemented correctly (e.g. the beginning of help screen always displayed, help text dependent on screen from which the help function is called?)	No	See 4.1
4.22	Are the help functions tested in substance or only the 'links' to help screens?	No	See 4.1
4.23	Sorted order on overview screens	No	See 4.2, less impact on functionality
4.24	Time dependent validations (day/week dependable functionality)	No	Not applicable
4.25	Product dependable validations	Yes	
4.26	User dependable validations	No	Not applicable (only one user type)
4.27	Alternative data input methods (via different screens, keyboard, mouse)	Yes	(Input via different screens only)
4.28	Other input validations/dependencies	Yes	
4.29	Completeness (are all buttons and fields present?)	No	See 4.1
4.30	Place on screen (are objects placed in the correct position?)	No	See 4.1

GRAPHICAL USER INTERFACE

	Aspect	Test?	Motivation
5.1	Screen resizing	No	Less impact on functionality
5.2	Screen displacement	No	See 5.1
5.3	Maximize window	No	See 5.1
5.4	Minimize window	No	See 5.1
5.5	Maximum number of windows opened at the same time	No	See 5.1
5.6	Opening the same screen several times	No	See 5.1
5.7	All windows closed at once	No	See 5.1
5.8	Arranging windows	No	See 5.1

GRAPHICAL USER INTERFACE (*Continued*)

	Aspect	Test?	Motivation
5.9	Operation of defined accelerator keys	No	Must be assessed by the end users
5.10	Operation of defined shortcut keys	No	Not applicable
5.11	List boxes/combo boxes – are all applicable values in the list? is the list sorted correctly?	No	See 5.9
5.12	For radio buttons, but only one radio button can be selected per screen	No	Is tested in the unit test
5.13	Use of check boxes – the selection and deselecting of one ore more check boxes	No	See 5.12
5.14	Scroll function – from left to right on the horizontal scrollbar, from top to bottom on the vertical scrollbar	No	See 5.1

MESSAGES

	Aspect	Test?	Motivation
6.1	Control messages	No	Low priority
6.2	Control warnings – are you sure yes/no	No	Low priority
6.3	'No paths' of warnings. If no, do not process – is the change saved in the database?	No	Not applicable
6.4	Control of special messages (show network messages, printer messages, etc.)	No	The functionality of the application is tested, not the behavior of the application in a network
6.5	Operation of help functions within messages	No	Is tested in the unit test
6.6	'Please wait' messages	No	Not applicable

INTEGRATION

	Aspect	Test?	Motivation
7.1	Interfacing with other systems – output from a system is the input for another system (internal or external to the organization). How are the interfaces to be tested, e.g. testing correctness of output format only, testing by using the applications interface? (A sequence of interfaces is also possible)	No	Tested during production acceptance test
7.2	Integration of several subsystems within the application	No	See 7.1
7.3	Testing broadcasts (internal messages) transmitted to other systems	No	See 7.1
7.4	Testing broadcasts (internal messages) transmitted from one subsystem to other subsystems within the application	No	See 7.1
7.5	At the same time interfacing with other applications	No	Tested during unit test
7.6	Use of different media – printers, tape, optical disk, hard disk, floppy disk.	No	See 7.1
7.7	Dependencies with other systems – how does the application respond to other systems having failures or being down?	No	See 7.1

PROGRAM FLOW

	Aspect	Test?	Motivation
8.1	Check coverage of all program code	No	Tested during unit test
8.2	Check correct use of variables in program code	No	See 8.1
8.3	Check efficient use of program language	No	See 8.1
8.4	Correct processing per program	No	See 8.1
8.5	Correct output per program	No	See 8.1

DATA PROCESSING

	Aspect	Test?	Motivation
9.1	Change record (via screen)	Yes	
9.2	Delete record (via screen)	Yes	
9.3	Deletion of several records at once (via screen)	No	Not applicable
9.4	Deletion of all records at once (via screen)	Yes	See 9.3
9.5	Can other status transitions occur to one/several records	Yes	
9.6	Deletion of 'parent' record while 'child' record exists	No	Is a standard DBMS function
9.7	Creating 'child' record while 'parent' record is not yet created	No	See 9.6
9.8	Configuring double keys (e.g. registering several identical loan parts)	Yes	
9.9	Check in a table if the key is saved in the database for the record added	No	Tested during unit test
9.10	Check that all fields of a record are saved correctly in the database	No	See 9.9
9.11	If a record with a certain key is deleted, is it possible to create a record with that key? Are the right fields assigned to the key?	No	See 9.6
9.12	Locking mechanisms – two changes on one record	No	Tested during unit test
9.13	Concurrent use – multiple read requests for one record are allowed	No	See 9.12
9.14	Archiving of records (save duration of logical deleted records, clean up of records)	No	See 9.9
9.15	Time-outs – how does the application respond when the database cannot process data requests fast enough?	No	See 9.9

OTHER

	Aspect	Test?	Motivation
10.1	Correctness of calculations	Yes	
10.2	Control of output lists (on paper)	No	Tested during unit test
10.3	Control of batch processes	No	Not applicable
10.4	Synchronization of batches, duration of batches	No	See 10.3
10.5	Traceability via audit trail	No	See 10.3

3.4   Clusters

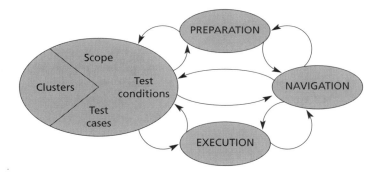

A structured test set must be capable of being divided into testable units – these are the clusters. During the Analysis phase, it is important to structure clusters in a logical way since the subdivision into clusters serves as a stepping stone for the test conditions and test cases. A clear division into clusters makes the test set more transparent, and easier to maintain. [Buwa 99] gives a concise overview of the cluster division. The clusters as defined in the test strategy are a starting point.

These clusters are, in principle, recorded in a single location such as a worksheet which is part of a workbook. The first sheet of the workbook contains general cluster information, drawn from the cluster card as described in Section 2.4. The second sheet contains the test conditions, which are defined on the basis of the cluster card specifications. The test conditions are then elaborated in one or more test cases – these are saved on the third sheet.

3.4.1   Division into clusters

The division into clusters should fit within the defined scope of the project. If certain parts of the system are not tested, there is no need to create a cluster for them. The fact that a particular cluster will not be tested must be recorded though, to state explicitly what will and will not be tested. A number of issues are important for the subdivision into clusters:

Test type

The test type to be executed has a significant effect on the cluster division. If a unit test is required, the division is often technical in nature. In such a division, a cluster may consist of the testing of a group of program modules, such as the effect of a sorting mechanism in an overview screen. For a system test the clusters are more likely to be divided according to functionality. An example is testing a number of different ways that data might be entered.

Independent clusters

It is important to set up clusters in such a way that they can be executed independently. Therefore, you should avoid relating clusters on the basis of content as much as possible – an error in the first cluster can lead to problems in the second because it failed to receive the correct input. Another advantage of cluster independence is that if there is no serial relationship they can be executed in parallel, reducing the time required to complete all of the test clusters. Clusters can be made independent by ensuring that they use different data. This implies that not all the clusters need to be executed by definition, but rather a selection can be made of the test parts that will actually be carried out for each test run.

Transparency of each system part

If insight into a certain system part is to be obtained as quickly as possible, this can be allowed for when the division into clusters is made. In the same way, the completion dates and the order of the system software should be taken into account. The divisions of the clusters will then be adjusted to the defined priorities and the completion schedule (i.e. the clusters for the main system parts, or those that need to be completed first, will be created first). When the test set needs maintenance, this division will have to be reassessed.

These issues are often addressed during the first set up of a cluster division in the test strategy. When a cluster defined in the test strategy is to be split into one or more clusters, the existing workbook is copied. This causes the information from the cluster card to be duplicated. Although most information will remain the same (e.g. stakeholder, test type, test department, etc.), some subjects will need modification:

- priority, which must be defined in more detail;
- timebox, where the time available for the original cluster must be divided among the newly defined clusters;
- specifications, since any subdivided clusters will need to be tested individually – check that all specifications are tested and divided among the clusters;
- acceptation criteria, which may be adjusted depending on the relative importance of the newly divided clusters, and any change in acceptance criteria;
- test approach, which may need to be adjusted to the more detailed specifications;
- test environment, which may need to be adjusted to the more detailed specifications and new approach.

All these considerations must result in a clear division into clusters that is comprehensible to everyone involved. It does not necessarily have to correspond with the layout of a detailed design, since the subdivision into clusters ideally parallels the business processes of the organization.

3.4.2 Recording clusters

A cluster should preferably be recorded with all the relevant information in one document, such as a workbook with several worksheets. Parts recorded in a cluster should include:

- general cluster information;
- test conditions;
- additional information (to help interpreting the content of the cluster);
- test cases.

Each part is identified by a header, indicating document type, version, cluster, author, etc. It is important for cluster files to be easily recognizable. Clusters should thus be given logical file names.

3.4.3 Cluster overview

A cluster overview provides a practical synopsis of all the identified clusters, with a brief description of what is tested in each cluster. This overview is then used as the entry screen to the entire cluster set.

Both the logical names of the clusters and the file names of the clusters should be documented in the overview. In addition, the general cluster content and the reasoning behind the cluster division should be listed. The latter increases the test's accessibility if clusters are added to the test set during maintenance, or if certain modifications need to be included in existing clusters. In line with the initial division, clusters are added or modified in the same way.

When all the test cases of a single cluster are specified in detail on several worksheets, the overview refers to them. Subsequently, specific test data can be included in the overview for each part. For example, the person responsible for drawing up the test cases and the status can be mentioned. Alternatively, the duration of the test execution, whether or not a start cluster is required, and whether or not a batch needs to be run may also be included.

The first column can indicate whether or not the cluster needs to be tested, since a cluster can be identified but not specified afterwards (see Section 3.3). In the overview, several documents, such as worksheets, may belong to a single cluster. If this is the case, the general cluster data in this overview (see Table 3.3) is not repeated in each specification of a document – only the first line mentions the data.

Table 3.3 Example test cluster overview

Test?	Cluster	Scope	Cluster Filename	Work-sheets	Worksheet description	Analyst	Status Maintenance Ready for review Tested Final
No	Product	This cluster relates to products	–	–	–	–	–
Yes	Basic applicant data	This cluster relates to basic data	BAS	BAS1	This worksheet tests basic data screens	RK	Maintenance
Yes	Mortgage	This cluster relates to mortgage data	BHY1	BHY1	This worksheet tests calculations	RK	Maintenance
Yes	–	–	BHY2	BHY2	This worksheet tests entry validations	RK	Final
Yes	Program data	This cluster relates to the program test of the FLIGHT system	FLY	FLY1	This worksheet tests screens and database tables	LD	Maintenance
Yes	–	–	–	FLY2	This worksheet relates to the testing and reviewing of program code	LD	Maintenance

3.5   Test conditions

The test conditions are drawn up before the test cases. Based on the list of test conditions, the adequacy of the coverage can be verified. The list of test conditions needs to be correct, complete, and within the scope determined.

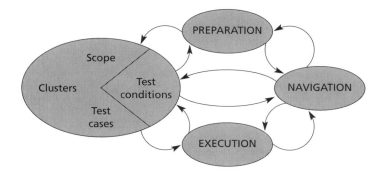

A list of test conditions is created for each cluster. A test condition is a concise statement indicating which demands are made on a particular aspect of a test object. Testing the condition proves whether the statement is correct. It is important to draw up a test condition with the appropriate rigor. [Buwa 99] discusses this issue in more detail.

For example, consider the condition 'only managers are allowed to access the strategic plans'. This indicates that non-managers are to be denied access, but that a distinction between managers within the group is not made. A test condition should be a concrete phrase – a phrase such as 'a manager is allowed to do more with the system than others' is far too vague to be useful. A test condition should always be as concise as possible, without losing any information.

The following rules can be applied to achieve this:

- include as many single test conditions as possible. This clarifies whether the feature to be tested in the test condition operates as expected. When several features are named in a test condition, it is more difficult to trace the reason for a particular finding;
- formulate test conditions in positive terms;
- do not include any complementary test conditions since they are redundant and create an unnecessarily large number of test conditions.

3.5.1 Creating the right test conditions

The test conditions are described on the second worksheet of the cluster, and are defined on the basis of the specifications (business requirements) described in the cluster card. Every test condition is a specific elaboration of a part of the specification. The test conditions are defined in accordance with, and with approval of, the stakeholder. The stakeholder also defines the priority of the test condition and the risk taken when a condition is not tested. This makes it easier to prioritize the test afterwards.

In order to create the appropriate test conditions, they should be drawn up by someone with both functional knowledge, and the ability to formulate logically. Ideally, experts in the field, as well as system documentation, should be consulted to obtain sufficient information on how the system should operate. Depending on the project situation, some projects can use the input of experts in the field, whereas for others the system documentation can serve as basic information.

Test techniques (see Section 3.7) can be used to draw up test conditions in a systematic way. This applies to situations in which documentation is available, as well as those where no usable documentation is available. However, test techniques are not used by default, only in situations where they can add value. The drawing up of a decision table to create test conditions for a function with only two decision moments requires a higher investment (in terms of time and money) than it yields (additional certainty with regard to the correct degree of coverage).

3.5.2 Recording test conditions

The test conditions, and underlying test cases (as discussed in Section 3.6), should be documented in a spreadsheet. This makes it possible to cross check the test conditions and test cases in a single workbook. However, the test conditions can also be documented in other ways, for example in a database or a word processor, provided that transparency and accessibility are guaranteed.

Each test condition is given a unique number. The number takes the form XXXNCn as described in Table 3.4.

Table 3.4 The unique number of a test condition

XXX	Cluster identification
N	The document number (e.g. of a worksheet in a spreadsheet) in which the related test cases are described. (When there are many test conditions, it is possible to document test cases belonging to one cluster on several worksheets – this must be documented with the test conditions)
Cn	Numbering of test conditions

Beside this number it is indicated whether or not the test condition is actually tested – because of the option of drawing up all the test conditions within the scope of the cluster, but then not testing some of them due to, for example, a relatively low priority. This indicates that test conditions have not been overlooked, but that a conscious decision has been made not to test some of them.

One way of defining the priority of test conditions is to question, per test condition, what the impact is of not testing it. Priorities should be defined on the basis of the so-called 'must have', 'should have', 'could have', and 'nice to have' requirements.

The following example, for the Flying High system, shows how the test conditions can be drawn up. In order to illustrate the differences between the test conditions for a unit test and a system test (which focuses mainly on functionality) test conditions have been specified in more detail for both types. In Section 3.3, the potential thoroughness of the Flying High system was elaborated. The following example is based on that material.

3.5.3 Example of test conditions for a test object

The following is a brief description of the functionality of the Flying High system. The aim of this description is to get a general idea of the way the system operates.

'Flying High' is a reservation system which operators use to book flights for particular dates. This Windows application displays various input and overview windows. The main window is the flight reservation screen (see Figure 3.2). The operator can enter new flight reservations, query existing reservations, modify, and remove them in this window. The operator can also enter the desired departure date, place of departure, and destination for a new reservation. When this data has been entered, a selection can be made from the available flights. Once the correct number of tickets has been specified, the application calculates the total amount of the order based on the ticket price. The operator can query the detailed data of the reservations made on an overview screen.

Table 3.5 shows the test conditions of the system test.

Table 3.5 Test conditions system test

Document	Test conditions: Test cluster FLY1 (flight reservation system, system test)
Version	1.0
Date	12-01-2001
Author	Tester

FLY1

Test?	Test conditions	Test condition description
Y	FLY1C1	A reservation can be created
Y	FLY1C2	An existing reservation can be changed
Y	FLY1C3	An existing reservation can be removed
Y	FLY1C4	An existing reservation can be opened
Y	FLY1C5	The place of departure must not be shown as an option in the destination list
Y	FLY1C6	The flight list should only display flights on the entered departure date, place and destination
Y	FLY1C7	The ticket price is determined by the selected flight
Y	FLY1C8	The list of available flights is determined by the selected departure date, place and destination
Y	FLY1C9	The total amount is the number of tickets multiplied by the ticket price
Y	FLY1C10	An operator can only query his own reservations in the reservation detail screen
Y	FLY1C11	The flight reservation overview should display the departure time, arrival time and airline – in addition, the total number of reservations, tickets, and the total amount should be displayed

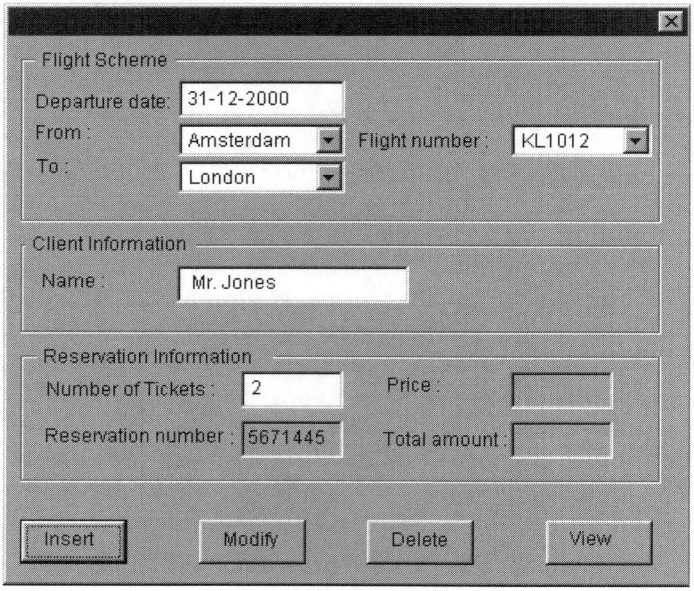

Figure 3.2 Flight reservation system entry screen

The system's test conditions can be derived from the operation of the Flying High system described above.

Test conditions FLY1C1 to FLY1C4 are related to database actions. Test conditions FLY1C5 to FLY1C8 concern the testing of the mutual relations between the fields. The single field validations that apply to the flight reservation system are not tested here since they will be dealt with in the unit test.

Test condition FLY1C9 is the test of the only calculation executed in the window. Test condition FLY1C10 concerns the completion of the authorization. Test condition FLY1C11 tests the list functionality. No test condition has been included to test the error messages for erroneous input. This is because such messages are assigned low priority – there would be a very small impact on the business process if this functionality does not operate correctly.

Based on the operation of the Flying High system described above, and the screen displayed, the test conditions for a unit test are derived as shown in Table 3.6.

As stated above, the test conditions for a unit test are somewhat different from those created for a system test. For example, test condition FLY2C6 requires examination of the database itself, which is not required for a purely functional test. In this unit test, the field types (test conditions FLY2C1 to FLY2C4) are also verified. There are similarities between the unit test and the system test, and this overlap means that some features may be checked twice.

Table 3.6 Test conditions unit test

Document	Test conditions: Test cluster FLY (flight reservation system, unit test)
Version	1.0
Date	12-01-2001
Author	Tester

FLY1	Screens and database test

Test?	Test conditions	Test condition description
Y	FLY1C1	No other destination except the destinations displayed in the relevant list box can be entered
Y	FLY1C2	No other place of departure than the places of departure displayed in the relevant list box may be entered
Y	FLY1C3	The 'tickets' field is a numerical field $\{0 < x < 100\}$

FLY2	Screens and database test	
Y	FLY2C4	When a reservation is entered, it must be correctly included in the database
Y	FLY2C5	When an existing reservation is removed, it has to be logically removed from the database (marked by 'd')
Y	FLY2C6	When an existing reservation is modified, the changed data has to be included in the database
Y	FLY2C7	Only the logically existing reservations in the database should be displayed in query functions
Y	FLY2C8	The flight date, place of departure, flight number, and name are mandatory fields
Y	FLY2C9	The flight list only displays flights that correspond to the entered departure date, place and destination
Y	FLY2C10	No other flight number can be entered other than those displayed in the relevant list box
Y	FLY2C11	When a flight has been entered, the accompanying data must be displayed in the flight reservation overview
Y	FLY2C12	The destination list must not display the place of departure
Y	FLY2C13	The ticket price is determined by the selected flight
Y	FLY2C14	The total amount is the number of tickets multiplied by the ticket price

Table 3.6 Continued

Test?	Test conditions	Test condition description
Y	FLY2C15	The fields in the flight reservation overview are execution fields and cannot be modified
Y	FLY2C16	The buttons in the flight reservation screen should accept shortcut keys
Y	FLY2C17	The tab order on the screen is from top left to bottom right
Y	FLY2C18	The place of departure and destination fields contain the first available value in the list
Y	FLY2C19	The departure date field contains the system date
Y	FLY2C20	The overview list is arranged in closing order of the reservation

3.5.4 Another way of drawing up test conditions

Test conditions are drawn up to clarify what the system is supposed to do in certain situations. In the execution of certain tests, it is often difficult to describe them by means of test conditions. For example, when testing calculations, calculation of the correct result using different combinations of parameter settings should be used. However, it is not necessary to write out fully every combination of parameters to be tested in the shape of test conditions. Another form is recording the parameter combinations to be tested (a variation on the decision tables) but without the specified actions.

For example, input screens are not used in a system that calculates pensions to be paid for clients. The system uses the client data that has been recorded previously using a client registration system. It is important that the pension calculation is verified for several clients with different profiles, since several parameters affect the calculation. For instance, the age at which a person wants to retire is of crucial importance for the calculation. In addition, other rules may apply if an individual works part-time, or if they have several jobs, or if they are partly retired.

In this system, the various schemes cannot be tested independently of one another. When you execute a system test, a client must be selected from the database. Each client's status is recorded (i.e. whether or not the client is working part-time, when they were born, etc.). Thus, it is always a combination of various schemes that is tested, even though a combination of schemes does not lead to an essentially different calculation. Thus, testing all the possibilities of each scheme usually suffices, and it is irrelevant which values from another scheme are used. In this way, the number of test cases required is equal to the scheme with the largest number of options. If the various combinations had been important, they could have been detailed according to the decision table method. This test technique will be described in more detail in Section 3.7.

In Table 3.7 the various options of the schemes that influence the pension calculation have been set out and compared with the test conditions to be tested. This layout creates a clear overview of which situations will be tested.

Table 3.7 Test conditions for pension calculations

Document	Overview					
Cluster	Pension calculations					
Version	1.0					
Date	12-01-2001					
Author	Tester	Test case no.				
Chapter from detailed design		PEN1C1	PEN1C2	PEN1C3	PEN1C4	PEN1C5
	Retiring date of person entitled to a pension					
C2.3.2	Insured retires at age >= 55 and age < 61	Y				
C2.3.1	Insured retires at age 61		Y			
C2.3.3	Insured retires at age > 61 and age <= 63			Y		
C2.3.4	Insured retires at age > 63 and age <= 64				Y	
C2.3.5	Insured retires at age > 64 and age < 65					Y
	Retirements					
C2.3	First retirement	Y		Y		Y
C2.3	Subsequent retirements		Y		Y	
	Work relations					
C3.1	One work relation	Y	Y			Y
C3.2	Several parallel work relations			Y	Y	
	Influence part-time factor					
C4.3	Part-time factor 1	Y	Y		Y	
C4.4	Part-time factor <> 1			Y		Y
	Retirement factor					
C 4.5	Retirement percentage 100%	Y	Y		Y	Y
C 4.6	Retirement percentage >=10% and <100%			Y		

3.6   Test cases

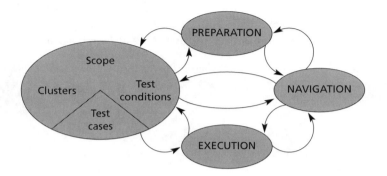

Drawing up the test cases involves detailing the test set. Each test condition can be further specified into one or more test cases, which instantiates a specific test condition. The test cases are described in such a way that they are easily comprehensible to the person who maintains the test set. The method for creating test cases described here makes the test cases appropriate for both manual and automated execution.

The main goal of the test strategy is to make optimal use of test capacity, in which the priorities of test conditions play a major role. Starting with the most urgent test conditions ensures that the most important risks are covered by the test.

Each test case consists of various actions that must be undertaken in the test, such as entering a client, or verifying their availability. Each action should be described in a single line on a spreadsheet. An action word is included at the start of the line indicating which action should be performed. In the remaining columns, the arguments required for the action are recorded, such as the name and address data of the client to be entered, or the number of the client to be queried.

When the test cases are drawn up, the syntax of the action words must be agreed on first. When two testers both want to use an action word in different clusters for logging onto an application, it is useful for them to use the same action word with the same arguments. This supports the reusability of the action words – if the login process in an application changes, only one action word needs to be changed.

This syntax of the action words (name of the action word plus arguments) is recorded in the action word documentation. When creating the action words for the test cases, a check should be done to determine whether the required action words have already been defined. New action words must also be added to any existing documentation.

3.6.1   Naming action words

An action word is a combination of actions, defined by the test analyst in consultation with the navigator, indicating how the test is to be executed. If the test is automated, the action words serve as input for the navigator, who programs them in navigation scripts (see Chapter 4).

If a series of actions is always executed together in a test, it is wise to group them together as a single action word. For example, when entering a client the following series of basic actions could be executed:

- select screen ABC;
- open window X12;
- press tab;
- enter 'name' field;
- open 'gender' list box;
- select from list;
- press tab;
- press 'OK' button;
- close screen ABC;
- return to main menu.

If each of these actions was defined individually, the test would be too difficult to read and the spreadsheet would be very long. In addition, each action would have to be entered individually in all the relevant test cases. Thus, it is more appropriate to group these actions together under a single action word, such as 'client entry', which defines all of the actions. Grouping also makes it easier to maintain test cases since only the definition of the action word needs to be adjusted (i.e. maintenance in a single location).

For example, in order to execute ten test cases that relate to the entry of an account, the same actions are performed – only the specified entry data is different. We can compare the differences between naming each action individually (Example A) and grouping related actions together (Example B). In Example A the actions are written out individually for each test case – 'open screen A', 'enter account number field', and 'press the OK button'. In Example B the action word 'enter account' is used in all the test cases, and this encapsulates the three actions ('open screen A', 'enter account number field', and 'press the OK button'). These definitions are then recorded centrally on the spreadsheet.

As a result of a modification request, the system is changed in such a way that after pressing the OK button, a newly introduced 'approval button' must be pressed in order to complete the operation. In Example A this means that the action 'press the approval button' must be added to each of the ten specified test cases, opening the possibility that one or more test cases may be overlooked. In Example B this adjustment is executed only once and in one location, namely the spreadsheet where the definition of the action words is recorded. Example B also reduces the data entry workload by a factor of ten.

Similarly, a series of actions that must be executed to start a batch job can also be included in a single action word. The actions of logging in as a system administrator, copying files, typing other commands after a prompt, and waiting until the job has been completed can all be encapsulated in a single action word.

Since the target group must be able to read the test set clearly, it is important that the action word indicates what must be executed in a comprehensible manner. In a function-oriented test, the action words usually represent business actions, whereas in a unit test the action words are more technical in nature.

A division of different types of action words is given in Table 3.8.

Table 3.8 Action word types

Action word type	Description
Low level action words	These action words are application independent and refer to the application's interface
High level action words	These action words are application dependent and relate to the application's functionality – a high level action word consists of various low level action words
Directive action words	These action words are application independent and are required for test control and documentation

Here are some examples of low level action words that can be used for a unit test:

- press tab;
- open window;
- press key;
- open file.

Examples of high level action words for function-oriented tests are:

- entry order;
- modify client;
- remove supplier;
- check product;
- start batch;
- login.

Examples of directive action words required to control and document the test are:

- start test case;
- author;
- document;
- date.

In addition to self-explanatory names for action words, the naming system should also be consistent – this maximizes their potential reusability and utility. For example, it is common practice to formulate action words as active, imperative, or singular. In addition, the language in which action words are formulated should be agreed upon, particularly for large projects involving a multinational (and potentially multilingual) development team. When an action word such as 'client entry' has been defined, it would be more appropriate to use 'product entry' than 'query product', 'entry of products' or 'enter product'.

In general, an action word relates to a single screen or file. However, it is crucial that action words are formulated in terms of business functionality. This may also cover part of a screen, or two or three screens. In a new version of a system, the screen layout is often modified, or screens are added or removed, but the basis of business functionality is modified less frequently. Action words defined on the basis of business functionality ultimately require less maintenance.

3.6.2 Naming arguments for action words

In addition to the action word itself, various arguments may also be registered in the test case spreadsheet. Their names are recorded using a header above the arguments. Table 3.9 shows an example of the arguments relating to the action words 'client entry' and 'check product'. The table also shows an example of its content.

Table 3.9 Test case arguments

	Family name	First name	Street	ZIP code	Place
Client entry	Jones	Elizabeth	12867 La Jolla Blvd	95472	Sebastopol

	Product no.	Product description	Color	Type	Weight
Check product	P124	Perforator	Red	PER43	900

The arguments allocated to an action word are the parts that are relevant for the test. They can be the fields on a screen, but also fields in a database, or on a list. If it is not important to test a particular field on a screen with the action word concerned, it will not be included as an argument.

The action word 'client entry' from the example above may be used for various test cases. For example, it could be used to test entry validation in the 'family name' field, as well as entry validation in the 'zipcode' field. When the 'family name' field is tested, the fields 'first name', 'street', 'zipcode' and 'place' are perhaps redundant. However, these fields are included in the action word 'client entry' since they are all entered once when the functionality is tested. In this way, an action word can be reused in various test cases.

The names of the arguments are usually identical to the names of the fields on the screen, or in the files, which makes the action word easier to understand. However, this is not, by definition, a fixed relationship. When field names change in a new version of the system, and it has been decided to use the names of screens consistently in the test set, this can result in an increased number of tasks required for testing. In such cases, it may be better to develop logical names for the arguments that will not require constant adjustment in every new version of the application.

When test cases are designed using action words and arguments, complicated situations can arise. Some of these situations and their proposed solutions are described briefly below.

Double field names on the screen

If the field with the name, address, and place of residence is displayed twice on the screen (such as a home address and a postal address) the argument names can be prefixed, as shown in Table 3.10.

Table 3.10 Double field names in a screen

	Supplier code	p_address	P_place	b_address	b_place
Supplier entry	L13121	20 Morris St	Foster City	25 College Rd	Carmel

Check box on windows screen, or yes/no option on an emulator screen

If a check box is displayed on the screen, its name must be included as the argument name to be able to identify the appropriate check box. This argument can then be further specified by the value selected from the check box, such as 'Y' or 'N'. In the example shown below, the name of the check box is 'additional insurance' – not taking out additional insurance is chosen ('N') as shown in Table 3.11.

Table 3.11 Use check box or select yes/no

	Name	Insurance type	Additional insurance
Insurance entry	Smith	VZO	N

Radio button on windows screen, or selecting from a number of options on an emulator screen

When a selection can be made from a number of options, the name of the argument will be the name of the class group. For example in 'print range', the selections 'all', 'current page', 'pages' or 'selection' are available, so the name of the group will be 'print range'. The selected option is then filled in as an argument. See Table 3.12. An alternative is to add each option as an argument name and then to fill in 'Y' or 'N' for each argument. However, this is a less efficient method since radio buttons only allow one of several alternatives to be selected making all other arguments redundant.

Table 3.12 Radio button use

	Print range	Number of copies	Printer name
Print document	Current page	2	HP LaserJet 4 plus

3.6.3 Documenting the action words

It is important that navigators and analysts are both informed of the defined action words and their meanings. For example, the navigator needs to know what should be programmed whilst the analyst must know how to use the action words in the clusters. Confusion can arise if the operation of the action words has not been documented correctly. For example, whether or not a screen is open at the start of an action word, whether or not to close a screen at the end of an action word, or which argument(s) should be used as the key(s) can all create ambiguity if they are not defined by their respective action words.

Once the syntax of an action word (its name and arguments) has been determined, it needs to be laid down in the action words documentation. This documentation is usually created in a spreadsheet. Various components must be maintained for each action word. Firstly, the spelling and order of the arguments must be maintained to ensure that the same syntax is used consistently. Secondly, the action words documentation must describe the action word method adequately. Thus, the action word's initial conditions (i.e. on which screen or in which situation should the system be before the action word can be executed), its basic actions, and its required state after execution should all be defined.

In addition to the items mentioned above, the name of the analyst who designed the action word must be recorded so that later users or maintainers can ask the designer to clarify any ambiguity in the definition of the action word. The current status of the action word should also be recorded – for example, has it only been devised on paper, or has it already been programmed (if an automated test is required)?

3.6.4 Example of action word documentation for a test object

Below is an example of the action words documentation for the Flying High application in spreadsheet form. The data has been recorded on two different sheets – the first worksheet contains the action words with their arguments; the second lists all other data for each action word.

In Table 3.13, the action words worksheet documentation shows the action words and their arguments. It also includes a category column to allow sorting the action words in the spreadsheet.

When action words are modified during maintenance, the documentation also needs to be updated. When a new argument has to be added to an action word, this does not automatically mean that the action word's arguments have to be relocated. The new argument could be put at the end of the existing arguments, for example. In the automated execution of the test cases, the arguments are sorted in the appropriate way in the navigation script, so that the arguments are put in the correct places on the screen.

The example in Table 3.14 gives a textual description of the operation of the action words. Although the person creating the documentation has a certain amount of freedom in describing the action word, it is also possible to formalize the action word description to improve clarity. The action word documentation would then resemble that shown in Table 3.15.

Table 3.13 Action word documentation

Document	Action words documentation – arguments									
Version	1.3.0									
Date	01-19-01									
Author	Tester									

Category	Action word	Argument1	Argument2	Argument3	Argument4	Argument5	Argument6	Argument7	Argument8	Argument9
General	Login	User name	Password							
Flight	Flight reservation entry	Reservation number	Departure date	Place of departure	Destination	Flight number	Name	Number of tickets		
Flight	Modify flight reservation	Reservation number	Departure date	Place of departure	Destination	Flight number	Name	Number of tickets		
Flight	Check flight data	Reservation number	Departure date	Place of departure	Destination	Flight number	Name	Number of tickets	Ticket price	Total amount
Flight	Flight entry	Flight number	Departure time	Arrival time	Ticket price					

Table 3.14 Action word documentation; action words description

Document	Action words documentation
	Action words description
Version	1.3.0
Date	01-19-01
Author	Tester

Action word	Analyst	Creation date	Status	Screen(s)	Clusters	Initial situation	Situation after action word execution	Comments
Login	RK	12-26-01	Concept	Login	FLY	Application started up, not yet logged in	User logged in	
Flight reservation entry	LD	12-26-01	Tested	Flight reservation	FLY	Main menu	Values entered, approve transaction using 'insert reservation' button; screen remains open	
Modify flight reservation	LD	12-30-01	Concept	Flight reservation	FLY	Flight reservation screen	Flight reservation screen is open, data has been modified	First search reservation in 'flight reservation overview' screen; then modify specified values; reservation number is key
Check flight reservation	LD	12-30-01	Concept	Flight reservation	FLY	Flight reservation screen	Flight reservation screen is open, data has been checked	First search reservation in 'flight reservation overview' screen; then check values; reservation number is key
Flight entry	LD	12-30-01	Concept	Flight	FLY	Main menu	Flight data processed; screen remains open	

Table 3.15 Action words template

Action words template					
Action word	Open file in Notepad				
Interface					
	File name	*File types*	*Directory*	*Stations*	
Open file in Notepad	File name	File types	Directory	Stations	
Design					
Action	Window				
Select menu item	Unnamed Notepad	File	Open		
Field entry	Open	File name	File types	Directory	Stations
Press button	Open	Open			

The subject 'Interface' is followed by the arguments that have been defined for an action word, and how the actual field names will appear on the screen. In the 'Design' section, the basic mechanisms of the action word are composed and recorded in predefined steps.

The action words documentation that creates templates using these action words is rather elaborate, and may seem over the top for simple action words. However, there is little room for ambiguity and this is essential for large projects, particularly if the designers of action words are not available for future consultation. The suitability of chosen documentation methods should be considered for each project, as should the requirement for additional information for each action word. The need for elaborate documentation increases exponentially with the number of people involved with the test.

The examples mentioned above are recorded in spreadsheet form. However, it is also possible to lay down documentation about action words in a manner consistent with local requirements.

3.6.5 Recording test cases

The test cases should preferably be recorded on a spreadsheet. If there is a large number of test conditions, the test cases of one cluster can be split into several worksheets. Each test case worksheet is given a name of the form 'Test cases XXXN', where XXX is the cluster identification, and N is the sheet number on which related test cases are to be documented.

For example, names given to worksheets containing the test cases for the cluster FLY might include FLY1 and FLY2. Alternatively, cluster PRO might have the test cases PRO1 and PRO2.

Test cases are always assigned a unique number. If several test cases are drawn up for each test condition, this should be indicated by a test condition number ('Ci') followed by a test case number ('Tj'), giving the form XXXNCiTj for the worksheet name. For example, the test condition FLY1C1 may have two test cases FLY1C1T1 and FLY1C1T2, whilst the test condition FLY1C2 might have three test cases FLY1C2T1, FLY1C2T2 and FLY1C2T3.

3.6.6 Example of test cases for a test object

Table 3.16 shows a partial example of a test sheet with test cases. It is a further specification of the test conditions for the Flying High systems test, which were drawn up in Section 3.5.

Table 3.16 Test cases for 'Flying High'

Document	Test cases Cluster							
	(Flight reservation system)							
Version	1.0							
Date	12-01-01							
Author	Tester							

	User name	Password						
Logon	Marvin	Football						

Test case	FLY1C1T1	Entering a new reservation must be possible						
	Reservation number	Departure date	From	Destination	Flight number	Name	Number of tickets	Ticket price
Flight reservation entry		12-01-01	Orlando	Salt Lake City	XY1322	Albany	2	
Check flight reservation	412	12-01-01	Orlando	Salt Lake City	XY1322	Albany	2	250

Test case	FLY1C2T1	Modifying an existing reservation must be possible						
	Reservation number	Departure date	From	Destination	Flight number	Name	Number of tickets	Ticket price
Flight reservation entry		12-14-01	Ft Lauderdale	New York	XY14333	Tucson	1	
Modify flight reservation	413						2	
Check flight reservation	413	12-14-01	Ft Lauderdale	New York	XY14333	Tucson	2	735

3.6.7   Drawing up test cases

Test cases consist of an input specification and an output prediction. For a relatively simple test case, two test lines are included in the spreadsheet – an input specification (such as the entry, modification, or removal of data), and an output check. For a complex test case as many as forty test lines with actions may be necessary. Sometimes data has to be searched for and further search actions carried out with the established values, before detailed data is entered. Thus, test cases can vary widely in their complexity.

To create test cases, the syntax of the required action words is copied from the action words documentation. Subsequently, the test analyst completes the arguments required for the test. For example, if an entry validation needs to be executed it could be like the one shown in Table 3.17.

Table 3.17 Example of a test case

Start test case	FLY1C2T1	The departure date must be higher than or identical to the system date					
	Reservation no.	Departure date	From	Destination	Flight number	Name	Number of tickets
Flight reservation entry		12-01-01					
	Message						
Check message	Invalid value, <departure date> field cannot be in the past						

The test case in this table is the specification of the test condition 'The departure date has to be greater than or equal to the system date'. To test this case properly, an incorrect value must be entered in the departure date field. Firstly, the run date of the test must be established to be able to predict what constitutes an incorrect value. Once the run date has been established, the value 'hard' can be recorded in the spreadsheet. If the run date has not been determined a priori, the date in the spreadsheet must be made relative, which ultimately eases the spreadsheet's maintenance.

In this example only the departure date has been entered. The system to be tested validates the integrity of entries for each field, which makes entering other values redundant. Some systems only validate entry data after all the fields have been entered, and after pressing the OK button or Enter. In this case, it is essential to enter all the other arguments with valid values, otherwise the cause of a possible deviation could not be established clearly.

A number of examples for drawing up test cases are listed below.

Not filling in all the arguments

It is not always necessary to fill in every argument that belongs to an action word. In an entry action, the arguments with a default value on the screen could, for instance, be omitted or could be made optional. In this way, what is being tested is whether the application has used the correct default values. In addition, it is better to specify only the relevant arguments for a particular test case as this supports transparency in the test cases.

In the example in Table 3.18 only a single reservation (number 645) is searched for in the first test line. No checks are performed on any of the record's other values, and only the availability of the record is verified. In the second test line, the name is specified along with the reservation number. When the test is executed the record will be searched first, after which the name recorded with the reservation is validated. The other values have not been specified and are, apparently, not relevant to the test.

Table 3.18 Not entering all the arguments of an action word

	Reservation number	Departure date	Place of departure	Destination	Flight number	Name	Number of tickets	Ticket price	Total amount
Check flight reservation	645								
Check flight reservation	892					Jones			

In this example, the irrelevant arguments are blank. A fixed value, such as the symbol '-', can be allocated to these fields as an argument which is irrelevant to this test. Using a marker in this way indicates that the field has not been overlooked, and a conscious decision has been made to exclude it.

Calculations

In the following example (see Table 3.19) a calculation is verified. The total amount needs to be equal to the ticket price, multiplied by the number of tickets.

In this example a new flight is entered in the first test line, for which a reservation is made on the second test line. Besides a number of mandatory fields, the key data for this test is entered in the reservation line. In this case the flight number decides the ticket price in conjunction with the number of tickets. The result of the calculation is predicted on the third test line.

Table 3.19 Recording a calculation in a test case

Start test case	FLY1C9T1	The total amount is the number of tickets multiplied by the ticket price						
	Flight number	**Departure time**	**Arrival time**	**Ticket price**				
Flight entry	XY1000	0615	1720	2005				
	Reservation number	**Departure date**	**Departure**	**Destination**	**Flight number**	**Name**	**Number of tickets**	
Flight reservation entry		12-01-01	Boston	Orlando	XY1999	Eastwood	2	

	Reservation number	**Departure date**	**Departure**	**Destination**	**Flight number**	**Name**	**Number of tickets**	**Ticket price**	**Total amount**
Check flight data	751						2	2005	4010

Removing data

In addition to testing whether particular records have been created, or data has been modified correctly, the non-existence of a record often needs to be verified. For example, if an operation to remove a record is executed, the actual deletion needs to be verified. One strategy is to use a 'check no' action word, as shown in Table 3.20.

Table 3.20 Recording the check if data is removed

	Reservation no.	**Departure date**	**From**	**Destination**	**Flight number**	**Name**	**Number of tickets**
Remove flight reservation	899						
Check no flight reservation	899						

After a flight reservation is removed, as shown in the first line, the second test line checks whether the flight reservation is no longer present. If the record is found, the test report will report an error.

Prolonged processes

System processes that take a long time to complete must also be taken into account. If such processes have been identified, they should be used sparingly. For example, a link between various purchasing and sales orders by means of a transaction will be tested. However, there are a number of different potential solutions. Two of these are shown in Table 3.21.

Table 3.21 Alternative ways of laying out tests for prolonged processes

Solution A		Solution B	
Login	User John	Login	User John
Order entry	1x	Order entry	1x
Logout		Order entry	2x
Login	User Gina	Order entry	3x
Order entry	1y	Logout	
Check transaction	1	Login	User Gina
Logout		Order entry	1y
Login	User John	Order entry	2y
Order entry	2x	Order entry	3y
Logout		Check transaction	1
Login	User Gina	Check transaction	2
Order entry	2y	Check transaction	3
Check transaction	2	Logout	
Logout			
Login	User John		
Order entry	3x		
Logout			
Login	User Gina		
Order entry	3y		
Check transaction	3		
Logout			

In Solution A user John logs in. He executes an order and subsequently logs out again. Then, user Gina logs in, enters her order, checks the transaction, and then logs out. This process is repeated three times.

In Solution B user John logs in, executes three orders, and logs out again. Then user Gina logs in, executes three orders, checks three transactions, and logs out again.

Suppose the login process takes a rather long time. In Solution A logging in happens six times in total, whereas in Solution B it only happens twice thereby taking much less time to execute. Solution B is the most efficient solution in this case. The method of entering a number of entry specifications, followed by a series of execution checks, is often used to test batch job functionality. Running a batch job generally takes a relatively long time and should therefore be used sparingly. However, at the same time, the transparency of the test cases must not be overlooked.

It is often convenient to keep the input specification and the output prediction close together. In this way, if the input specification of the test cases is modified by maintenance, the affected output prediction can be traced. It is sometimes difficult to find such a link in input series, followed by a batch and execution series. These issues must be clarified by means of additional documentation, or by clear test case numbering.

Number of test cases per worksheet

Worksheets containing the test cases should not be excessively long. If there are more than 500 lines, specifying them on several worksheets must be considered – long sheets lead to lack of clarity and boredom for the reader.

Alternatively, there can be a temptation to skimp on test cases, and this must be avoided for completeness. A report is generated for each worksheet and, if there is a large number of worksheets with few test cases, a large number of reports is created making it even more difficult to analyze the test results. A benchmark figure of 150 lines per worksheet is commonly used in industry.

Testing using test scenarios

If the aim of the test is to simulate a user's actions as closely as possible, normally only positive tests are executed. A scenario follows a client through the system. In this case, it can be very beneficial to make test cases interdependent. In this test type, many different test conditions are combined into a 'soap opera' of events. One test condition can also recur in several soaps, although this requires a separate administration within the test documentation.

Table 3.22 shows an example of part of a scenario test, which registers a number of actions central to calculating a pension. Various test conditions can be used for this registration, three of which are mentioned here.

Table 3.22 Example of a scenario test

Test condition no.	Test condition	Soap 1	Soap 2
PSS1C1	It must be possible to register a participant's children	Y	Y
PSS1C2	It must be possible to register a participant's spouse	Y	N
PSS1C3	It must be possible to register a participant's divorce	Y	N

Two 'soaps' are involved here. In Soap 1 the record of a participant with children who experiences a divorce is tested, whilst Soap 2 concerns an unmarried participant with children. The example given in Table 3.23 shows how test cases are specified for Soap 1. Since almost every test line concerns a different test condition, the numbers of the test conditions are not registered in each individual test line. Otherwise, half the sheet of test cases would consist of test condition numbers making it difficult to read. All affected test conditions are registered at the top of each soap. In addition, the test conditions state which conditions are tested in each soap, enabling test cases to be traced when they are maintained. To clarify the course of events in a soap, comments may be inserted between the test lines where necessary.

Table 3.23 Example of 'soaps'

Cluster	Screening participant's life						
Version	**1.0**						
Date	**1-07-01 0:00**						
Author	**Tester**						

Section	Starting the application						
Restore database Start application							
Scenario	1	Divorced participant with children					
Test conditions	PSS1C1	PSS1C1	PSS1C1				

Section	**Entry primary registration employers**						
	Company name Standard mandatory	*Reason*	*Sector*	*Steet name*	*House number*	*Place*	*Employer no*
Display employer	Employer 1	adm	ME	Indiablv	10	Harlem	12421
	Employer no.	*Employed*	*Group wzh*				
Display activities	12421	01011950	1				

Section	**Entry primary registration participants and employment**								
	Personal reference number	*Employer no.*	*Name*	*Initials*	*Gender*	*DOB*	*Street*	*House no.*	*Place*
Display person	1223	12421	Jones	BA	M	04-03-1950	Schoolrd	3	San Jose
	Hours	*Occupation*	*Number*	*Sort*	*Amount*	*Work council*			
Display employment	38	004	1	S	3100	N			

Section	**Display participants' relations**						
	Display spouse						
	Pers. reference	*Name*	*Initials*	*DOB*	*Gender*	*D (divorced)*	*Type*
Maintain relations	1223	Spouse a	exa	12-12-50	2	n	1
	Display child						
	Pers. reference	*Name*	*Initials*	*DOB*	*Gender*	*D (divorced)*	*Type*
Maintain relations	1223	Anna	exa	22-08-77	1	n	4
Maintain relations	1223	Yvar	exa	30-12-79	2	n	4
	Display divorce						
	Pers. reference	*Name*	*Initials*	*DOB*	*Gender*	*D (divorced)*	*Type*
Maintain relations	1223	Spouse a	exa	19-03-51	2	n	1

Table 3.24 A test line without an action word is a documentation line

	Reservation no.	Departure date	From	Destination	Flight number	Name	Number of tickets
Flight reservation entry		12-13-01	Orlando	Salt Lake City	XY1431	Lee	1
Flight reservation entry		12-15-01	Los Angeles	San Diego	XY1421	Wilson	4
Check flight reservation	1412	12-13-01	Orlando	Salt Lake City	XY1431	Lee	1
Check flight reservation	1413	12-15-01	Los Angeles	San Diego	XY1421	Wilson	4

3.6.8 Documentation lines

The spreadsheet line showing the names of the arguments (header) is not a test line – thus, there is no action word on the first line in the first column. The header only serves for documentation purposes – it makes the test much easier to read (see Table 3.24). In the same way, additional text can be added to the test sheet by way of documentation, so long as the first column on this line remains empty. This implies that all the items in the first column can be regarded as action words. Thus, items such as clusters, versions, and dates are also action words, but are only stated for documentation purposes and can be copied to the report. In an automated test execution, no navigation script will be invoked, if there is no action word in the first column.

The line containing a header for action words is usually not repeated when a test line follows another test line with the same action word, or an action word that has the same arguments. This improves readability greatly.

New flight reservations are entered on the first two test lines, whilst the data entered is checked on the final two lines. All the test lines contain the same arguments and therefore require the same header. The header is therefore not repeated.

3.6.9 Making optimal use of spreadsheet functionality

It is sensible to make best use of the spreadsheet program's features to store the test cases. Using references between cells can save a great deal of work in maintaining the test cases. For example, the required product codes can be defined at the top of the spreadsheet and referred to in the specification of the action word's arguments. If the same test needs to be executed again, but with different product codes, only the product codes at the top of the spreadsheet would need to be modified. Thanks to the references, the entire worksheet will be adjusted. References can also be made between different worksheets in a workbook within the spreadsheet. However, it is not recommended to make references between different workbooks since links may be lost when files are moved to other directories.

The spreadsheet's functions can also be used to calculate the output predictions. Having a calculation result produced dynamically by the spreadsheet program can be highly effective for maintenance. When a parameter in the calculation is modified, it can be adjusted in the formula, after which the spreadsheet will calculate the new output prediction dynamically.

Other spreadsheet functions can enhance the worksheet layout. Background and text colors can be used to highlight important parts of test cases, based on agreements about the color combinations used for different situations. This prevents excessively colorful spreadsheets and enhances the test products' transferability.

Using the filter function, the spreadsheet program can be made to display only the lines that match a specific search string. Thus, only the lines containing a particular action word can be displayed if wanted. This is particularly convenient when undertaking maintenance activities.

3.6.10   Argument commands

Argument commands can be useful, especially when field values are difficult to predict, cannot be predicted at all, or contain values that you do not want to record in a set way since they need to be modified regularly.

An argument command is assigned a special sign, such as an ampersand '&'. Examples of commonly used argument commands are described below.

&Keep and &Refer

These argument commands are used when a certain value is unknown prior to execution, and is only generated by the system as the test is actually being run. For example, a reservation number is generated automatically following a reservation entry. Such a number is often required to query data on the next screen. &Keep is then used as an argument to retain the value concerned. &Refer is used as an argument to refer to the retained value. For an example, see Table 3.25.

Table 3.25 The use of &Keep and &Refer

	Reservation no.	Departure date	From	Destination	Flight number	Name	Number of tickets
Entry flight reservation	&Keep[nr1]	11-17-01	Orlando	Bar Harbor	XY142	Salinger	2

	Reservation no.	Departure date	From	Destination	Flight number	Name	Number of tickets
Check flight reservation	&Refer[nr1]					Salinger	2

The reservation number generated is retained in the first test line (i.e. stored in memory). The reservation is queried in the second test line using the retained value as the key.

&Empty and &Notempty

The command often used for a check action is &Empty, which is the equivalent of an empty argument, and is used to improve the readability of a cluster.

A product is entered in the first test line without specifying its type, as shown in Table 3.26. If the screen displays no default value, the field must remain empty. This outcome is tested in the second test line by means of the argument command &Empty. If a value is seen in the 'type' field this error will be reported. The argument command &Notempty is used in the same way, except that the check is based on a field being populated. As long as the field is populated an error will not be reported.

Table 3.26 The use of &Empty

	Product no.	Product description	Color	Type	Weight
Product entry	P2423	Stapler	Black		222
Check product	P2423	Stapler	Black	&Empty	222

&Spaces and &Anything

&Spaces is used for input actions in which a space is entered instead of text in the argument concerned. This can be used for checking whether spaces are permitted as field input. Again, the argument command format is more readable than if a space was inserted in the spreadsheet. The argument command &Anything indicates that every value is correct so long as something is entered.

&Cont

This is used to interrupt a long test line which contains many arguments, even continuing with subsequent arguments on the spreadsheet's next test line, as shown in Table 3.27.

Table 3.27 The use of &Cont

	Loan type	Effective date	Expiry term	Principal sum	Term	Interest type	Payment method	
Loan entry	Redemption in full	11-01-01	Monthly	100,000	24	Fixed	Invoice	&Cont

	Interest	Interest effective date	End date	Expiry date	Savings type
&Cont	6.00	11-01-01	11-01-03		Single – BEF

In this example, &Cont is placed at the end of the first test line. In the line where the arguments are continued, &Cont is placed in the action words column. This allows all arguments that belong to a particular action word to be grouped in a visually acceptable way.

&Snap

This command is used to predict output for the current system based on an older version. This establishes whether any conversions provide the same functionality as before. In this way, any errors which have been corrected (or at least identified) in the old version do not need to be re-examined. It is often convenient to use this assumption when the test is drawn up.

The &Snap function operates as follows – the worksheet containing test cases is drawn up as usual, except that only the key values are recorded for the output predictions. &Snap is then entered as an argument in the other fields.

In the test case shown in Table 3.28, only the product code has been specified as input. The action 'check product' verifies whether the product exists, and whether the default values for this product displayed on the screen have been stored properly.

Table 3.28 The use of &Snap

	Product no.	Product description	Color	Type	Weight
Product entry	P2423				
Check product	P2423	&Snap		&Snap	&Snap

Instead of using this sheet for a test execution, a so-called 'snap run' is first executed on the application's old version. In this run, data specified on the test cases sheet is entered in the system but no data is checked. Instead, it is retrieved from the application, using the key value, and placed in a snap file. The text &Snap is overwritten with the real value, yielding both input and output predictions. This test sheet can then be used to test the new version after the conversion, and would look like the example shown in Table 3.29.

Table 3.29 Test cases after executing &Snap function

	Product no.	Product description	Color	Type	Weight
Product entry	P2423				
Check product	P2423	Chisel	Blue	BEI66	1

Thanks to the snap function, the tester does not need to find and enter values that can be retrieved from the application's old version. This saves an enormous amount of time if only a few functions have been modified in the new version of the application.

3.7   Test conditions and test techniques

Existing test techniques can be used to create the various TestFrame analysis products. Depending on the situation within the organization and the type of test executed, various techniques can be chosen, as shown in Figure 3.3. In this book, the decision table technique and the entity lifecycle technique are described as the recommended test conditions for translating clusters into test techniques. For additional information on existing test techniques, see [Hetz 88], [KitE 95], [Mors 93], and [Beiz 90].

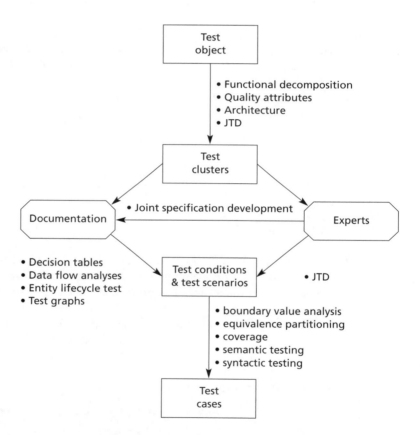

Figure 3.3   Test techniques

A functional decomposition can often be used to break a system into clusters. In that case, each cluster covers a functional part of the system. This method of division is often used for functional-oriented tests (i.e. systems test and user acceptance test). If an integration test has to be executed, a division based on architecture is suitable. Where a division is based on quality attributes, clusters are created to test aspects such as performance, user friendliness, and durability.

Basic information is one of the factors that determine which method is best for translating the cluster division into test conditions. If there are proper specifications on which the test can be based, traditional techniques such as decision tables, test graphs, data flow analysis, or entity lifecycle tests can be chosen. The use of decision tables and the entity lifecycle test are specified in more detail later in this chapter. If adequate specifications are lacking it will clearly be difficult to apply these techniques. However, this does not imply that the test can only be conducted with a complete specification. Which set of test conditions provides sufficient coverage may also be determined in a systematic way using experts in the field.

Various scenarios are possible, including the development of appropriate system specifications using the 'joint specification development' method. The specifications drawn up in this way are then used as a basis for applying traditional test techniques. Another option is to draw up the test conditions directly on the basis of the experts' knowledge. This working method, known as the 'joint testware development' method, relies on intensive interviews with experts. This technique will also be discussed in more detail later.

In addition to test techniques, supporting techniques for translating test conditions into test cases can also be used to create test conditions. Depending on the thoroughness of the test techniques, boundary value analysis, equivalence classes, semantic testing, and syntactic testing can all be used.

There are many other test techniques that can be used within the TestFrame method. It is important to apply these pragmatically. Test techniques do not always have to be used for designing analysis products. For example, it would be an exaggeration to set up a decision table to chart test conditions for a function in which only a few decisions were made. The use of test techniques must be justifiable in terms of computing and human resources. Making use of certain test techniques is not in itself a goal – rather, these techniques support the set up of the appropriate test set.

3.7.1   Decision table technique

The decision table technique is used for charting a test object's functionality systematically, in order to assess its processing completeness and correctness. In this technique, a description or design (usually in the shape of a narrative) is traced back to the principles on which it is based – combinations of conditions and the resulting actions. Using decision tables in this way enables you to uniformly create test conditions.

A decision table is a concise notation method that represents the results of the analysis. Composite conditions must be divided into single conditions. Subsequently, all possible combinations of these conditions are set against the accompanying actions in a decision table. The theory underlying decision tables is elaborately discussed in [Mors 93].

Decision tables are eminently suitable for use in combination with the TestFrame method. They are mostly used for drawing up test conditions, although a decision table may also clarify how to create relevant test cases for a particular test condition. This would apply when a decision has been made to draw up the test cases in rather general terms. Decision tables are often created in a spreadsheet file, on an additional worksheet, with the test conditions and the test cases.

Table 3.30 A simple decision table

| | Test condition number | | | |
	1	2	3	4
Condition 1	N	N	Y	Y
Condition 2	N	Y	N	Y
Action A	X	–	–	–
Action B	–	–	X	X
Action C	–	X	–	X
End routine	X	X	X	X

A simple decision table is shown in Table 3.30. Each column in the table corresponds to a single TestFrame test condition. In the example presented, test condition number 3 can be described as follows: if condition number 1 is true, and condition number 2 is not true, Action B is executed, after which processing is terminated.

Although used mostly for black-box tests (functional tests) in which complex functional situations are charted, the decision table technique is also suitable for white-box tests. An additional advantage is that basic information can be tested this way. By using all the logical (and illogical) situations as a basis, a decision is forced about the actions resulting from them. Contradictions can also be effectively traced in this manner. Using decision tables can contribute to the completeness and consistency of basic and detailed design. They can also be beneficial in situations where no adequate design is available. Instead of analyzing knowledge that is available on paper, the relevant conditions and actions which could play a role in the testing are recorded from introspection. The resulting decision tables form the basis of the conditions formulated in TestFrame.

For consistency purposes, and also to demonstrate progress, it is important to indicate explicitly in the decision tables which situations will not be tested. For example, an extra line can be included that indicates whether the column concerned will be tested. The reasons for not testing particular situations must also be stated.

3.7.2   The decision table technique's working method

Having a large number of conditions and actions with all the possible combinations of the true/false nature of conditions can generate a large number of situations. Thus, in practice the number of test situations must be limited as much as possible by using a subset of all available options.

The number of test situations can be reduced in various ways. The following describes how the decision table technique can be applied in full, as well as in a reduced form, using a simplified decision table.

Systematic approach

The basic principle of the systematic approach is that all the possible combinations of decision table conditions, and all the actions relating to them, are described. The following rule can be used to calculate the number of combinations – the number of possible combinations is equal to 2^n, where 2 is the number of values a condition can have (Y or N), and n is the number of conditions in the table. Thus, for a table with 3 conditions, $2^3 = 8$ columns have to be specified, for a table with 4 conditions this is $2^4 = 16$ columns.

When dealing with large numbers of conditions, it is recommended that they are divided into smaller decision tables if possible. References to other decision tables may be included in the decision table. For example, if a cluster has been defined for orders (enter, view, modify, and remove), the entry screen for the order header would resemble that shown in Figure 3.4.

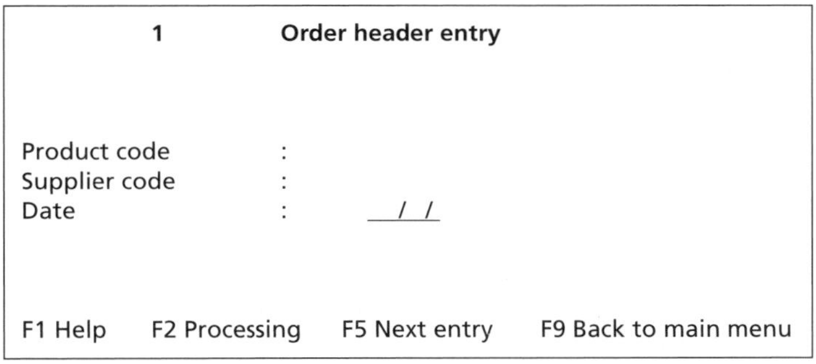

```
┌──────────────────────────────────────────────────────────────────────┐
│          1              Order header entry                             │
│                                                                        │
│                                                                        │
│                                                                        │
│   Product code        :                                                │
│   Supplier code       :                                                │
│   Date                :        / /                                     │
│                                                                        │
│                                                                        │
│   F1 Help    F2 Processing    F5 Next entry    F9 Back to main menu    │
└──────────────────────────────────────────────────────────────────────┘
```

Figure 3.4 Example of an entry screen

This results in the decision table shown in Table 3.31. There are three conditions, which leads to $2^3 = 8$ columns.

Intuitive approach

In the so-called intuitive approach described in [Mors 94], the tester decides which test situations are relevant, either on the basis of the available documentation or knowledge of the system's functionality. Such an inventory is usually incomplete but gives a clear description of the relevant test situations. The intuitive approach can be applied, for example, when all key practical cases have been described, and if the number of test cases increases disproportionately due to exceptions in the table.

Table 3.31 Decision table based on entry screen of Figure 3.4

Table BST1 Entering order header								
Test condition number BST1C	1	2	3	4	5	6	7	8
Product code is valid	N	N	N	N	Y	Y	Y	Y
Supplier code is valid	N	N	Y	Y	N	N	Y	Y
Date is greater than/identical to current date	N	Y	Y	N	N	Y	N	Y
Display error message 'product invalid'	X	X	X	X	–	–	–	–
Display error message 'supplier invalid'	–	–	–	–	X	X	–	–
Display error message 'date invalid'	–	–	–	–	–	–	X	–
Display order header	–	–	–	–	–	–	–	X
Go to decision table BST2 (order lines)	–	–	–	–	–	–	–	X

Such an approach is not obvious, since the tester requires a thorough insight into both the system's functionality and its use. However, due to the limited time, money, and resources available for testing, this approach is often selected in practice.

Simplifying decision tables

Systematically written decision tables in which all the combinations have been identified can often be simplified by eliminating irrelevant, less likely, or even impossible conditions. For example, if several columns contain identical actions the condition values in a specific condition may be compared. If they are identical the other condition values are redundant. In that case, the Y/N value can be replaced by a dash as described earlier. In this way, identical columns are created one of which can be removed. Table 3.32 shows an example of this method.

Table 3.32 Simplified decision table

Table BST1 Entering order header				
Test condition number	1	5	7	8
Product code is valid	N	Y	Y	Y
Supplier code is valid	–	N	Y	Y
Date is greater than/identical to current date	–	–	N	Y
Display error message 'product invalid'	X	–	–	–
Display error message 'supplier invalid'	–	X	–	–
Display error message 'date invalid'	–	–	X	–
Display order header	–	–	–	X
Go to decision table BST2 (order lines)	–	–	–	X

In this example, columns 2, 3 and 4 have been removed (relative to Table 3.31), since if the product code is invalid an error message always appears, irrespective of whether or not the other fields have been entered correctly. This is a result of the order in which the fields are checked on the screen (i.e. from top to bottom). In addition, test condition numbers 5 and 6 have been combined – if the supplier code is invalid an error message will appear, irrespective of whether or not the date has been entered correctly since that is always checked last.

The columns in the decision table display all the relevant test conditions concisely. They cannot always be understood at a glance, which is why it is useful to write out the test conditions in a form that is easy to read. The TestFrame test conditions form, described in Section 3.5, may be used for this purpose.

3.7.3 Example of a decision table for a test object

Travel agency 'Flying High' has a frequent flyer program for clients who regularly book flights with them. If someone flies over twice a month, for example, one bonus point is added to the 'Frequent Flying High' (FFH) card for each $500 of the total amount. When someone books a flight for the tenth time in the same calendar year, ten bonus points are awarded on a one-off basis. FFH card owners receive a 1% discount on the total amount. The system is required to execute these checks and calculations. A decision table can be created in order to chart the situation properly. These results are shown in a simplified form in Table 3.33.

Table 3.33 Decision table for FFH functionality of the Flying High system

Test conditions FLY	1	2	3	4	5
Client has an FFH card	Y	Y	Y	Y	N
Client has already flown twice this calendar month	Y	Y	N	N	–
Client flies for the tenth time this year	Y	N	Y	N	–
1% discount on total amount	X	X	X	X	–
1 FFH bonus credit for each $500 of total amount	X	X	–	–	–
10 FFH bonus credits	X	–	X	–	–
No action	–	–	–	–	X

A peer-to-peer review of the table is undertaken to ensure that no scenarios have been overlooked. The reviewer observes that if a client does not have an FFH card and flies for the tenth time, an application form should be sent to them automatically. This action must be added to the decision table, and hence a new column must be added – someone may or may not fly for the tenth time, in combination with having or not having a card. This results in the decision table shown in Table 3.34.

Table 3.34 The adjusted decision table for FFH functionality of the Flying High system

Test conditions	1	2	3	4	5	6
Client has an FFH card	Y	Y	Y	Y	N	N
Client has already flown twice this calendar month	Y	Y	N	N	–	–
Client flies for the tenth time this year	Y	N	Y	N	Y	N
1% discount of total amount	X	X	X	X	–	–
1 FFH credit for each $500 of total amount	X	X	–	–	–	–
10 FFH credits	X	–	X	–	–	–
Send an FFH membership form	–	–	–	–	X	–
No action	–	–	–	–	–	X

3.7.4   Entity lifecycle test

This test technique charts the lifecycle of data in a system to check its scope. This test technique is easy to apply, and suitable for drawing up test conditions. The entity lifecycle test is often used to complement test techniques that focus on the processes formulated around the logical entities. Furthermore, it can be very useful if functional specifications are lacking. Alternatively, if usable specifications are available, the entity lifecycle test can be used as a complementary test for scope and correctness of the data's lifecycle. For more information on the entity lifecycle test see [Beiz 95].

3.7.5   Working method for the entity lifecycle test

Identifying the processes and data

The entity lifecycle test can be divided into two phases – identification and analysis. In the analysis phase, the scope of the test and a division into test subareas or clusters is firstly defined. Next, the relevant processes and data collections are charted, on the basis of the entities described in the data model for example.

Recording the lifecycle in a CRUD matrix (create, read, update, and delete)

When the entities that are crucial for the test have been defined, the processes that manipulate these entities are reviewed. For example, this may involve presenting, modifying, reading, and removing data. In the example shown in Table 3.35, such a matrix has been devised for the entity 'product'. The table shows the CRUD matrix defining the operations for a product which can be entered, updated, deleted, and viewed. When a product is deleted, the available stock needs to be checked – if stock is available, this action is not permitted. When an overview is created of all the outdated articles, the entities 'product' and 'stock' are consulted. Table 3.36 shows a completed CRUD matrix for the Flying High application.

Table 3.35 An example of a CRUD matrix

	F301 Create product	F311 Update product	F321 Delete product	F521 Read/view products
PRODUCT				
Product code	C	R	D	R
Product	C	U	D	R
Color	C	U	D	–
Type	C	U	D	–
Weight	C	U	D	R
Outdated	C	U	D	R
STOCK				
Product code			R	R
Location code			R	R
Number in stock			R	R
Number allocated			R	R

Table 3.36 The CRUD matrix for the entity 'Reservation' of the 'Flying High' system

	Reservation entry	Modify reservation	Remove reservation	Reservation overview
RESERVATION				
Reservation number	C	R	D	R
Flight number	C	U	D	R
Tickets	C	U	D	R
Client name	C	U	D	R

Analyzing the CRUD matrix

After recording the reviewed data's lifecycle in a matrix as comprehensively as possible the analysis phase is initiated. The presentation, review, and removal functions are verified for each data collection. If the result is negative, whether the lack of such a function is correct must be determined.

Drawing up the test conditions (for each entity)

After analyzing the CRUD matrix, the results can be transferred to the test conditions on a one-to-one basis. The following three rules are applicable.

1. The order of the test conditions is crucial. Although the test conditions must be as independent as possible, the read/review action can be used for data entry and modification, as well as removal.

2. Test conditions, such as consistency checks for testing the relations between data collections, must be defined. One example is a test condition where an attempt is made to remove a product which is still in stock.

3. The initial loading of the database must be described, and which test conditions (and test cases) have data included should be indicated. The initial data collection is decisive for the selection of the test cases. Therefore, this data must be referred to when the test cases are recorded.

3.8 Test cases and test techniques

Test conditions form the basis of all test cases. Typically, one test condition results in several test cases. The application of certain test techniques can contribute to the systematic (and therefore responsible) reduction of the number of test cases, and the optimization of the test set. In this book, the techniques known as equivalence partitioning, boundary value analysis, syntactic testing, and semantic testing are further specified as the recommended techniques to translate test conditions into test cases.

In the equivalence partitioning technique, test cases are divided into classes in such a way that the result of one test value from that class is representative of all the other test values of that class. More test cases from the same equivalence class hardly provide more certainty. Table 3.37 shows an example of the application of the equivalence classes technique to Flying High system.

Equivalence class: Flying High

In the Flying High system, the number of tickets ordered must be entered in reservations. Of course, there must be at least one, but the maximum is 100. Please note that if a reservation is made for over 50 tickets, a 10% discount applies to the price to be paid. Thus, there are two classes:

Table 3.37 Equivalence classes for the 'tickets' section in the reservation screen of the Flying High system

Number of tickets	Total price
1 to 50 (inclusive) tickets	Tickets * price
51 to 100 (inclusive) tickets	0.9 (Tickets * price)

In the above table, this results in two test cases if equivalent classes are used – one in which a reservation with 25 tickets is displayed (i.e. no discount), and one in which a reservation with 75 tickets is displayed (i.e. a discount)

Boundary value analysis focuses on the boundaries distinguishing the classes. Test values must be selected in such a way that they lie on, and are on either side of, the value defined as the boundary. [KitE 95] and [Myer 79] review these techniques in detail.

Therefore, three test cases must be defined for each boundary to be tested:

- one test value that is identical to the boundary value;
- one test value just below the boundary value;
- one test value just above the boundary value.

Table 3.38 shows an example of the application of boundary value analysis to Flying High.

Boundary value analysis: Flying High

In the Flying High system, the number of tickets ordered must be entered in the reservation screen. Of course, there must be at least one, but the maximum is 100. Please note that if a reservation is made for over 50 tickets, a 10% discount applies to the price to be paid. Therefore, there are four classes:

Table 3.38 Boundary value analysis for the 'tickets' section in the reservation screen of the Flying High system

Number of tickets	Total amount
Less than 1 ticket	Impossible
1 to 50 tickets	Tickets * price
51 to 100 tickets	0.9 (Tickets* price)
Over 100 tickets	Impossible

In the case above this results in no test cases, using the boundary value analysis:

- reservation of 0 tickets (not allowed);
- reservation of 1 ticket (no discount);
- reservation of 2 tickets (no discount);
- reservation of 49 tickets (no discount);
- reservation of 50 tickets (no discount);
- reservation of 51 tickets (10% discount);
- reservation of 99 tickets (10% discount);
- reservation of 100 tickets (10% discount);
- reservation of 101 tickets (not allowed).

3.8.1   Syntactic testing

Syntactic testing provides insight into the test objects' quality, with regard to the design and structuring of screens (online) and overview (on paper). In addition, this technique can be used to test entry checks systematically. More information on the subject can be found in [Beiz 90].

The execution of a syntactic test addresses the following issues:

- entry checks (categories on screens);
- design and structure of screens (online);
- design and structure of overviews (online or batch processing);
- function keys;
- shortkeys (e.g. using the key combination 'Control' and 'd' instead of clicking the 'execute' button with the mouse);
- filling in list boxes;
- browse functions within an application;
- tab order on screens;
- cursor position;
- link to help functions (has the correct link between the application and the help function been defined).

This list is not comprehensive and has to be assessed, or even complemented, for each test process.

The results established by a syntactic test are often regarded as being less important than those from other tests. For the test object's functionality, it makes very little difference whether a field in a screen can be accessed by means of a tab key, or by clicking the relevant field with the mouse – especially when the test object is used only a few times a day. On the other hand, the functionality of the test object is critical for the business operations. In a small number of cases, the incorrect operation of syntactic elements can completely disrupt business operations. For example, if a data entry application lacks a correct tab, order processing within the application wll be processed more slowly and this does have an impact on business operations. Similarly, the incorrect operation of entry checks increases the risk of incorrect output, due to processing speed and the number of orders to be processed.

3.8.2   Syntactic testing working method

Using basic information (such as documentation, input from experts, and analysis of the running system) an overview is created of syntactic tests which can potentially be executed. The characteristics (such as the screen/field/overview) which must be met according to the specifications (e.g. tab order, field length, alphanumeric/numeric, etc.) are also determined here.

Subsequently, it must be decided whether or not to execute a test. It is crucial to remember that, due to the often large number of categories on screens and overviews, the number of test cases can be very, very large. Thus, it is usually necessary to justify why a particular part needs testing. With a view to consistency and demonstrability, it is also important to explicitly define which parts will and will not be tested. The overview of the parts that will be tested and those that will not is subsequently included in a spreadsheet workbook.

During the Analysis phase, tests are laid down for both the numeric and the alphanumeric values, from which the input is derived during the execution of the test. For example, the test strings '1234567890' (numeric) and 'abcdefghijklm' (alphanumeric) lead to the following input during the test execution of test case PRO1C2T3:

product code	=	123
product	=	abcdefghij
color	=	abcdefgh
type	=	abc
weight	=	12345

The action word 'check field' forces the test to check whether this input is valid. Using this set up, the test can be executed in a simple way either manually or automatically. Table 3.39 shows an expansion of test cases that can arise from syntactic testing.

Table 3.39 Example of test cases in the execution of syntactic testing

Document	Test cases Cluster PRO1 Product entry			
Version	1.0			
Date	01-11-2001			
Author	Tester			
Test case	**PRO1C1T1**	**Check tab order 'Product Entry' screen**		
	Screen name	Field order		
Check tab order	Product entry	Product code, product, color, type, weight		
Test case	**PRO1C2T1**	**Entry check of fields in 'Product Entry' screen**		
	Screen name	Field name	Field length	Field type
Check field	Product entry	Product code	3	Numeric
Check field	Product entry	Product	10	Alphanumeric
Check field	Product entry	Color	8	Alphanumeric
Check field	Product entry	Type	3	Alphanumeric
Check field	Product entry	Weight	5	Numeric

Note: function keys in 'Product Entry' screen are explicitly NOT tested.

3.8.3   Semantic testing

Semantic testing provides insight into the test object's quality, with respect to the relationships between data, during the input process. They are carried out if it has been determined that one or more of the following parts need to be assessed:

- relationships between input data on the same screen;
- relationships between input data on different screens;
- relationships between input data and data which is already available in the system.

The execution of a semantic test can involve the following:

- checking whether all the mandatory fields have been entered;
- by entering a field, the initially optional field becomes mandatory. For example, 'partner name' field can become mandatory if the 'prefix partner name' field has been entered;
- there is a limited number of input possibilities for field B once a particular value has been entered in field A. For example, if field A = 'girl', field B will only accept 'Ann', 'Mary' and 'Lena', etc. Alternatively, if field A = 'boy', field B can only contain names such as 'Edwin', 'Henry' and 'Andrew';
- as a consequence of a particular selection on screen 1, categories will or will not be displayed on screen 2. For example, if an adult client has been selected on screen 1, the categories 'passport number' and 'driving licence number' are displayed. If a client of a minor age is selected, the categories 'father's name' and 'mother's name' are displayed on screen 2;
- errors in data relations. For example: processing the entry of a client number that already exists, and is supposed to be unique; selecting an adult client for a junior savings account; or entering a client with a birth date in the future (if it has been specified that birth dates always have to be in the past);
- errors in message format because of relationship checks;
- authorization issues. For example: are the applications allocated to an employee, indeed made available to this employee; is an employee given access to the applications allocated to him;
- security issues. For example: can an authorized employee log in with the correct password; what is the response if an incorrect password or user identification is used.

This list is not comprehensive, and needs to be assessed for each test process.

3.8.4   Semantic test's working method

Using basic information (such as documentation, input from experts, analysis of an operative system) the semantic tests to be potentially executed are charted. This results in an overview showing the existing relationships, their details, and which will and will not be tested.

The required initial loading of the test database is also based on this information, if this is necessary for testing the relationships between input data and data that already exists in the system. The description of this required initial load of the test database is part of the test documentation created during the Analysis phase.

The overview of the relationships that will and those that will not be tested is subsequently included in a spreadsheet with the worksheets 'general', 'test conditions', and 'test cases', on the basis of which the test is executed. An example of these worksheets are shown in Table 3.40.

Table 3.40 (part 1/3) Worksheet for test cases of cluster PRO2

Document	General information cluster PRO2: semantic testing for Product Entry
Version	1.0
Date	01-11-2001
Author	Tester

Scope of cluster PRO2:

In cluster PRO2, only the situations and relations are tested in which an entry of a product *fails*

Situations in which they are realized are recorded in Cluster PRO3

Test environment:

Database PROD has to be loaded to execute PRO2

This database contains the product with the following elements: product code = P2, product = nail, color = black, type = AAX, and weight = 1

The color parameters need to be set in such a way that only black, gray, white, beige, red, green, and blue are accepted as input

Table 3.40 (part 2/3) Worksheet for test cases of cluster PRO2

Document	Test conditions cluster PRO2: semantic testing of Product Entry
Version	1.0
Date	01-11-2001
Author	Tester

This document contains the test conditions of cluster PRO2: relation test for Product Entry

Each logical test case is indicated with the cluster number (PRO1 for this cluster) followed by the test condition number

Test condition no.	Test condition description
PRO2T1	Product codes must be unique
PRO2T2	A weight must be > 0
PRO2T3	Only the colors black, gray, white, beige, red, green, and blue are allowed

Table 3.40 (part 3/3) Worksheet for test cases of cluster PRO2

Document	Test cases cluster PRO2: semantic testing of Product Entry			
Version	1.0			
Date	01-11-2001			
Author	Tester			

Test case	PRO2C1T1	Product codes must be unique			
	Product code	**Product**	**Color**	**Type**	**Weight**
Enter product	p2	Nut	Gray	AAX	1
Expect message	The value in the product code field is not allowed				

Test case	PRO2C2T1	Negative value in weight field is not allowed			
	Product code	**Product**	**Color**	**Type**	**Weight**
Enter product	p5	Sandpaper	Beige	TEXA	−1
Expect message	Negative value or 0 not allowed				

Test case	PRO2C2T2	Value 0 in weight field is not allowed			
	Product code	**Product**	**Color**	**Type**	**Weight**
Enter product	p5	Sandpaper	Beige	TEXA	0
Expect message	Negative value or 0 not allowed				

Test case	PRO2C3T1	Purple is not an allowed color			
	Product code	**Product**	**Color**	**Type**	**Weight**
Enter product	p8	Sandpaper	Purple	TEXA	2
Expect message	The value in the color field is not allowed				

Test case	PRO2C3T2	Pink is not an allowed color			
	Product code	**Product**	**Color**	**Type**	**Weight**
Enter product	p8	Sandpaper	Pink	TEXA	2
Expect message	The value in the color field is not allowed				

Using this set up, the test can be executed both manually and by computer. Table 3.40 gives a detailed overview of test cases created by semantic testing.

3.8.5   Joint testware development

JTD is a test specification technique used to develop test set products using workshops. This technique is often used when system documentation is incomplete or outdated and cannot be used for the analysis. Thus, it is necessary to rely entirely on the knowledge of experts and others involved in the test project. Through discussions and workshops, sufficient insight can be gained to enable the creation of a cluster division with the set of appropriate test conditions. More information on JTD can be found in [Jans 00].

The system documentation, on which the test can then be based, can also be created jointly – this process is called joint specification development (JSD). This step can be skipped and test documentation can be created directly using the JTD method. In many cases, this test documentation is used later as an alternative for system documentation.

JTD is an iterative and creative process, and not all participants enjoy using it. JTD can only be executed by a group of people who are willing to discuss and specify ideas and products in a structured way. The following products can be created via JTD:

● prioritization of parts of the test object;
● test conditions;
● division into clusters;
● acceptance criteria for the system;
● requirements with regard to the required test environment.

JTD is especially suitable for determining the division into clusters and defining the test conditions. Expert knowledge is required to create these products. The aim of JSD sessions is to obtain these products. JTD is less suitable for drawing up test cases, as this is usually too specific an activity to be undertaken by one group.

3.8.6   Joint testware development working method

The working method of a JTD process is comparable to that used for rapid application development (RAD) processes. RAD processes are iterative and incremental, and continuously repeat the entire cycle from beginning to end. This incremental aspect ensures that the entire application is developed and completed in phases. This is very similar to a JTD process where the various parts are specified step-by-step. For example, in the first session the different perspectives for the test conditions are gathered, and in the next the test conditions can be drawn up.

A JTD session should always achieve an objective that has been agreed on in advance. If it has been decided that a division into clusters will be made – one that everyone agrees with and can work with – this has to be laid down by the end of the session. If the session's objective is to create test conditions, these must be recorded as they are formulated at the meeting.

An important factor in a successful JTD process is the group dynamism, which forces better ideas to be produced as workshops progress. Together, the participants discuss what is important to test, and the best way of doing it. An important feature of jointly specifying test products is that everyone immediately knows how and why decisions have been made, which creates better support for the final result within the organization.

A JTD workshop is a very suitable means of controlling the process and achieving results in a timely manner. For that purpose, it is important to decide in advance which products will materialize from the workshops and which will be produced by other techniques. The various test products are often created at different workshops (unless they are minor ones), with a substantial amount of overlap. In such cases, it is worth considering discussing them all at the same session. However, test environment requirements and the determination of the test conditions should always be discussed at separate sessions.

Discussing the various products at different workshops also makes it easier to ensure that appropriate participants are present at the right time. It is more important to have experts present in a session at which test conditions are drawn up than when discussing the technical aspects of a test environment.

Thorough preparation is essential for workshop success. The contributions expected from participants must be clear before the workshop starts. In addition, they must have been given all the available information well before the workshop if they are to prepare adequately. Furthermore, it is important to have appropriate facilities (such as a conference room, whiteboard, coffee/lunch, etc.) so that the workshop process is disturbed minimally.

The workshop must be chaired by an experienced moderator/process supervisor who is familiar with the JTD process, and has the authority to make decisions. This process supervisor is responsible for moderating all discussion and for the ultimate creation of the products. A key issue, in this respect, is that the final result envisaged should always be kept in focus – thus, repetitive discussion should be minimal, and all participants should be encouraged to contribute in a positive way.

The workshop will be composed of various participants with different roles – these are listed in Table 3.41.

As mentioned earlier, the composition can differ from workshop to workshop. Furthermore, participants can take on more than one role. Alternatively, there may be several representatives from one discipline or department. It is important that the persons involved have the authority (and a mandate) for undertaking their role. It is the task of the process supervisor to ensure the appropriate composition of the group.

Table 3.41 Key JTD workshop participants

Minuter	To relieve the facilitator, the presence of a minuter is recommended
TestFrame expert	The TestFrame expert knows how products must be documented, and can advise from his test knowledge and experience
Application expert	An IT expert with (functional) knowledge of the application can advise about automation
Domain expert	A team member with knowledge of the problem domain is needed to develop the test set – someone with knowledge of business processes is needed to indicate the importance of aspects and prioritization
Internal organization expert	The presence of a team member with broad knowledge of the internal organization is crucial
Customer	The presence of customer, or a representative, is required when formal decision making is undertaken

3.9   Data dependency

The final section of this chapter discusses the issue of data dependency, another factor that must be taken into account when setting up a test set. Data dependency complicates the development and management of test cases and test execution. Therefore, at the start of a test process close attention needs to be paid to the existence of dependencies and how to deal with them. There are two types of data dependency – order dependency and reference dependency.

Order dependency is when the result of one test case affects the next test case – thus, if the first test case is not executed correctly then the second cannot be executed. An example of this dependency is testing the functions 'display client', 'modify client', and 'remove client'. In this example, the second and third test cases depend on the correct processing of the first.

Order dependency can have a negative effect on the execution of the test set. Consider the example mentioned above. It appears that test cases 2 and 3 cannot be executed if test case 1 has not been processed correctly – if client 'Jones' is not displayed, he obviously cannot be modified or removed. An entire test process can fail due to this order dependency. In a manual test, the problem can be avoided sometimes by improvising, but intervention of this kind will reduce the test's reliability. In addition, improvisation is very labor intensive. During automated test execution, the entire exercise can be brought to a halt if a test case has not been processed correctly. Often, the test cannot be reproduced consistently and unambiguously, thereby diminishing the test's reliability.

Reference dependency implies that a test case's output prediction depends on the data available in the test database at that point in time. However, since this data is unstable, and may change over time, it may not be completely representative. Take a booking system, for example. A certain cluster may contain the conclusion of a forward contract for a client as a test case, followed by a prediction of that conclusion. However, the exact nature of the prediction depends on the relevant quotations available in the test database at that time.

If there is reference dependency, no prior defined output predictions may be drawn up. For that reason, the test cannot be identically reproduced with the same data and values (i.e. the reference data is *non-stationary* in statistical terms). In the example described above, it appears that the output prediction with regard to the value of the concluded contract differs if an exchange rate of $1.50 is used in one case, and a rate of $2.00 in another. Executing a regression test, with a stable, predefined test set, is no longer possible since the test set has to be adjusted to the data available in the database each time. An unambiguous and consistent test execution can then no longer be guaranteed. Incidentally, data dependency cannot always be avoided. The following examples represent some common (and difficult) situations.

- When the lifecycle of an entity is tested, it must be possible, according to the specifications, to display an account, modify it, and remove it on the same day. To test this, test cases must be drawn up that depend on each other. This is an example of order dependency.

- If converted data has to be tested during the test, a fixed, predictable database cannot be used since that section of the test determines whether the application may cooperate with recent, converted data. This is an example of reference dependency.

- If the client demands that the most recent production data be used for the test, it is not possible to draw up fixed output predictions. This is also reference dependency.

- There are also test types with less data dependency. Two examples are production–acceptance tests (PAT), and performance tests. These are rather technically oriented and few substantive functional matters will be tested. The exact test data is less important in such tests.

3.9.1 How to counter data dependency

Fortunately there are ways of reducing the impact of data dependency which involve using a test database load that has been predefined. This test database is known as an initial database – it holds a minimum collection of test data and enables the functionality of an application to be tested separately.

For example, consider the entry, modification and removal of a client. A database containing the clients 'McKellar', 'Jones' and 'Kennedy' can be created to reduce data dependency. The following test cases are defined:

1. 'enter client Jones';
2. 'modify client McKellar';
3. 'remove client Kennedy'.

Even if the display of client 'Jones' fails, test cases 2 and 3 can still be executed because they have been set up independently using the clients 'McKellar' and 'Kennedy' respectively.

This example makes it clear that analyzing the data wanted in the initial database is an important determinant of successful independent execution of test sets. It is the analyst's task to determine which data is required and this is recorded in the test plan, or a separate design document. The basic principle is that the data mentioned is ready in the test database before starting the execution of the test.

It would be easy to use a copy of a production database as an initial database. However, this is not always the appropriate solution, given that some situations may need testing but are not available in the production database. If a test case demands a specific situation (such as a client with a foreign address) and it is not available in the initial database, then it must be added to it. A basic test database must always meet the following conditions:

● each table must have sufficient records to be able to test all the different clients, products and other data elements relevant to the test (e.g. for a performance test it is unnecessary to include every data element in the database);

● the relationships between the records in the different tables (such as keys) must be consistent;

● the database structure's version must fit the application's version, since the modifications of the system to be tested have to be followed;

● the data in the database should not be out of date (e.g. date fields must match the data used for the test).

The test database must be managed and maintained to enable regression tests to be performed successfully. When the initial database is set up, several decisions can be made that consider this:

● the database structure;

● the data to be used;

● how dates are synchronized.

In addition, various decisions about test case structure can be made in the spreadsheet. Several alternatives are described below, including discussion on their strengths and weaknesses.

3.9.2   Database structure

The database structure used in the production environment must be followed. Installing new versions of applications, or other related applications, can lead to modifications in the database structure. Two alternatives are worth considering.

The first is to copy the structure from the production environment at the start of each test process. The advantage is that it is easy to automate, reducing the test environment manager's workload.

A potential weakness is that if several new applications are expected, the production environment can be different from the scenario encountered by the application to be tested when it is installed.

A second alternative is to copy the structure from the production environment just once. Subsequently, the modifications in the database structure, followed by the conversions applied to the production environment, are also performed in the test environment. The advantage of this approach is that the conversion programs may be tested in the test environment first, before they are used in production. Also, the application can be tested in an environment identical to that in which it is implemented. However, the disadvantage is the extra time required to update these test activities and to schedule them properly.

3.9.3 Contents of the initial database

The tables must be populated with relevant data before the tests can begin. Static data (such as code tables) and dynamic data (such as client information) may be required. It is important that all the different types of test data are included and that the mutual relationships are correct.

There are three ways to create this database:

- data can be copied from the production environment each time;
- data can be entered directly into the database tables;
- data can be entered via the applications themselves.

If the data available in production is copied, subsets can be defined to reduce the amount of data. Sometimes, a form of scrambling will be required to ensure the data's confidentiality. However, the copied data's content must be sufficient to execute in the test set. The advantages of this approach are that the procedure can be automated easily, and that a physical test database (including records) is conveniently available each time. The disadvantage is the loss of control compared to manual data entry, based on the initial database design. In addition, checking if all the data mentioned in the initial database design is available entails a lot of work.

The second option is to create the database by using direct input. Most test processes require only a limited amount of data in the initial database and this could be entered using a standard SQL database client. In addition, conversions of the production database must also be executed on the test database. The advantages of this approach are that a minimum required data set can be created for use as the basis for all the project's test cases, and that conversions can be trialled in a test environment. The disadvantage is that a lot of work is required to build the database, particularly since the consistency between data must be retained. In addition, updating all later conversions involves a lot of effort.

The third option is to build an initial database from scratch refraining from entering data directly in the tables. In this case, data is only inserted using the application to be tested. The structure of the new environment can be set up, for example, from spreadsheets and navigation scripts via the application concerned. This must be executed before starting the actual test run. Thus, there are two separate activities and the physical building of the initial database is not part of the test execution. The advantages of this approach are that conversions in the production database are never followed up and so long as applications can work with the new structure, the data will always be entered correctly. The disadvantages are that navigation scripts must be written for a number of input functions in the applications, and that the input must be executed manually each time.

3.9.4   Date synchronization

When tests are run, the dates used in the test cases must be identical to the dates in the test database. If, for example, tests are executed for an insurance company's policy administration system, you need to be certain that the policy used in the test cases has not expired. When tests are defined for a stock exchange system involving the trading of options contracts, the validity of the test cases dependends on the expiry date of the options. Synchronization is therefore critical and can be achieved in two ways.

The first option is to use fixed dates, and to set the system date. To this end, an 'interesting' date can be selected (such as 23rd December) to test how the system behaves around national holidays. The test can then continue for a few days, while the system date shifts one day at a time. The advantage of this approach is that tests have to be structured only once, as far as the dates are concerned. The disadvantage is that the system date itself must be shifted – or that all the programs must be able to use a date retrieved from a table. In addition, problems can arise in tests with linked, external systems that do use the current date.

A second option is to shift all the dates in the test cases, and the test database, by means of update programs. A small SQL module is created in the initial database for each of the tables – this adjusts date dependent fields before a test is run. A direct reference to a date parameter in the spreadsheets can be included in the cluster. This approach works with relative dates rather than absolute ones. There are several tools developed specifically for shifting dates in large files. The advantage of this approach is that a reference can be included in test cases to day 0, day 1, etc. This can be clearer than using exact dates. The disadvantage is, of course, that update programs must be created and maintained for all the tables. This also applies to conversions.

It is not always possible to determine the contents of an initial database. For example, if the client requests that data is regularly refreshed from production, there are other options available for setting up a thorough, maintainable test set by laying out the spreadsheet in an appropriate way. The option selected depends on the number of system properties to be inserted.

3.9.5   Loading the database via a spreadsheet

If the application permits direct data entry, there is a way around specific data dependencies in the test database – data is entered using a spreadsheet with action words and arguments. This alternative is also discussed as a variant in Section 3.9.3. The input data is contained in a cluster spreadsheet, together with the test cases, input specifications, and the expected output, or is stated in a separate initial cluster.

Using the workaround

Sometimes data can be entered using the application's screens, but the output in the application itself cannot be checked. In such instances, the output can be obtained by carrying out database queries. The queries can be defined beforehand (e.g. in the spreadsheet with the test cases that need the output) and executed by query tools. In the worst case scenario, the output must be obtained using customized solutions.

Programming in the spreadsheet

If the dependency is relatively simple, the relationship may be included in a spreadsheet for the cluster itself by making use of native spreadsheet functionality (using formulas, references, labels, etc.). If the expected output depends on whether it is a weekday or a weekend, for example, this can be built in using a spreadsheet function. In principle, this method can only be used for relatively simple dependencies – otherwise, the entire application would be rebuilt, incorporating any potential errors!

Using the parameter spreadsheet

If data dependency is limited to certain parameters and constants, the current values can be recorded in a separate cluster spreadsheet. The other cluster test sheets then refer to this parameter list. This can be useful, for example, if a test case refers to the current date, the machine name, directory structure, etc. The parameter spreadsheet should be updated before running a test.

Using table control

An alternative to the parameter spreadsheet is table control. In complex data dependency environments, the parameter mechanism can be expanded to include references to a local table. If the cluster is based, for example, on the name and address data of persons with a mortgage, this can be recorded in the spreadsheet as a reference to a 'name and address' table that lists this data. The table must be populated with appropriate and current data before the test is run. This can be executed manually, or by a computer running a preprogrammed query.

The decision tree diagram shown in Figure 3.5 can be used to indicate the best solution method.

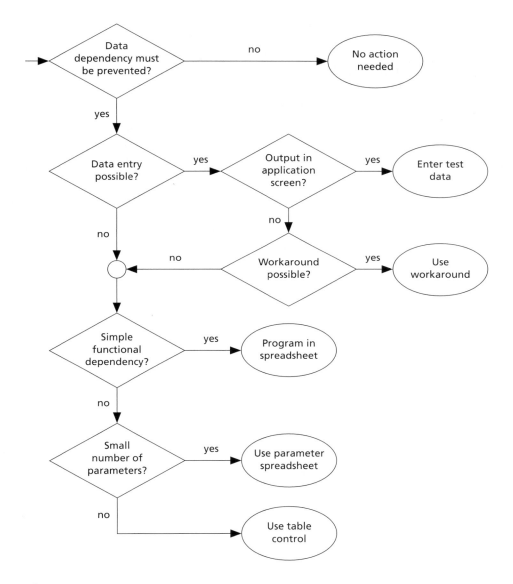

Figure 3.5 Decision tree diagram for data dependency

Summary

The aim of the Analysis phase is to set up a comprehensive and reusable test set. To this end, a clear delineation is made to indicate what will and what will not be tested. The required basic information, such as the available sources from which the analysis will be composed, is also assessed. Subsequently, the test object's parts to be tested are divided into clusters. In this way, the test object is divided into logical, verifiable units that have the greatest possible degree of independence.

Subsequently, test conditions and test cases are set up for each cluster. A test condition is the translation of a system specification into a verifiable requirement, and the test case is the further enumeration of this. A test case consists of one or more test lines, each consisting of an action word and its arguments.

To create the appropriate test conditions and test cases, test techniques are used where appropriate. This can occur in situations where complete and updated documentation is available, and also in situations where this is not the case. Data dependency must also be taken into account. This method of systematic analysis ensures that the Analysis result contains as few gaps and overlaps as possible, and that the envisaged test coverage is achieved. Using action words, and a clear and unambiguous documentation method, makes the analysis accessible, transferable and maintainable. This ensures optimal reusability of the analysis for the execution of regression tests.

4 Navigation

4.1 Introduction

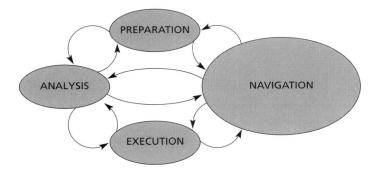

One of the advantages of the TestFrame method is the option of automating test execution fully or partially. Whether or not this is useful depends on a number of factors. Developing the navigation material, for example, requires a substantial investment of time and effort. The advantage of not having to test manually must outweigh this. The frequency with which the test has to be repeated should also be considered, along with the availability of experts to execute the test manually and the number of different action words required for the execution of the test. This latter factor is interesting if, for instance, a large number of test cases are needed to test a limited number of functions – in this case, the input data varies greatly, while only a limited number of action words is required. In such a scenario, the relative cost of the test execution's automation is low. Automated testing is an important part of the TestFrame method. Using the method, a form of automated testing may be set up for flexible use within the entire test process. More information on the subject of test automation can be found in [Dust 99] and [Fews 99].

This chapter starts with a discussion of the advantages of automated testing over manual testing and the process of Navigation is discussed in detail. In contrast to other chapters, some technical knowledge is required here.

4.2   Opting for manual or automated test execution

Earlier chapters have already mentioned that test sets (set up with TestFrame) can be executed manually or by computer. This section compares the advantages of automated testing to manual testing. It also shows how TestFrame differs from the traditional technique of automated testing using record & playback.

Automated testing is appealing – instead of a person having to test an application manually, an automated test tool does the work. This saves valuable human resources and makes the best use of computing resources. Instead of undertaking routine (and very boring!) testing activities, the tester can concentrate on other jobs.

A schematic representation of action word use is shown in Figure 4.1.

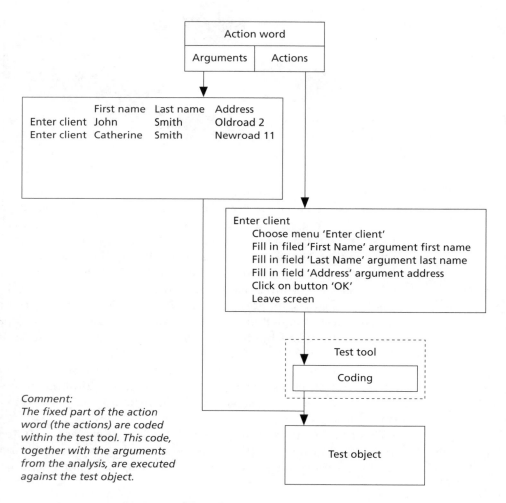

Figure 4.1   Schematic representation of action word use

4.2.1   Advantages of the traditional automated testing method compared to manual testing

There are several advantages of traditional automated testing method with record & playback over manual testing and these are discussed below.

Improved use of time

This is the most common reason for using automated testing. Actions such as keystrokes and mouse movements, which are usually executed by a tester during a manually executed process, can be undertaken by a test tool. These actions can be repeated many times without the tester's involvement. The tester can concentrate on other activities during that time.

Fewer routine activities

Testing applications manually soon induces boredom in the tester. Few people are eager to execute a test repetitively. When record & playback are used, the test tool executes repeated activities without manual intervention. The tester is free to focus on more creative tasks.

Consistent test execution

In automated testing, the chances of human error are virtually eliminated. When a person executes a test, not every action will be the same as the others because of variations in data entry. This variability can lead to errors in the tester's input, and trivial differences early in an input sequence can have dramatic consequences later on.

Improved result reliability

As mentioned above, routine testing activities are boring. This means that the results are less reliable than those of an automated process, since a human tester may unwittingly overlook errors in the results.

Easier test process planning

When planning, a team member's unexpected absence can have an impact on a project's timeline, which may already be short. If a test tool takes over the team member's actions, this risk is eliminated. The knowledge of the system (such as the actions to be performed) have already been laid down in the scripts.

Fewer concessions in execution thanks to time savings

After modifying an existing system, only the functions that have actually been modified are tested manually. This restriction is often imposed because retesting unmodified code increases the overall cost of the test process, in terms of both time and money. However, it should be noted that a modification in one part of the system may have a negative effect on the operation of another part. When automated test tools are used, a full test can always be run since this requires only marginally more time than testing just the modified code.

4.2.2   Advantages of automated testing using TestFrame compared to traditional automated testing methods

Action words occupy a central position in the TestFrame method. An action word is a combination of actions, defined by the analyst, which must be performed for a specific test case. In this way, a direct link can be created between the analysis products and the automation of the test. The worksheet containing the test cases is read from top to bottom. Each action word initializes a script which executes the appropriate action.

Less maintenance

In traditional automated testing, using the record & playback method, the entire test is recorded sequentially. When something changes in the test run (e.g. because of a change of focus by the tester, or a modification to the system) the entire test must be recorded again.

This repetition can be avoided using the TestFrame method. The test's contents are determined by the clusters' contents. For each action word software is written. If the tester's insight changes, only a single cluster will be changed. If the test object changes, only the software linked with the action word concerned needs to be modified.

Testware is more accessible

Test tools store all the information needed in scripts, including all navigation actions and all the data required for the test. In many cases, staff with functional knowledge maintain the data while technical staff focus on the software. In traditional automated testing, the information contained in scripts is generated in random order making it difficult for functional and technical staff to filter the information. TestFrame clearly separates the test data (analysis) from the software (navigation scripts) improving access for both functional and technical staff.

Scripts are easier to read (systematic set up)

A test set is divided into action words, each with its own code fragment. These small pieces of code are easier to read than tests that have been recorded in full. In addition, these action words are grouped by mutual characteristics, and the set up is systematic making the code more accessible.

Full link to the test cases

When tests are executed according to the traditional automated method, doubts may arise about their reliability. This is mainly caused by the fact that non-technical staff tend to regard a test tool as a magical entity that operates autonomously. Demonstrating that the test tool does nothing more than execute the instructions contained in the test cases can alleviate this misunderstanding substantially. In traditional automated testing, this link is difficult to demonstrate, since the test data is included in the scripts. Using TestFrame, this link is very clearly included in the report to show that the testing has taken place exactly according to the description in the test case.

Reports that fit the rest of the method

In the traditional automated testing method, the test tool itself often generates reports. The report's content can then only be defined to a limited extent. In addition, the standard report is highly technical – in TestFrame, the report is separate from the test tool and can be customized to have a specific form and content.

4.2.3   Reasons for opting for a manual test with TestFrame

Of course, TestFrame is not a panacea for resolving all test automation problems. Some reasons for using a full or partly manual execution of the test within TestFrame are given below.

Too many technical problems

Sometimes, there are so many problems involved in automating a test that the solution is too time consuming (e.g. no object recognition, synchronization, etc.). This can be a valid reason for executing a test manually.

One-off test

An important advantage of an automated TestFrame test is the testware's reusability. Energy is expended only once on its development, effort that is not required for the next test. A one-off test cannot take advantage of this benefit, which can be a valid reason not to automate the test.

Unstable system

If the system's responses are completely unpredictable and vary each time, it can be more efficient to execute the first tests manually.

If there are doubts about automating the tests, it is usually wise to defer the decision until clusters have been identified in the test analysis. Subsequently, the advantage of automation can be considered for each cluster. Such considerations are often easier to make at the level of individual clusters than for a complete test.

After a decision has been made to opt for a full or partly automated test, the navigation set up can be initiated. The next sections discuss what this involves and what steps must be taken.

4.3   Technical test using record & playback tools

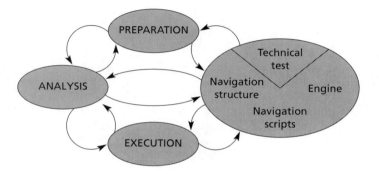

Before a record & playback tool is used to execute an automated test, a technical test must be performed to determine if the tool can work with the test object. This must be done at the start of the project in order to minimize delays arising due to unexpected technical problems during the test process. Experience has shown that this type of technical problem will cause serious delays in a project. However, if a technical test is executed at the start of the project, all possible problems involving the record & playback tool and the test object can be identified.

A technical test is executed by a navigator who has sufficient knowledge of the record & playback tool's options, and the platform on which the test is executed. It is critical that both an expert in the field and an analyst are available alongside the technical expert, who can demonstrate the application and call up any difficult screens so that they can be included in the technical test.

When a technical test is executed, the record & playback tool's limitations must be taken into account. For example, all kinds of settings for recognizing specific classes of scheme objects ('controls') that must take place within the tool, or must be delivered in a separate module (an 'integration') by the supplier. These add-ons must be ordered separately sometimes, and then support a separate development platform such as PowerBuilder, SAP/R3, etc. Therefore, it is important to determine, in advance, which type of development platform was used to create the application to be tested so that the supplier of the tool can be queried about the available support for that development environment. The integration could use up some delivery time, or require additional costs that have not been itemized in the project's budget.

A technical test involves the following specific key issues:

- the test tool's ability to read the test object's required data, and convert it into variables;
- being able to read objects ('controls') that are not recognized as standard;
- data presentation in the application, often displayed in spreadsheet-like tables on the screen (called grids) – they are often difficult for a tool to access;
- being able to read all pop-up windows, and other specific sub-windows;
- being able to deal with a full screen application, which may not allow test tool actions;
- being able to send data reliably to the application to be tested;
- reliability in very fast data entry – can the application cope with a test tool that can enter data many times faster than a user;
- being able to select and activate the application's various objects;
- being able to synchronize and wait for a certain state of the various screen elements – for example, entry elements that can only be activated again after the application has completed an operation;
- speedy execution of a test – in certain screen elements the test tool waits for a long time, with synchronization (or input processing) being unnecessarily slow.

When problems occur in technical tests, it is necessary to determine possible workarounds. At the very least, it is wise to contact the test tool's supplier and explain any problems that arise. Ultimately, a different tool might have to be selected. Clearly, it is best to discover any incompatibilities or inadequacies at the beginning of the project.

The results of the technical test should be recorded in a report, which has a clear conclusion. If problems are difficult to solve, the client commissioning the test must be contacted as soon as possible to minimize any delay in the project. If there are serious problems, another test tool should be considered. A fallback position is to execute the tests manually.

4.4 Navigation structure

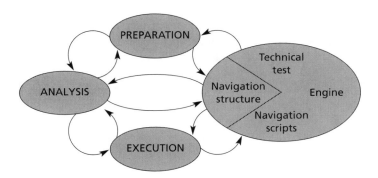

The navigator's environment consists of the test tool, the functions developed with it, and any related files (such as clusters, generated reports, and documentation). The environment undergoes constant change as new test tool versions are released, functions are adjusted because of modifications to the test object, and new clusters are set up.

In order to respond rapidly, simply and reliably to the changes, it is important to give consideration to the structure of the navigation environment. Questions such as where do we install the test tool, where do we store the functions, and how do we deal with the clusters must be addressed. The answers to these questions naturally lead to the design of the navigation environment. It should be noted that the environment's layout is dynamic and may change over the course of time.

This section discusses the navigation environment and its layout in greater detail. In addition to the navigation environment, there is a test environment which contains the test object. There is a close relationship between these two environments and this will also be discussed.

4.4.1   The functions

Navigation development is a form of system development. A navigation system is developed to interpret clusters, and execute the actions specified in them, on the system to be tested. This implies that the rules for rational system development also apply to navigation. One of the most important rules involves the program's modular set up. For navigation, this suggests that, in the case of overlap between the various functions, the mutual part is encapsulated in a separate subfunction. The newly created separate subfunction is then invoked from the original main function. Overlap can arise again between these functions, which results in the creation of yet another new function. In this way, multiple functions can be created that are not directly called from the spreadsheet.

A logical structure is required to organize these functions. A frequently used structure is the division into high level and low level functions. This division is comparable to the difference between functional and technical design. In general, high level functions have a close relationship with the functional description of the system, whilst low level functions concern the technical implementation making them dependent on the platform and interface. In addition to these high level and low level functions, there are also directive functions. These are functions directly linked to, respectively, the high level, low level, and directive action words derived from the Analysis phase.

A test language is used for the description of low and high level functions that has been specifically developed for this book. It is called TestFrame Virtual Language (TVL) and its sole purpose is to provide the navigation examples in this book. There is no test tool available that can work with TVL. It has been designed to be read easily, rather than operate in a production environment – see the Appendix for a detailed description.

High level functions

A high level function is usually the implementation of a high level action word. These functions define a user's programmed actions, ensure that the test data from the test sheets is placed correctly on the screen, and that the application's output data can be verified. This is done by 'navigating' through the system's various screens.

It is recommended that a standard structure is selected for high level functions. If, for example, a test object is structured according to a fixed structure of menus and screens, the start or end location of a high level function is an important consideration. One could opt to have each function start in the main screen, and to navigate from there to the screen concerned. The function would then have to end with a return to that main screen.

```
Function EnterClient()

        Menu("relations,clients,enter").Select
        gi_Input(…)
        gi_CheckConfirmation("client entered")
        gi_BackToMainMenu()

End Function
```

Example 4.1

The `gi_CheckConfirmation()` function shown in Example 4.1 is a completeness check of the function `EnterClient()`. This should not be confused with a check, since `EnterClient()` is not a check action word.

The action word in Example 4.1 assumes that the start is always the main screen. In some situations, it can be desirable for the action word to remain on the screen in which the last action took place – if this action word has to check a message, for example. If it had returned to the main screen, this message would have been lost. In that case the function, `gi_BackToMainMenu()` could be removed. The function `Menu().Select` would have to be replaced by a function that – before selecting the menu elements – checked whether the system to be tested displays the main screen. If this was not the case, actions would have to be performed to return to the main screen.

Low level functions

The functions `gi_CheckConfirmation()` and `gi_BackToMainMenu()` from Example 4.1 are low level – they operate directly at the level of the test object's interface. This can, for instance, be a standard (GUI) Windows application, but also a mainframe system that can be accessed via a terminal emulator on a PC. Examples of other low level functions are `SelectOption()` and `PressButton()`.

If these functions are used at cluster level, they are called low level action words. Low level action words are primarily used in tests with a low level of detail (such as unit tests) whereas the high level variant is used in functionality-based tests.

In GUI applications, the number of low level functions is usually smaller than in character-oriented systems, since the test tool already supplies many functions. The aspects of the user interface in automated testing will be discussed in a separate chapter.

Directive functions

In addition to high and low level functions, directive functions can also be implemented. They are not related to the application to be tested and are not concerned with the interface. Directive functions are used to control the test process. If these functions are used at cluster level, they are called directive action words. Examples of directive functions are:

- adding extra information (cluster author, time of the test, etc.) to the generated report;
- reading an external file;
- writing error messages to the report.

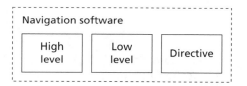

Figure 4.2   Navigation software set up

4.4.2   Using libraries

All the developed functions (high level, low level and directive) together comprise the navigation software. They can all be included in a single script, but it is advisable to subdivide them into various scripts known as libraries. These libraries are grouped on their functional characteristics. This grouping can be based on the division into high level, low level and directive functions, but a grouping based on the parts of the test object is also possible. If, for example, a test object consists of four modules, four libraries can be set up on the basis of these modules. If a screen in the module changes, the related function can be retrieved easily. Usually, a combination of characteristics is the best basis for grouping, such as one library of high level, low level or directive functions per module.

With a clear and systematic division into various libraries, the navigation software can be maintained rapidly, simply and reliably. In this way, changes in functions only need to be introduced at a single location. The following issues must be taken into account when subdividing into libraries:

- the test object or part of the test object to which a function pertains;
- the function type (high level, low level, directive).

4.4.3 Physical structure

The physical layout and location of the navigation software make up an important part of the navigation environment's design. A clear and structured environment can contribute to rapid, simple and reliable maintenance. The physical structure depends on a test project's characteristics, and that is why there is no generic way to plan for it. However, it is advisable to store the clusters, the generated reports, and the navigation scripts separately in different locations.

To set up an environment at the start of a project, there are several options – three examples of which are shown in Figure 4.3. Option A shows the clusters, the generated reports, and the navigation scripts clearly separated from each other.

Sometimes a new version of the test object is released during the project. The navigation software then has to be adjusted, and the old version has to be retained. The set up shown in option B is designed for this situation.

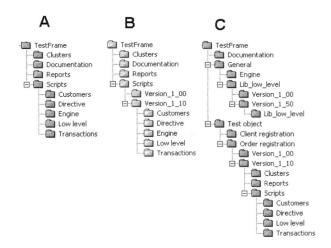

Figure 4.3   Physical structure of navigation software

If there are several versions of the test object, a navigation environment as shown in option C can be chosen. The general libraries and the test object libraries have been clearly separated. The general libraries contain functions that can be used for several test objects. Since an engine only contains directive functions that are interface independent, it can be used for various test objects – this turns it into a general library.

Other libraries can contain low level (e.g. `gi_OpenWindow`, `gi_PressButton`) and directive functions (such as the functions in the engine), but high level functions can also be included – for example, logging onto the test object or starting a batch procedure. This set up enables the optimal reuse of functions.

The test environment's physical location also requires attention. The entire environment can be placed centrally on the network, so that it can be accessed from several workstations. However, it may also be necessary to install the environment locally on only one workstation. A combination of centralized and local installation is also possible for test objects that have a different setting for each workstation, and therefore require different navigation software. For further information about laying out the test environment, see Section 2.6.

4.4.4   The starter motor

The navigation environment structure plays a role in the set up of the test's 'starter motor'. A starter motor is a function that initializes the test execution – it is called the MainScript. This script loads the specific libraries, selects the appropriate cluster, and starts the engine. Like the engine, this MainScript will be used for several test objects and therefore has to be set up in general terms with only directive functions.

4.4.5   The test tool

The test tool plays an important role in the navigation environment and where it is installed is very important. For example, this location issue will have to be taken into account if working on several workstations simultaneously. The test tool can be installed locally on all the workstations, or it can be made available from one central location. In general, the supplier of the test tool will be able to assist in making this choice. In some cases, the organization prescribes a particular location. In order to maintain a clear distinction between result (functions) and means (test tool), it is recommended that the test tool is not installed in the same environment as the functions and libraries that have been developed.

4.4.6   External tools

Other software is sometimes required for the test process, in addition to the test object. For example, software to start batch jobs, or a tool for effecting a time change may be essential. Another possibility is that part of a test object has to be tested when the rest of it has not been completed. If the test object must be fully operational to achieve this, certain measures will have to be undertaken, including simulating the parts of the test object that have not been created. These devices are called stubs and drivers. A stub is that part of a simulated test object where data is destined to go; a driver is that part from which the data originates. In other words, the existing test object invokes a stub, and a driver invokes the existing test object.

Sometimes, external tools take on the roles of both drivers and stubs. For instance, a database script can play the role of a driver, or a batch job that of a stub

– this way, they operate at the same level as the test object. If this situation occurs in the automated test process, separate high and low level functions will have to be developed. The location of the tools also plays an important part since they can either be stored in the test object environment or included in the navigation environment.

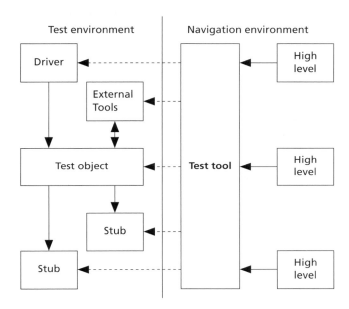

Figure 4.4   Coherence between the test environment and navigation environment

4.4.7   The test environment

As mentioned above, the relationship between the test environment and navigation environment is critical. When the test environment is set up, the existence of the navigation environment must be taken into account. A clear option will have to be created to approach the test environment from the navigation environment. Only then can the test tool be used for the test. In addition, the test environment must provide the option of testing the navigation script. This implies that the navigation libraries that have been developed constitute software in themselves, and therefore need to be tested before being put into operation. One option is to set up a completely separate 'test-the-test' environment, which is only used to test the navigation that has been developed.

4.4.8   Documentation

Documentation is an important part of the navigation environment's maintenance and management. The nature of the environment has to be described ('scope'), how it is structured ('structure') and how it is used ('procedures'). Documentation is not usually held in a single physical document, since the various subjects are documented in different places and ways. What follows is an overview of the subjects that need to be addressed in the test environment's documentation and the aspects of it that have to be described.

The parts of the environment and the scope of the navigation's responsibility have to be clearly defined. The parts of the entire environment are shown in Figure 4.5.

- test tool
- engine
- developed functions
- composed libraries
- clusters
- generated reports   ***Navigation environment***

- test object   ***Test environment***
- various databases for the test object (0-cluster, initial situation, etc.)
- other software needed for the test path (batch software, drivers and stubs)

Figure 4.5   Parts of the entire test environment

The structure of all these parts and how they are used must be recorded.

The test tool

The test tool is delivered by a supplier and it is important that the information about it is available at all times (e.g. help desk telephone number, settings, possibly executed adjustments, etc.). Agreements about the supply of updates and new versions must be established.

The engine

The engine acts as the hub within the navigation and it must be comprehensively documented. Characteristics such as its functionality and the technical specifications must be described, in addition to how modifications are introduced and how new versions of the engine are implemented.

The developed functions

The function documentation should be located near the functions themselves. The best approach is to have each function preceded by a comment block containing the following information:

- the action word, if applicable;
- the function's purpose and a brief description;
- the test object to which the function relates, if applicable;
- the function's author;
- the function's version;
- the function's modifications.

Another option is to create the documentation outside the functions. This creates an overview of low level functions, which is also available for other test objects or projects.

The composed libraries

The documentation of a library can be placed in the library itself, as with the functions. For example, at the top of the library there can be a list of the functions in the library, stating the reason for this grouping. However, it is also recommended that this documentation is created outside the libraries, since the various libraries can be connected by a number of relationships – for example, high level functions can invoke low level functions in another library. This dependency can be described in a meaningful way in the documentation. In addition, issues such as the physical location, the structure of the libraries, and the procedures for modifications of newly built libraries can also be recorded.

The clusters

The clusters occupy a separate place in the navigation environment. They fall within the scope of the Analysis *and* Navigation phases. Clear agreements must be made about the delivery and maintenance, from the analysis phase.

The generated reports

The reports also occupy a separate place in the navigation environment. They also fall within the scope of the Analysis and Navigation phases and agreements must be made about the supply and maintenance from navigation.

The test object

In general, a test object can operate with various profiles and settings. This often happens at user level. For example, the toolbars offered by many applications can be adjusted according to user preference. If there is a test script that makes use of such functionality, it will be necessary to document the settings of the system to be tested.

Various databases for the test object (0-cluster, initial database, etc.)

The test environment must be transparent. To this end, all the databases, both local and central, are charted. Links to other systems must also be described.

Other software needed for the test process (e.g. batch software)

If software other than the test object is required for the test process, it must be documented. For instance, separate functions may have been developed and put in a separate library with a specific structure for this additional software. This software can also have its own settings and its own initial configuration. All additional software must be treated and described in the same way as the test object itself.

4.5   The engine

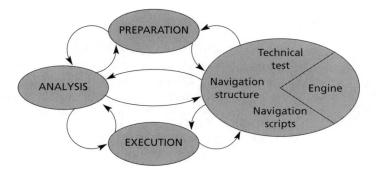

Automated testing within TestFrame has a number of standard functions that are always required. For example, reading in a cluster, linking an action word to the related function, and generating a test report. These routines can be brought together in an 'engine' module.

   To start a test, the test tool must run a script. The main script is responsible for completing the tests in the test framework (navigation structure). This script activates the engine. Since the engine is the hub of the navigation, it is one of the most important components of TestFrame's test framework implementation.

4.5.1   Routines which can be carried out by the engine

The engine can effect standard routines including:

- reading the cluster file;
- recognizing and executing the standard (directive) action word functions;
- recognizing the actions defined by the navigator (for the test-specific action words);
- performing checks and processing the results;
- creating the reports.

A summary of the functions of an engine is given in Figure 4.6, with an overview in Figure 4.7.

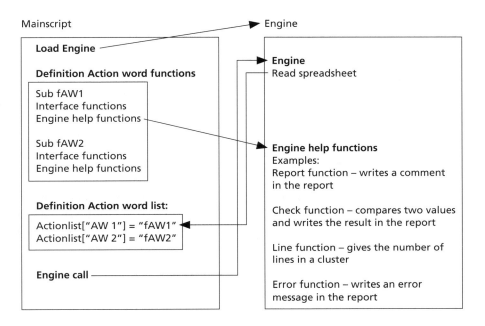

Figure 4.6   Engine functionality

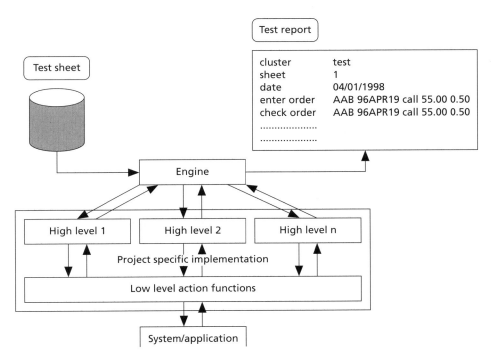

Figure 4.7   Position of the engine within navigation

4.5.2   Recognizing action word functions

The engine does not know in advance which action word functions the navigator has defined. This means that the navigator has to indicate which functions have already been written, and for which action words. Therefore, an action word needs to be linked to the function that relates to it. There is a function available in the engine which identifies action words and connects them to the related functions.

4.5.3   Check function

The check function ensures that the values retrieved from the screen are compared to those mentioned in the spreadsheet, and will state this in the report. Since the engine already knows the expected values recorded in the spreadsheet, the navigator only has to supply the actual values.

4.5.4   Commands of arguments

The engine can support various special commands, used by an analyst in the spreadsheets, in the arguments of an action word. The arguments can be given a special meaning using commands. For instance, there are commands to store data during the test, and also commands that indicate that a field must be empty. Examples of this type of command are:

- &Keep;
- &Refer;
- &Empty;
- &Not Empty;
- &Spaces;
- &Anything;
- &Cont.

4.6   Developing an action word function

This section describes how to set up navigation scripts. An action word function (navigation script) is a function that is written in the test tool, and constitutes the implementation of an action word. This details the test's automation. The overview is illustrated by a concrete example of how this can be set up using TVL.

It is assumed that Chapter 3 (Analysis) has been studied. This knowledge and the examples in that chapter will be reused here. The interface shown in Figure 4.8 will be used.

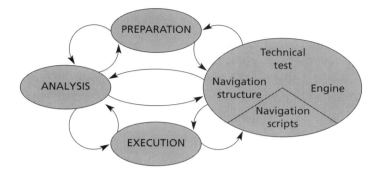

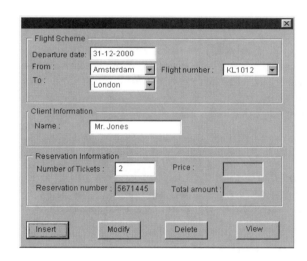

Figure 4.8   Example of test object's user interface

4.6.1   Feasibility

The first task is to determine if the action word created by the analyst is technically feasible. It is important that the application itself is reviewed to confirm that the arguments contain sufficient data associated with the action word. It is important that the arguments have been described, that they are included in an example, and that the order of the arguments has been recorded. If not, consultation with the analyst will be required.

The action word's start and end points must also be determined. An action word must be capable of being executed completely independently, on the basis of an assumption of a particular initial position. It should be possible for the action words to appear in the cluster in random order. It is important that the application's start and end points are correct, otherwise running the cluster may cause the navigation to fail.

4.6.2   Preparation

A number of preliminaries must happen to ensure that the navigation system runs smoothly. A navigation system consists of a test tool, an engine, and self-developed scripts. The preliminary preparation includes the following activities:

- installing the test tool;
- installing the engine;
- access to the test object;
- navigation system settings;
- selecting action word functions.

Installing the test tool

Typically, a test tool is used to automate a test and it must be installed correctly to operate correctly. Generally, this can be achieved easily if vendor support is provided. If there are new test tool versions, it is wise to install the new tool version after uninstalling the old one. Remember to store the user settings and other self-developed data (scripts) in another location.

Installing the engine

The engine must be placed in the right location within the navigation structure (see Sections 4.4 and 4.5). The engine should operate in such a way that application-specific navigation can read clusters or create reports easily.

Access to the test object

The system to be tested must be accessible to be able to develop and test the navigation fully. The test object needs to be installed and configured correctly so that it operates as reliably as possible. It is also useful to examine the test object in combination with the test tool to assess the test tool's support.

Navigation system settings

Many types of settings are required for the combination of navigation scripts, engine, test tool, and test object. An automated test often stops as soon as it encounters a single incorrect setting – therefore, it is important to check that all the settings are correct. The documentation plays an important role in this respect. It is recommended that standard settings are used as much as possible, and that any deviations are documented.

Selecting action word functions

The engine reads the spreadsheet line-by-line, and invokes the action word function belonging to the action word on the line that is being read in. Let's examine how this works in practice. The test object in this example is the Flying High flight reservation system used earlier. Two action words will be specified here – 'flight reservation entry' and 'check flight reservation'.

Specifying an action word function's selection is not difficult since it uses a translation table. The engine invokes the (fixed definition of the) function `gi_Action words()` (see Example 4.2). In this example, action word function names have not been determined according to particular rules. In bigger test projects, it makes sense to standardize them. See the Section 4.7 for more information about this subject.

```
Function gi_Action words(Action word As String) As String
Dim b_Found As Boolean

 b_Found = True
 Switch Action word
  Case "flight reservation entry"
   gi_EntryFlight()
  Endcase
  Case "check flight reservation"
   gi_CheckFlight()
  Endcase

  Default
   b_Found = False
 Endswitch

 If b_Found = True Then
  gi_Action words = Action word
 Else
  gi_Action words = "  "
 Endif
 Return gi_Action words

 End Function
```

Example 4.2

4.6.3   Specifying action word functions

The starting position of the first action word 'flight reservation entry' (as defined in Section 3.3.3) is the main menu. The action word description shows that a new flight reservation must be selected first. After that, all the data recorded with the action word must be entered in the user interface, using the 'arg' list (array) as it is often defined in the engine. This will comprise all the arguments stated after the action word in the spreadsheet. The action word is stated in `arg[1]` and the arguments start with `arg[2]`. Example 4.3 shows the specification into TVL for the action word 'flight reservation entry' in the function '`gi_FlightEntry()`'.

```
Function gi_FlightEntry() As Boolean

  If Window("Flight reservations system - Mainmenu").Shown = True Then
    Window("Flight reservations system - Mainmenu").SetFocus
    Button("New flight reservation").Push
  End If

  Window("Flight reservation system").SetFocus
  Edit("Departure date:").SetCursor(1,1)
  Type("[Home][sEnd]")    "Select all the existing characters in the field
  Type(arg[2])

  List("From:").Select(arg[3])
  List("Destination:").Select(arg[4])
  List("Flight number:").Select(arg[5])

  Edit("Name:").SetCursor(1,1)
  Type("[Home][sEnd]")    "Select all the existing characters in the field
  Type(arg[6])

  Edit("Number of tickets:").SetCursor(1,1)
  Type("[Home][sEnd]")    "Select all the existing characters in the field
  Type(arg[7])

  Button("Entry").Push

  Return OK

End Function
```

Example 4.3

When this function is started, it checks whether the main menu screen is active at that time. The analysis prescribes that the screen has to remain open after this action word has been completed. If the previous action word was also 'enter flight reservation', the application's starting position is not the main menu. The check intercepts this.

The next function we specify is 'check flight reservation'. It is very similar to the previous function. However, this action word focuses on validation so there is little input. Besides 'arg', the array 'rectable' is also used here. The engine in this example will compare the entire 'arg' list with the 'rectable' list, and indicate the differences detected in the report (the function `Check()` is used for this purpose). Example 4.4 shows the specification in TVL for the action word 'check flight reservation' in the function `gi_CheckFlight()`.

```
Function CheckFlight() As Boolean

  Window("Flight reservation system").SetFocus
  Button("Overview").Push

  Window("Flight reservation overview").SetFocus
  Edit("Reservation number:").SetCursor(1,1)
  Type(arg[2])
  Button("OK").Push

  Window("Flight reservation system").SetFocus
  rectable[3] = Edit("Departure date:").GetText()
  rectable[4] = List("From:").GetSelection()
  rectable[5] = List("Destination:").GetSelection()
  rectable[6] = List("Flight number:").GetSelection()
  rectable[7] = Edit("Name:").GetText()
  rectable[8] = Edit("Number of tickets:").GetText()
  rectable[9] = Edit("Price:").GetText()
  rectable[10] = Edit("Total:").GetText()

  Check()

  Return OK

End Function
```

Example 4.4

This function has not taken into account the fact that the reservation number entered may not occur in the database, and will cause an error message to appear in the application. In other words, the spreadsheet must be perfect in order to perform this function correctly. In practice, it is desirable to have error handling take place in navigation.

4.6.4 Testing the action word function

When action word functions are created, it is necessary to test them appropriately. Of course, it is very inconvenient when a test stops after reading only two lines from a spreadsheet (or even worse, after 100 lines!) because there is an error in the navigation. If some error situations remain uncorrected, this implies that the test cannot be executed appropriately by the computer.

When an action word function is tested, it is important to try to imitate lifelike situations, without using the whole spreadsheet. The navigator can set up a small cluster containing the action word to be tested. It makes sense to do this in cooperation with the analyst. Remember the error situations, and try to test them as much as possible.

4.6.5 GUI-based systems

When the navigation is set up, the test object's interface must be taken into account. Often, a division is made into test objects that use a GUI, and test objects that use a CUI (such as a terminal). GUI and CUI systems are technically different and this means that the navigation needs to be set up individually for each type of interface.

Several issues must be monitored when a GUI application is tested. The main issue is that such an application has many different independent screen objects, whereas a CUI application screen displays only one object. In practice, the analysis differs very little (since functionality is detached from the technical implementation) but a GUI application's navigation is much more complex.

A clear risk when testing a GUI application is that too much attention is paid to obtaining and checking all sorts of details from the various screen elements (e.g. x-, y-positions, width, height, etc.). This is often exacerbated by the test tool's technical ability to do so. Testing these features are, however, not usually a priority. The following issues are typically the most important.

Synchronization

Synchronization is required if applications vary in their responses to input with respect to timing. This variation can be caused by delays in the system itself (because several applications are running at the same time), or by external factors (network delays, etc.). A test tool can usually automatically compensate for this, but not in every case. This section first discusses the automatic synchronization provided by test tools, and then synchronization that may need to be programmed.

In some cases, the test tool is simply too fast to elicit an appropriate response. For example, the test tool may attempt to read values on screen while the application is still refreshing them with new values. The test tool then synchronizes on the basis of the availability of the screen data, and not on the basis of the values being refreshed on screen. Often, one of the problems is that the screen values look all right (i.e. the timing problem cannot be observed with the naked eye), whereas the required values are quite different. In this case, the value observed must be cross checked against the old and expected values.

Automatic synchronization by the test tool

Test tools are usually able to compensate for time variations automatically. These are called 'time-outs' and they can be set through the test tool's options. A time-out is the maximum amount of time the test tool will wait for a certain event. If the event occurs before the time period has lapsed, the test run is immediately resumed. An extra waiting period can usually be inserted for each occasion on which a screen is opened. Often, it is unwise to set the standard too high. If the implementation of input always needs to be checked, for example, or if no error message appears, the test tool will wait for the set time period each time. This has a major impact on a test's execution time. Therefore, it makes more sense to set the standard waiting period to be short and to use explicit extra waiting periods when required.

Additional synchronization

Functions must occasionally be written for additional synchronization, to make the test wait for the object to complete a certain operation. In general, the application reflects this waiting visually, by displaying an extra window or by turning the fields grey during that time. It is more problematic if the application does not give any feedback when it has completed its operation. In that case, there is simply no other choice than to wait for a set period of time. It must be made clear that it is not always necessary to write your own function if the test tool can solve this automatically. It is only necessary when a waiting period needs to be longer than usual.

In order to create an additional synchronization function, you must first determine what feedback the application shows when it has finished processing. This feedback must always be used in the function's implementation. In Example 4.5, a situation is used in which the fields temporarily turn gray until the application has completed a particular processing operation (in this case, data is retrieved via the network). It is wise to create a low level function for which the maximum waiting period can be set. In this way, the function can be used at different points during the navigation. The function must also state the screen element that is being waited for. In other cases, the expected value in the function could also be entered.

Keyboard versus mouse

In a GUI environment, both a keyboard and a mouse can be used. Most test tools immediately convert this type of action into mouse operations, since their application function is 'listening'. The actions can be executed correctly, but using the mouse instead of the keyboard. One of the main advantages of this approach is that mouse-oriented commands are synchronized automatically and no additional synchronization actions are required.

Sometimes, a GUI environment has to be explicitly navigated using the keyboard. For example, keyboard input may constitute an essential part of the test object (e.g. data entry applications). The test script may then need additional synchronization, otherwise the screen elements may not be ready for the input. In general, the test tool interprets keyboard input as analogue, or 'raw input', which is executed without synchronization.

Most test tools have two ways of approaching the GUI – object-oriented, or via the analogue (raw input) method. An object-oriented approach means that the test tool is familiar with the various screen elements, and it approaches them without the user having to indicate the element's location. The analogue approach means that the test tool is not familiar with the various screen elements, but only undertakes action at certain locations. Most test tools can combine the two methods in a single script. The test requirements will determine which of the two methods is appropriate – the navigation produced by the object-oriented method is easier to maintain.

```
Function gi_ExampleFunction () As Integer

      Window("Flight system").SetFocus
      Button("Update").Press

      'Synchronize: wait maximum 60 sec. until the field name is available again
      gi_WaitForNetwork("Name:", 60)

      Return OK
End Function


Function gi_WaitForNetwerk (s_ObjectName As String, i_TimeOut As Integer) As Integer
Dim i_MaxWaitTime As Integer, b_EditEnabled As Boolean

      'Determine maximum period in seconds by adding the entered time-out to
      GetSeconds (catches up on current time 'seconden to)
      i_MaxWaitTime = GetSeconds() + i_Timeout
      b_EditEnabled = Edit(s_ObjectName).GetAttr("Enabled") 'Initialise the
      edit status

      While (i_MaxWaitTime > GetSeconds()) And (b_EditEnabled = False)
            b_EditEnabled = Edit(s_ObjectName).GetAttr("Enabled")
            If b_EditEnabled = False Then
                  Pause(1) 'Release system short while
            End If
      End While
      If b_EditEnabled = False Then
            Return TIMEOUT               'Maximum waiting period exceeded
      Else
            Return OK                    'Network ready in time
      End If
End Function
```

Example 4.5

Custom objects and mapping

Custom objects are objects that the test tool does not recognize as standard. In such cases, the test tool only registers mouse clicks and keyboard actions while it is recording. If the test tool does not recognize specific objects as standard, it usually has an option to treat the object as standard – this operation is called 'mapping'. However, the technical processing of this type of object in the operating system must be identical to the standard screen element. It can only be determined if this is the case by evaluation. If the custom objects cannot be 'mapped', the input can be entered using mouse movements, mouse clicks, and keyboard input – checks can be performed by retrieving text from the screen. It is then best to put them in low level functions.

Screen elements that cannot be compared to standard objects in any way are trickier. Common examples include drawing objects within a drawing application, and worksheets in a spreadsheet program. In order to test these screen elements properly, low level functions must be written so that these elements do not obstruct testing. This can even lead to having to perform certain actions manually. A technical test carried out at the start of the project will indicate this.

Integrations / add-ons

Integrations (also known as add-ons) are expansions of the test tool to enable it to deal with specific environments. Screen elements that the test tool did not recognize before can be recognized as standard objects by complementing the tool in this way. This eliminates the need for low level functions to be written. The tool supplier usually applies an additional charge for these add-ons but they may also be included in the delivery on the installation CD. Some integrations can be downloaded from the vendor's web site. Before commencing a project, it is a good idea to ask whether add-ons are available to avoid having to write low level functions. An advantage of using these lies in the fact that the tool supplier maintains them and, thus, the navigator does not need to do it.

Unexpected screens, error windows and application errors

A hindrance in the execution of automated tests is the fact that error messages can appear at unexpected points and it is difficult to determine what to do with these messages. If the application ends up in an 'error situation' that requires it to be restarted, this will halt the execution of an unattended test run. The entire test environment can become unstable due to this halt. Clear agreements must be made about these types of problems. Some error situations can be resolved automatically by the navigation. Others can be so serious that the test run must be stopped immediately and the error situation reviewed by experts (who may be the developers).

Expected error messages have to be intercepted, and it is recommended that the development team is asked which error messages will appear and when. Naturally, this also needs to be recorded in the information system's design documentation. However, practice has proven that the error message list indicated by the development team is not always exhaustive. One possible solution is to have the test tool ignore all unexpected error messages. Most test tools are equipped with standard features to do this automatically. It is important to print the encountered message in the test report, otherwise the tester does not know what happened.

Impact of version modifications

Modifications of test objects can arise in various ways – new functionality, modified functionality, and modified data. If only the layout of GUI screens has been modified, this has little impact on the existing navigation. However, one requirement for this is that the screen elements are located on the same screen. If new screen elements have been added, these also need to be tested and a new piece of navigation will have to be created. Between the different versions, the identifying names of the elements may have changed. The navigation will have to be adjusted accordingly. For test tools that use an interim table of objects and their attributes, only the modified objects need to be adjusted in that table.

4.6.6 Character-based systems

CUI systems are usually those in which one computer (often a mainframe) is connected to a number of terminals with text only display capabilities. The behavior of these terminals can be emulated on a PC, by using a 'terminal emulator' application that meets a specific standard (such as VT100, VT52 or ANSI). These programs can be used by a test tool just like any other program. The set up of this terminal emulator's interface is rather simple.

CUI systems usually have a text screen of 24 by 80 characters. Input is entered mostly in tab order. Some test tools have special expansions that support various terminal emulators – a great advantage of this approach is that the synchronization with the host (server or mainframe) can be executed in a standard way by the tool. If the selected test tool does not support the terminal emulator, it is the navigator who will have to take care of the synchronization. It is best to do so using low level functions which retrieve the information from the screen. The test tool must determine if the system has completed the processing operation before the text is read. For example, text output indicating that the system is 'busy' might disappear, or text output indicating that the system is 'ready' might appear.

Highly generic low level functions can usually be written for a CUI system and the use of such functions has many advantages. If, for example, only one function is written to read the screen, only this function needs to be adjusted when the terminal emulator is modified. This modification will, therefore, only have a minor impact on the developed testware's maintenance. All the other low level functions that require information from the screen will have to invoke this function. Example 4.6 shows low level functions used with CUI systems.

Retrieving text from a screen

This `gi_GetScreen` function can be used to retrieve information from a terminal emulation screen or a command prompt window. The screen information is stored in a general variable `gas_Textlines[]`. This is an array which contains the lines from the screen. `gas-Textlines[1]` contains line 1 of the screen, `gas-Textlines[2]` line 2, and so on. All the functions that require information from the screen invoke this function. The advantage is that if you switch terminal emulators, only the function `gi_GetScreen` needs to be adjusted.

To improve performance, you can choose to read the screen only if it has been changed since the last reading action. A screen changes, for example, when input has been entered after which the screen needs to be reread. A specification of this is the use of the flag `gb_Refresh`. For a function which enters data (such as the function `gi_Input()`) this is set to `True`, so that new screen information is read in the function gi_GetScreen. When the screen has been read, the flag is reset to False so that nothing new is read on the next pass.

```
Function gi_GetScreen () As Integer
Dim s_Text
If gb_Refresh=True Then                        'only retrieve screen information if
                                               'there was
                                               'input between this and the
                                               'previous screen display.

    Window(application).SetFocus               'a test tool needs to know in which window
                                               'follow-up actions will be executed.
    s_Text=Window.GetText                      'get the text from the active window and put
                                               'that in the variable text.
    TextToArray(s_Text,gas_Textlines,eol)
                                               'put the text, per line in an array. This
                                               'array is a general variable, so that the
                                               'screen information can be used by the
                                               'other functions
    gb_Refresh=False                           'Indicate that the screen no longer needs
                                               to be retrieved if there was no input.
End If

Return OK

End Function
```

Example 4.6

Checking whether a particular text is displayed on the screen

In Example 4.7 the gi_StringOnScreen function searches the screen to find a string. If the string is found, the line number is returned. If the string is not found, the value not_ok is returned. This function can be used for checks.

```
Function gi_StringOnScreen ( s_Str As String ) As Integer
Dim i_line As Integer

        gi_GetScreen ()
        For i_line=1 To 24 Do
                If (Index ( gas_Textlines[i_line], s_String)) Then
                        Return i_line
                End If
        Return NOT_OK

End Function
```

Example 4.7

Selecting an option

In Example 4.8 the `gi_Option` function expects the option's text as input. Based on this string, the option number is searched on the screen, and typed in. This reduces the dependency of adding and omitting options (and as a consequence, the number change).

```
Function gi_Option ( s_OptionName As String) As Integer
Dim i_OptionLine As Integer, i_OptionNumber As Integer
i_option_regel = StringOnScreen ( s_OptionName)          'find the line on the
                                                          screen 'that contains the
                                                          option.
        i_OptionNumber = GetOptionNumber ( i_OptionLine )  'get the number of the
                                                          option on that line.
        Type(i_OptieNummer)                               'type the number followed
                                                          by enter
        Type(gs_Enter)
        Return OK

End Function
```

Example 4.8

Checking whether certain text is on a certain line

In Example 4.9 the `gi_StringOnLine` function searches `s_Str` in a specific line. If `s_Str` is found on the line, the value `OK` is returned. If `s_Str` is not found, the value `NOT_OK` is returned. This function can be used for checks.

```
Function gi_StringOnLine ( s_Str As String, i_line As Integer ) As Integer
        gi_GetScreen ()
        If (gb_Index ( gas_Textlines[i_line], s_Str)) Then 'Check if s_Str is on the
                                                              line
                        Return OK
        End If

        Return NOT_OK

End Function
```

Example 4.9

Retrieving error messages

The `gs_GetMessage` function in Example 4.10 will return the text of the last line, which was retrieved by the function `gi_GetScreen` as a return value. In most terminal emulators, this is the message line. If the message is in another line in a particular application, only this function needs to be adjusted.

```
Function gs_GetMessage () As String

        gi_GetScreen ()                                 'get the text from the screen

        Return gas_Textlines[24]              'return the text of the last line

End Function
```

Example 4.10

Returning to the main menu

The gi_GoToMainMenu function shown in Example 4.11 ensures that the system to be tested is taken to a standard start position for the next action.

```
Function gi_GoToMainMenu () As Integer

If StringOnLine("Mainmenu",1)=NOT_OK Then    'if the system is not in the main menu

        TypeKey(F3)                          'press F3. In this example the
                                             'screens have only one level. In most
                                             systems
                                             'more actions need to be executed
                                             'to get to the main menu.

        End If

End Function
```

Example 4.11

Entering arguments from the cluster in tab order

In Example 4.12 (overleaf) the `gi_Input` function ensures that the arguments from the cluster are typed to the terminal emulator screen.

Symbols in generic functions in CUI systems

The following symbols can be used in the function `gi_Input()`.

Table 4.1

Symbol	Meaning
1,2,…,n	Arguments from test cluster
'string	Text
R,r	Enter
Rx,rx	x times 'Enter'
Fx	Function key
T,t	Tab
Tx,tx	x times 'Tab'

```
Function gi_Input ( s_Parm ) As Integer

Dim as_Arr[MAXLEN] As String, ai_parm[MAXLEN] As Integer
Dim s_ArgumentNumber As String, i_Counter As Integer
Dim i_Num=0 As Integer, i_NumberOfElements As Integer
Dim i_RepetitionCounter As Integer, i_Repetitions As Integer
Dim i_ParmCounter As Integer
Dim s_Input=" " As String

      i_Num=SplitStringToArray(s_Parm, as_Arr,";")
      For i_Counter=1 To i_Num Do
       s_ArgumentNumber=as_Arr[i_Counter]; 'First argument for input
       Select Case (ToLower(Left(s_ArgumentNumber,1)))
        Case "t"      'tab
              i_Repetitions=Left(s_ArgumentNumber, 2)
              If i_Repetitions="" Then i_Repetitions=1
              For i_RepetitionCounter=0 To i_Repetitions Do
               s_Input=s_Input & "<kTab>"
              Next
        Case "f" 'function key
              s_Input=s_Input & "[F" & Right(s_ArgumentNumber,2) & "]"
        Case ""     'Text
              s_Input=s_Input & Right(s_ArgumentNumber, 2)
        Case "r"              'return
              i_Repetitions=left(s_ArgumentNumber, 2)
              If i_Repetitions="" Then i_Repetitions=1
        For i_RepetitionCounter=0 To i_Repetitions Do
                 s_Input=s_Input & "<kReturn>"
      Case Else 'arguments from the cluster
              i_NumberOfElements=gi_SplitStringToArray(s_ArgumentNumber, ai_Parm,"-")
              If i_NumberOfElements=1 Then
                s_Input=s_Input & ga_Arg[ai_parm[1]]
               Else
               For i_ParmCounter=ai_Parm[1] To ai_Parm[2] Do
                s_Input=s_Input & ga_Arg[i_ParmCounter]
               Next
              End If
       End Select
      Next
      Type(s_Input)
      gb_Refresh=True
      Return OK

End Function
```

Example 4.12

The navigator can add other keys to the function `gi_Input()` in the low level library.

The arguments are entered in the active screen in tab order. For example, `gi-Input('2-6;f2')` enters arguments 2 to 6 (inclusive) in tab order, and subsequently presses f2. The same effect can be achieved by the statement `gi-Input('2;3;4;5;6;f2')`. The main advantage of this working method is that screen modifications need minimal maintenance effort on the navigator's part. If, for example, fields 4 and 5 are switched, this will have the following effect on the script of the function – `gi_Input('2;3;5;4;6;f2')`.

4.7   Navigation standards

It is the navigator's task to think about the results – is this readable and comprehensible for others? Is there sufficient comment in the sources, so that the justification for certain choices are also clear at a later stage? Comments explaining what a standard command does can be omitted since this can be read in the tool's user manuals. The layout of the sources can be used as a guideline and is less important that the quality of the contents. These standards are a means of achieving higher quality. This section contains directives for the names, and programming in navigation scripts for TestFrame.

TVL is used in the examples. This document can be used as a guideline for test tools using other languages (where the TVL language is replaced by the language used for the navigation). Take the comment sign for example – in TVL it is a single quote', but may be a semi-colon; or a hash# in other languages. What are called functions in this document may be procedures, methods, or other modular entities in the test tool concerned.

The reasons for standardizing navigation programming are as follows:

- maintainability of scripts;
- common approach for mutual exchangeability of navigators;
- creating reusable (generic) parts;
- promoting the reusability of scripts;
- readability of scripts;
- reducing the risk of programming errors;
- clarity during navigator training.

4.7.1   Variables

Names

In order to enhance the readability and maintainability of the navigation scripts, variable names are given a prefix, from which each variable's type can be derived directly:

```
<area of application><type><_><name of the variable>
```

Area of application (scope)

A distinction is made between general, local, and function variables. A general variable is defined with the `public` statement, the scope of which is the entire program. A local variable is defined with the `dim` statement, the scope of which is the library in which it occurs. A function variable is defined within a function (procedure), the scope of which is that function.

Table 4.2 Area of application of the function

Area of application	Prefix	Scope	Definition
General	g	Entire program	`Public`
Local	l	Within module	`Dim`
Function or procedure	(none)	Within function	`Dim`

For example, the scope of the variable `gs_OrderNumber` is the entire program.

Type

The type of variable determines which form of value it can contain – for a function, the type indicates which kind of value the function returns. The prefixes used in TestFrame navigation are shown in Table 4.3 and are based on standard prefixes used in programming languages (based on the Hungarian notation).

Table 4.3 Type of variables

Type of variable	Prefix	Description
Array	a	The indication 'a' precedes the type of the variable
Boolean	b	Value True or False
Exponent	e	Figure in scientific notation, e.g. $-3.14e7$
Float	f	Figure with decimals, e.g. 78.07623
Integer	i	Full figure, value can also be negative
String	s	One or more characters, text

For example, the variable `gs_OrderNumber` is a general variable (g) and a string variable (s).

Name of a variable

A variable's name starts with a capital letter. If the name is composed of several words, each word also starts with a capital letter. The name should be useful and functional, ensuring that it indicates the meaning of that which it denotes. For example, `gas_NameList` is a general variable (g), consisting of an array (a) of strings (s). Note the two capital letters in NameList.

Explanation and examples of type variables

The examples in Table 4.4 are presented to explain the TestFrame name notation in more detail.

Table 4.4

Name	Type	Description
as_NameList	Array of strings	This local array contains strings only
lb_Passed	Boolean	This local variable can contain TRUE or FALSE only
gs_Char	String	This general string contains zero or more characters
f_Amount	Float	Real, local figure
e_Exponent	Exponent	Exponential (part) figure
i_X	Integer	Full figure

4.7.2   Constants

There are two types of constant. The first consists of constants the value of which is used in action words and functions. The second type are the error codes. These are discussed in the next sections.

Value constants

Value constants and variables differ as far as their use is concerned. The form of their names differs only slightly – to mark a constant, the character 'c' is added to the prefix as shown below:

`<area of application><c><type><_><constant's name>`

For example, `gci_TimeoutPeriod` is a general (g) constant (c) of the type integer (i).

Error codes

System functions return error or status codes. These codes are general constants with numerical values. Numerical values should be avoided in favour of the constant. For example, '0' should not be used in place of 'OK'. Often the test tool's documentation can be used to find the appropriate constants.

4.7.3 Action word names

A programmed action word's name has a specific structure (see Table 4.5). The name is, by definition, identical to the action word from the analysis it belongs to, with spaces removed, and the initial characters of words are replaced by capital letters. The analysis standards prescribe that these names must be written in lower case.

Table 4.5 Action word format

Action word	Program name
select menu	`SelectMenu`
enter relation	`EnterRelation`
print relations overview	`PrintRelationsOverview`

The same applies to action words as for variables and constants – ensure that the name is useful and functional, and that it corresponds with what it has to do. The analyst determines action word names, but the navigator should authorize them. This is to prevent overlap between action words, and the same name being used for different action words. If, during the building of an action word, it appears that the name chosen is not a good description of the executed actions, the navigator should consult the analyst to find another name for it.

4.7.4 Function layout

Comment header

Each function must be supplied with a comment header (see Example 4.13). It can include the following data:

- author – maker's name;
- version – (optional) version number of the function;
- last update – date of last modification;
- arguments – the input and output parameters of the function;
- return value – the possible output value of the function;
- general variations – (optional) use of general variables (only included if general variables are used);
- description – the function description;
- changes – (optional) various past modifications.

```
'------------------------------------------------------------------
'
'Author   : TestFrame Navigator
'Version  : 1.1
'Last Update : 03 sep
'Arguments  : in : s_Text
'      in : s_FindText
'      in : s_ReplaceText
'Return value : Replace text
'Description : Replace in text s_Text the characters in
'      s_FindText by the characters in
'      s_ReplaceText and return as return value
'        .
'
```

Example 4.13 Function header

Return value of functions

Functions always return a value – indeed it is sensible to have them give a useful value. For example, a function returns a `True` value if it has been completed correctly, and a `False` value if it has been completed incorrectly. This is not only easier to read, but it also prevents errors. Another option is to name a variable at the start of the function and to supply it with a start value. An example is presented in Example 4.14.

```
Function gi_Function(in s_InputFile As String, ..) As Integer

Dim i_Ret = OK As Integer
  ...

  ...
  'If s_InputFile does not exist, discontinue processing
  If (s_InputFile= " " ) Then

    ...
    i_Ret= E_FAIL
  Else

    ...
  End If
  ...

  Return i_Ret
End Function
```

Example 4.14

4.7.5   Agreements about programming

Unambiguous programming enables code to be interchangeable and transferable. To achieve this, each navigator must code in the same way. Simply having agreements about the names is not sufficient to achieve this goal. Agreements must also be made about issues such as:

- code layout;
- statement use.

These aspects are discussed briefly below.

General

Using 'hard coded' values in scripts should be avoided. In addition, the following must be used where possible:

- constants;
- cluster information.

General variables should be avoided since they create dependencies in the test scripts and increase the risk of error situations. Functions should be used as much as possible – they prevent redundancy, are easier to read, and increase ease of maintenance.

Comment

Source documentation is mandatory and must be carried out by inserting comments in the code. For example, when a window is closed using `Window().Close`, a comment should be inserted explaining why this approach has been chosen and not the Escape key. In the event of modifications, the comment must be inserted immediately after modifying the code. If it has to be done at a later stage, the programmer often forgets what has changed – adding comments then becomes a difficult and error prone process.

4.8   Alternative scripts for navigation

In this chapter, we have developed all the navigation functions in the test tool's script language. We have used TVL as an example language. An easily maintainable and effective navigation system can be created in a well designed script, with high level and low level functions. For major test projects, a number of additions to this working method are possible. The objective of these additions is to record as much of the target system information needed in the navigation outside the functions. Here are some examples:

- which type of objects (such as entry fields, buttons, check boxes, etc.) does a certain window contain?
- which screens need to be opened successively and entered to display, for example, a client?

Using this approach, no technically trained navigator is needed to maintain the data. In addition, preparing the navigation at an early stage of system development is easier – especially in situations where there are no operating operative software versions available, for example.

In Section 4.4 a navigation structure was presented consisting of two layers – low level and high level. It is often sensible to insert a medium level between them to enable recording navigation information outside the script. We will call this medium level the 'intermediate level'. These intermediate level functions focus on the system's technical implementation, just as the low level functions do. However, where a low level function focuses on an individual element of, for example, a screen (such as entering one field or pressing one button) the intermediate level function operates one level higher. Examples include entering all the fields in a window or displaying a complete record in a batch file.

The two layer model of Section 4.4 is now a three layer model – high level functions use intermediate level functions, which in turn call low level functions. Two new mechanisms can be added to this navigation structure that enable information to be stored outside the scripts. These two mechanisms are 'table-controlled navigation', and 'template-based navigation'. Table-controlled navigation is relatively easy to support technically. Template-based navigation is only possible if the engine provides this option.

Table-controlled navigation implies that specific information about the system interface to be tested is included in external tables. Often this is a list of objects that can be displayed in a particular window. There are also other examples, such as a table containing fields of a transaction record which can be sent to a transaction processing system through a network connection. In fact, such a table is a kind of 'repository' (i.e. a structured set of data about an information system). Tables are a suitable vehicle for building intermediate functions from low level functions. We can then write, for example, `entry window address data <value 1> <value2>`... The intermediate level function's navigation queries the table to see which fields occur in the window 'address data'. Subsequently, it determines the type of each field (e.g. a text entry field or a list box), after which the appropriate low level function can be invoked to enter the data.

Template-based navigation is another way of defining action words. Using this working method, an action word is not built into the script language (as described in Section 4.6) but is defined by means of a 'template', which can be compared to the action word template in Section 3.6. This definition happens in a cluster using a special directive action word – 'define template'. The new action word and its parameters are the arguments of 'define template'. The lines following 'define template' determine what should be done if the new action word is used. They contain actions and checks, as usual in a cluster. The difference is that the arguments of the new action word start with the '&' symbol.

Take a client entry in a functional acceptance test, for example. To this end we create a new action word 'client entry'. Using a template, this could look like as shown in Figure 4.9.

DEFINE TEMPLATE	CLIENT ENTRY	&FIRST NAME	&SURNAME	...
PUSH BUTTON	NEWCLIENT			
DATA ENTRY	FILE CLIENT	&FIRST NAME	&SURNAME	FEMALE
PUSH BUTTON	FINANCIAL			
...				
END TEMPLATE				

Figure 4.9   Template

The action word 'client entry' is defined using the parameters 'first name' and 'surname'. Firstly, pressing the 'new client' button opens the screen 'client data'. Various data is then entered. The first and surname are the new action word's parameters. Subsequently, the new client's gender must be entered – this action word always selects 'female'. This value has not been defined as an argument and, therefore, all the clients that are created in the tests using the action word 'client entry' are entered as female. This apparently suffices for this examplar test.

After interpreting the cluster with the template definition, the new action word can be used (Figure 4.10):

CLIENT ENTRY	DANIELLE	ORWELL
CLIENT ENTRY	MARILYN	MARSH
...		

Figure 4.10

First, the template's lines are executed with 'DANIELLE' instead of &firstname and 'ORWELL' as &surname. After that the template is executed again with the values 'MARILYN' as &firstname and 'MARSH' as &surname.

The template approach is generally applied to create new action words rapidly. They can be used to express high level words in intermediate level words.

4.9   Summary

This chapter has explained the automated side of TestFrame (Navigation phase). Automated testing is an important part of the TestFrame method. It offers the opportunity of setting up a form of automated testing that can be applied flexibly throughout an entire test process. However, whether or not to automate a test must be reconsidered every time a test project is started.

Since tooling is important in automated testing (it is the third column of the Greek temple metaphor), a technical test is recommended for the test project. This examines the extent to which the test tool can communicate with the test object. This needs to be done at the start of a project to avoid unexpected technical problems later.

How do the principles of automated testing work within TestFrame? The TestFrame method uses action words – they consist of a variable part and a fixed part. The variable part concerns an action word's arguments – they contain the data required for the test case and their content can differ for each action word. The fixed part concerns the actions (keystrokes, mouse movements, etc.) that execute the actions relating to the action word. These actions are always the same for each action word.

This set up creates a situation in which the action word can be programmed into the test tool (action word function). The constant actions are recorded in the test tool code, and the arguments are read from the analysis clusters during the test's execution. This makes the test software easy to maintain, easier to read, and more accessible.

A navigator operates in a navigation environment that is constantly changing. For that reason, it is very important to provide it with a sound structure. By setting up test software in modules, a logical division is created based on three types of functions – high level, low level, and directive functions. In a large navigation, it is sensible to record some of the information elements (such as objects in a screen) outside the scripts.

It is recommended that functions are divided into different libraries based on common characteristics, to be able to deal with modifications rapidly, simply, and reliably. The standards within the functions themselves must also be adhered to – consistent names, layout, and comment are the first step towards proper maintenance.

In addition to the test software, issues such as script documentation, test tool and external tool management constitute part of the navigation environment.

The engine is the heart of automated testing within TestFrame. Since it is the hub of the navigation, the engine is one of the navigation environment's main components. In general, the engine is a library which consists of a number of directive functions that are a standard feature of TestFrame. The functions are entirely project and test object independent. The engine's main functions are:

- reading the cluster file;
- recognizing and executing the standard (directive) action word functions;
- invoking the specifically defined action word functions;
- executing the checks;
- creating the report.

When an action word is programmed into an action word function, it is always important to check if the analyst's wishes and demands are technically feasible.

Consultation between the navigator and the analyst is also required to refine, or sometimes completely change, action words.

Another key issue with action words is that they always have (documented) fixed start and end positions within the test object. This is because an action word must be capable of being executed entirely independently, based on the assumption of a particular start situation. Therefore, action words always have to be tested extensively in different orders before they are actually used in real test runs.

The difference between GUI test objects ('windows') and CUI test objects ('terminal') also leads to a difference in the way action word functions are specified. GUI's have the option of communicating directly with the various objects (buttons, entry fields, etc.) on the screen. This is impossible in CUI test objects where, usually, the entire screen is seen as one big object. For that reason, synchronization is different and more low level functions must be programmed for CUI systems.

5 Execution

Introduction

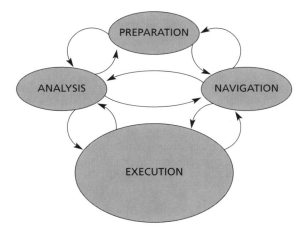

The actual dynamic testing of information systems is realized in the Execution phase. Based on the analysis, test cases are executed against the test object, with the predicted results being checked against the actual results. If the predictions do not match the results, the cause of the deviations must be determined. Possible causes include an error in the test products, a fault in the test environment, or that the test object operates differently than expected. This latter category of issue is, of course, of most interest to testers and developers.

In addition, it is important to take measures during the Execution phase to ensure that the developed test products are managed appropriately. This is an important precondition for guaranteeing a test product's reusability. All too often, due to a lack of management, test products cannot be reused when tests are repeated. Thus, the transition of a TestFrame project from the test development phase to the test management phase is an important process. This chapter describes the factors which play a role in a structured test run, including various scenarios for executing repeat tests. The result management process is also described and, finally, the management of test products during a test process is addressed.

5.2 Start position of the test run

The test environment must be complete before the test run can commence. This implies that the required infrastructure and the test object must be correctly configured and available. If an automated test run is concerned, the required test tools must also be installed. This can be established before the test run is started by using a checklist (i.e. comparing available components with the components recorded in the test plan). If some of the required components are not available, the start of the test run should be postponed. It is important to report the delay (including reasons and solutions) to all stakeholders in a timely manner. The initial database, defined during the Analysis phase (basic files for executing the test), must be installed in the test environment. A backup of this initial database should always be available since it must be possible to reset the start situation each time the test is repeated. If it is impossible to restore from a backup, a different procedure must be designed to achieve an unambiguous initial position. This condition must be met to guarantee a consistent test run.

Often, agreements must be made with the operations department, or the computing center, concerning the availability of staff and system capacity before a test is executed. This concerns activities that the test team executes itself, for instance, running batch jobs. This communication is important to avoid delays in the test run due to the unavailability of the required processing capacity.

If a shared test environment is used (i.e. several test teams using the same testing environment), the teams must also be attuned to one another. Test teams need to know when it is possible to execute a test without adversely affecting other test runs. An example of this is when one test team cleans up a test database, while another is executing a test. This problem is easily detected, but it disrupts and delays the execution of the test. A problem that is more difficult to trace arises when two test groups start a test run independently. If the test cases to be executed affect each other, expectations and results will not match. Often, a large amount of (search) time is required to determine that the observed mismatch is not caused by a program error, but by the test not being executed consistently.

Prior to the structured test run, it is advisable to get an impression of the quality and stability of the system to be tested by using a random test. This pretest is not executed on the basis of prior documented test cases, but on the personal insight and experience of the tester. The aim of this test is to detect major errors that may obstruct the test run (affectionately known as 'showstoppers') as rapidly as possible to solve them before the actual execution of the structured test begins. The ability to reproduce results is a key issue in this respect, and therefore the initial position, and each action that leads to the result, must be recorded.

5.3 Planning the test run

The test run takes place on the basis of the analysis results – the test scenario, the test conditions, and the test cases. If the execution is automated, unambiguous and consistent execution is guaranteed. A test tool will not skip any test cases, unless a system error occurs. In a manual test, there is often a temptation to skip a test case that has previously led to a correct result several times. However, one condition for a valid test run is that it starts from the same initial position each time. Automated test runs result in automatically generated test reports which indicate deviations from expectation.

In a manual test run, clarity, consistency, and objectivity are more difficult to guarantee. It is very important to make it clear to the testers that if the test is not executed on the basis of the analysis, the test results would lose a great deal of their value. One measure to enhance the clarity, consistency, and objectivity of a manual test run is to ensure that the test cases designed by one tester are executed by another tester. The test reports are generated manually – testers indicate on the test sheet whether the test was successful or whether it failed.

The test cases will usually be executed several times during a test process. Issues are established during the test run, after which the tested system is adjusted by the development team. Therefore, several test runs must be planned to be able to retest. There is no hard and fast rule for the number of test runs that should be planned within a test process. However, it is unrealistic not to plan any repair activities (or repeat tests) within a test process, since issues are established in each test process.

A number of aspects are beneficial for charting the required number of test runs. The following factors play a role in the determination of the number and timing of test runs to be executed during a test process.

The expected quality of the test object

The higher the expected quality of the test objects after the test, the lower the number of expected issues. This leads to shorter required restore and retest time. Therefore, fewer test runs are planned than for test objects with a lower expected quality.

Acceptance criteria

Depending on the defined acceptance criteria, more or fewer test runs can be scheduled. If the client defines lower acceptance criteria, fewer repeat tests are necessary. This reduces the total number of test runs to be executed.

Time required for fixing errors

During test runs, a period of time must be anticipated for the development team to repair errors. Typically, this can be executed simultaneously with the test run, but sometimes the test team will have to wait for the development team. Which activities the test team must execute during such periods should be stated.

Scope and complexity of the test set

A test set containing many test cases takes longer to complete than a test set with fewer comparable test cases. The more complex the test set, the more time the test run will take to complete. Testing the user interface of an online complaints registration system requires less time and coordination than testing the lifecycle of a savings account, in which various end-of-day (batch) processes must be executed.

Availability of parties outside the test team

If such parties are required for the test run, capacity must be planned. Examples include the operations department and external suppliers.

Availability of the test environment

To realize the test run, a test environment is required. If it is not permanently available to the test team, agreement should be reached on when the test runs can be executed. This concerns both internal coordination (e.g. when several test teams within one organization use the same test environment) and external coordination (e.g. if an interface needs testing that is connected to an external party). An issue that should not be underestimated when test runs are planned, is the potential reorganization of the test environment. If it has to be reset to its initial position for the execution of a test run, the time required to do so should be anticipated.

Batch and online tests

If both batch and online tests have to be executed, it is advisable to set up the test runs in such a way that the batch and online functions of the system are not tested simultaneously (i.e. sequential rather than parallel execution). The test runs for these two parts can often not be executed together – for example, because a batch program blocks tables that the online program is trying to update or delete.

Automated or manual test run

The completion time of automated test runs is shorter than that of manual test runs. Therefore, more automated test runs can be executed in the same period of time.

In addition to the points described above, it is important to select an appropriate approach to the execution of the test runs. The following sections describe a number of possible approaches.

5.4 Test run strategies

Several test run strategies are possible – three types are described below:

- type A – run full test set each time;
- type B – run test to first blocking error, with resumption from the error;
- type C – run test to first blocking error, with resumption from the start.

5.4.1   Type A – full test set each time

In this situation, the entire test set is executed on the test object during the test run. Errors that have been detected are reported. The entire test set is repeated on each new completion of the test object. Repeat tests are executed implicitly in this approach.

Example

Test set A comprises 30 test cases. All are executed on version 1.0 of the test object during the first test run. In response to the test reports that arise from the test run, issues are reported. After the error analysis and repair, the new test object's new version 1.1 is delivered by the development team. The entire test set A is executed on this version again. The results and a new version of the test object (version 1.2) arise from this test run. After the third full run of the test set it appears that there are no more errors that need to be resolved, after which no more test runs are executed.

Figure 5.1   Test run type A

Advantages:

- all the test cases are executed on the test object, ensuring the greatest possible certainty about the test object's quality – new errors are detected rapidly;
- it is clear which tests have been run.

Disadvantages:

- the complete test cannot be run if an error is encountered that blocks the test – an error that blocks the test is, for example, a complete part of the system that cannot be started. All the test cases that apply to this system part cannot be executed. In practice, this can be solved by temporarily skipping certain test cases;
- time consuming, especially if it is executed manually.

5.4.2   Type B – run to first error; resume from there

If type B is chosen, the test set is executed until the team detects an error that blocks the test. A new version of the test object is then delivered in the short term, in which the error causing the block has been corrected. Another option is to wait until the development team is ready to supply a new version of the test object. However, the new version has to be relevant and at least able to correct some errors with 'urgent' or 'high' priority.

The execution of the test set continues with the next test runs, from the point where the test run stopped last time around. In addition, the corrected errors are subjected to a retest. Test cases that did not lead to an error are skipped in this variant.

Example

Test set B comprises 30 test cases. During the first test run, an error causes the test to block in test case 11. Test cases 1 to 10 have been successfully completed on version 1.0 of the test object. In response to the test reports arising from the test run, errors are reported. After an error analysis and correction, the development team delivers the new version 1.1 of the test object. Test cases 11 to 20 are executed on it, since an error that blocks the test occurs in test case 21. Specific repeat tests based on the processed errors are also included in this test run. New errors, and a new version of the test object (version 1.2) also arise in this test run. During the third test run, test cases 21 to 30 are executed, plus specific repeat tests based on the processed errors. After the third test run no more errors arise, after which no new test run is executed.

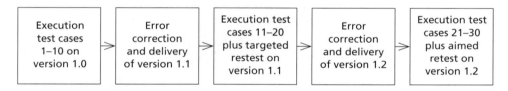

Figure 5.2   Test run type B

Advantages:

- this approach provides a solution for dealing with errors that block the test;
- more rapid retesting – feedback of errors is not postponed until the final test case has been executed;
- requires less execution time (suitable for urgent projects).

Disadvantages:

- new errors that arise in parts of the test object that have already been tested, and operate correctly at that moment in time, are not observed. The eventual quality of the test object is guaranteed to a lesser extent because of this.

After the final planned regular test run, a run can be executed in which all the test cases are executed once more to counter the disadvantage of type B testing. This provides the necessary insight into whether the test object parts that operated as expected (before the modifications of the test object) still do so after the modifications. Naturally, adding such a test run requires more time.

5.4.3   Type C – run to first error; resume from start

If type C is chosen, the test set is executed until the team detects an error that blocks the test. Subsequently, a new version of the test object is supplied in the short term, in which the error causing the blockage has been corrected. Another option is to wait until the development team is ready to supply a new version of the test object. However, the new version has to be relevant and able to correct some 'urgent' or 'high' priority errors. The test is then re run from the start of the first test case. Therefore, repeat tests are implicit in this approach. Type C only deviates from type B with regard to the retest. In type B, only the test cases that contained errors are executed again, whereas in type C all the test cases are always executed again after errors have been detected.

Example

Test set C comprises 30 test cases. In the first test run, test cases 1 to 10 are correctly executed on version 1.0 of the test object. An error occurs in test case 11 that blocks the test. In response to the test reports that arise from the test run, errors are reported. After an error analysis and correction, the development team supplies the new version 1.1 of the test object and the test is run again from test case 1. Then test case 21 causes an error that blocks the test. This also gives rise to error analysis and a new version of the test object (version 1.2). During the third test run, test cases 1 to 30 are executed. After this run, there are no more implementation errors and no more test runs are executed.

Figure 5.3   Test run type C

Advantages:

● all the test cases are executed in the latest version of the test object, which creates more certainty about its quality – new errors are rapidly detected;

● the approach accommodates the occurrence of errors that block the test.

Disadvantages:

● time consuming, especially in manual test runs.

5.4.4   Testing under pressure of time

Often, tests must be delivered in a shorter time than planned (or allocated). To address this problem, priorities must be assigned to tasks and low priority tasks cancelled. Priorities and risks are determined for each test condition. Conditions with the lowest priority should be crossed off (i.e. those which are 'nice to have', 'could have', 'should have', finishing with 'must have'). If any 'must have' tasks are to be cancelled, the risk to the client must be assessed. The deletion of some parts of the test execution and the accompanying risks should always be reported directly to the client. Ultimately, the client must make an informed decision about any test cancellations.

5.5   Analysis of test results and test report

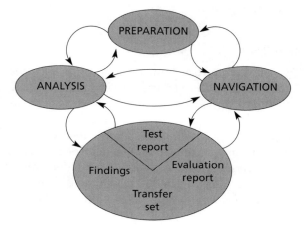

Using the test report, the correspondence of the test results with the predictions can be established. Any deviations are detected and registered as errors, which must then be analyzed.

If the test has been executed by computer, a test report will automatically be generated by the navigation during the test run. Depending on the person for whom the report is intended, different layouts can be used. For example, management is generally more interested in summaries, whilst the test analyst needs more information to analyze the report, and to record any possible errors.

The analyst must check if the test tool has succeeded in executing all the actions. In addition, any deviations must be compared to the predicted values and assessed. These assessments can only be properly executed if the navigation has recorded the relevant error messages (and any other messages) in the report. The navigator implements the way in which error situations must be processed after consultation with the analyst. This includes determining the exact text of the error messages and the situations in which they have to be displayed.

Data should be included at the top of the test report to identify the test. This includes cluster data (i.e. what is contained in the header of each test sheet), and also data about the version of the navigation used. In addition, it can be useful to log the directory paths of the relevant files in the report, as well as the time of the start of the test. The reports can also include details of the test environment and which version of the system was tested. In this way, it is possible to trace which versions and under what conditions the test was run. If the test tool fails to find an entire record during a search operation, this needs to be reported in a different way.

Analysis of the reports can show various types of errors:

- An error may have been made in the test specifications – such as a typing error or an erroneous assumption;

- Errors could also have been made in the programming of the navigation script – the tool may be searching in the wrong screen, or the order in which the values from the spreadsheet have been entered in the screen is incorrect. This type of error should not occur when the test sheet is run, but should have been intercepted by the navigator when the navigation script was tested. Either the test sheet with the test cases, or the navigation scripts needs to be amended to solve these errors.

- If both the navigation script and the contents of the test are correct, the test may still fail due to environmental factors. For example, the application may be temporarily inaccessible due to network problems, meaning that the test tool is unable to execute the specified checks resulting in an error. If the test is rerun at another time, chances are that the error will no longer occur, which sometimes makes it difficult to analyze the situation.

- Besides the above mentioned errors, there can also be actual errors occurring within the system being tested.

The analysis of the deviations is executed by the test team, in collaboration with experts in the field concerned. In addition to assessing the nature of the problem, the risk of the established errors is also assessed. Factors such as how frequently an error situation occurs, and the implications for the business of not correcting the established error, play an important role. The development team attempts to define the cause of the error, supported by the test team where necessary.

The test has been set up by determining the test conditions from the requirements. For every condition, a risk is linked by not properly executing the test. This set up is a combination of risk-based testing and requirements-based testing.

The test reports typically contain the results of the test. An alternative approach reports on the basis of which risks have been covered, and which requirements have been approved.

In this way, confidence in the system grows on the basis of its test reports (i.e. every time more risks are covered and requirements approved). While reports on the basis of the actual results can increase confidence in the system, these results may not be valuable in risk determination if they are of a trivial nature.

If the test cases from the test sheets are executed manually, a test report must also be prepared manually. A printed version of the sheet with test cases can sometimes be used for this purpose. The deviations for each test case should be recorded clearly and unambiguously. If the test case can be executed without problems and deviations, it can be ticked as having passed.

5.6 The transfer phase

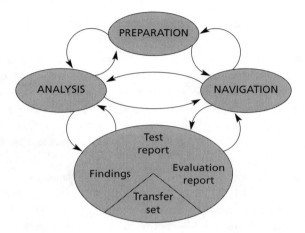

In the transfer phase of a TestFrame project, the test manager delivers a final report. This final report acts as a release document for the client. The final report must at least contain the following.

- Deviations compared to the defined test plan – the test plan includes a description of the TestFrame project execution. All deviations observed during execution must be described and reasons for the deviations must be given.
- Test process evaluation – the final report must indicate how the selected test strategy fitted the actual test process execution.
- Test results – the final report must contain a summary of the test results generated during the test process.
- Error overview – the final report provides an overview of all the errors registered during the test process (for example, by means of a matrix that compares the error's priority with its type). A trend analysis of issues registered should also be included. This can be displayed on a chart, for example, showing the number of registered issues in each time period. An important part of the issue overview is an indication of the issues that have not yet been remedied (including their priorities) since this is one of the factors used in giving advice about its release to the next phase. If possible, errors still to be dealt with are also indicated.

- Metrics of the test process – the collected metrics are included in the final report based on the subsequent recalculation.

- Test process evaluation – including an assessment of the parts of the test process which have been executed successfully, and which could have been executed more efficiently or appropriately. Where appropriate, a separate document can be prepared for the evaluation of the test process.

- Advice with regard to the release of the test object to the next phase – such transfer advice (e.g. system test to user acceptance test or acceptance test to production) is derived from the uncorrected errors, based on the current quality of the test object. The risks of these errors need to be charted.

In the transfer phase, the party responsible hands over all the test products of the previous TestFrame phases to management. This can be the test organization itself (sometimes part of the test organization is specifically set up for this) or a management organization external to the test team. The test plan prescribes to whom the test products will be transferred. The final report and the test products, which are to be transferred together, constitute the transfer set.

5.7   Issue management

Issues must be registered during the test run. The logging of deviations, compared to expected results, forms an important part of the reports generated in the test process. It is important to know who undertakes actions in response to the issues, and when the solution is to be provided. Insight into an issue's status ultimately leads to a better view of the test object's quality. This can be translated into a decision to take a system into operation or not. Appropriately organized issue management also provides the basis for effective communication between the test and development teams. More information on this subject can be found in [Kane 99].

An issue during the test process is a deviation from an expected result. This applies to deviations found in both the software and infrastructure (dynamic testing), and to deviations in the documentation, such as basic and detailed designs (static testing). All issues must be registered and should be easily accessible.

Many tools are available on the market for supporting the issue management process. It is also quite easy to self-administer issue management using a spreadsheet or database. The advantage of automating issue administration, over a manual solution, is that it offers superior options for tracking, monitoring, accessibility, and reports. If issue management is not automated, a written issue form can be used. However, in that case, it is important to ensure that proper procedures are set up for the paper flow – this prevents forms getting lost or piling up.

Issue management also serves another important purpose – it can be used to communicate reported issues to the clients via the help desk. In this way, a large audience will be informed about known problems, and will be notified when solutions are available for which test cases.

Sometimes, testers are offered the option of recording a 'wish list' via issue management, such as deficiencies identified in application logic. Naturally, agreements must be made about the scope of such a list, and how items in it can be acted on appropriately.

5.7.1 Consultation arrangement

A good consultation arrangement is important in issue management. An arrangement is often used where the test team's contact consults the developer's contact. This can be its own development team, or the supplier's. In this chapter, we assume that the coordination of the test team is taken care of by the test manager, and by the technical project leader on the part of the development team.

In a test process, consultation between testers always happens. This process involves checking whether established issues have already been included in the administration. New issues are passed on to the test manager. This consultation is informal in nature, and usually happens during a normal working day. In contrast, consultation between the test manager and the technical project leader is formal. New and outstanding issues are addressed, and target dates for new versions of the application are discussed.

Consultation also takes place between the developers themselves. The transferred issues are assessed and allocated. These consultations are usually informal. Figure 5.4 shows a summary of this arrangement.

Other groups may also be included in decisions concerning how issues are to be dealt with. For example, a product management department could participate in these discussions if they are involved in the development of the project.

If a production acceptance test is executed, consultation takes place between the development team and the management team. The above mentioned consultation arrangement also applies here.

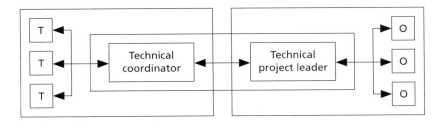

Figure 5.4   Consultation arrangement

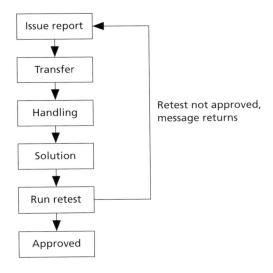

Figure 5.5   Issue management diagram

5.7.2   Issue management procedure

Figure 5.5 schematically displays the steps involved in issue management. Issues are reported as soon as the tester observes them, and are only registered in full if a new issue is encountered.

Issue status is preferably reviewed in regular consultation between the test manager and the technical project leader. At these consultations, the nature of the issue must be clarified. Some of the issues should be transferred – those with priority status must be reported to the technical project leader immediately. Other issues can be rejected, withdrawn, or deferred. Changes in the status or classification of the issues usually lead to a change in their administration.

The technical project leader discusses the transferred issues with the development team. Most issues are dealt with by assigning them to a developer. These issues are allocated the status 'taken on'.

It is sensible to hold issue consultations regularly, preferably on a daily basis, at the start of the project. During the rest of the test process the number of meetings can be reduced, especially when the number and importance of the issues decreases.

Once a solution has been found for an issue, it can be corrected. Firstly, the developer reports the solution to the technical project leader. The project leader records the most recent state of affairs in the administration. The status is changed from 'taken on' to 'completed, not transferred'.

During one of the regular consultation meetings, and after updating the administration, the technical project leader reports which issues have been dealt with to the test manager. The supply date of a new version of the test object is then determined, in conjunction with a retest. This scheduling is the test manager's responsibility, and returns the decision to the test team. As soon as the new version has been installed in the test environment, the technical project leader changes the status from 'completed, not transferred' to 'retest'.

After the new version has been supplied, the test team executes the retest. For each issue that has been solved, the retest shows whether the solution is approved or not – approval implies that it has been corrected; rejection means that a new message is created bearing the same number. This ensures that the history of the issue is retained. The issue is 'taken on' again by transferring it to the technical project leader at the consultation meeting. The process is repeated as necessary.

5.7.3 What has to be recorded?

In order to execute issue management effectively and efficiently, at least the following issues must be registered.

Unique identification

Issues should always be identified with a unique number. It is also important to indicate the application's version. Since an issue can reoccur at a later stage, it is also useful to record the release with the issue.

Person involved, date and time

The person who reported the issue, and also the date and time of observation, are recorded. This makes it easy for the parties involved to act as the elapsed time since identification and the issue observer are readily available.

Description of the issue

It is the tester's task to describe an issue carefully so that it is transparent for the developer. A description such as, 'Some aspects of the client registration process fail' provides insufficient detail. It would be much better to say, 'the system displays a foreign client in the client registration system, and an issue code 212, after which the process is aborted, and the data is not stored (entered data: T. Tester, 21-6-2001, Antwerp, Belgium)'. Function and screen identifications, screen printouts, and trace files are also examples of useful information. This enables an effective search for the issue that has occurred. It is also possible to refer to further information recorded on paper.

Type of issue

The classification of an issue provides useful additional information since it indicates the type of issue concerned. Issues can, for example, concern different parts of the system, such as the user interface or the database. Using this information, testers and developers can anticipate further possible issues during the process. Suppose the classification shows that 100 database issues and one user interface issue have been found – the development team and the test team know that relatively greater attention must be paid to the development and testing of the database, rather than the interface.

Priority

The importance of the issue is denoted by indicating its priority. The following classification could be used:

1. 'must have' – this issue has financial consequences for all our clients;
2. 'should have' – this issue has financial consequences for one of our clients, or has non-financial consequences for all our clients;
3. 'could have' – this issue has non-financial consequences for one of our clients, or has consequences for a client's department, and no workaround is possible;
4. 'nice to have' – this issue has some consequences for a client's department, but there is no easy workaround.

It is the test manager's task to continuously monitor whether the development team corrects the issues within the term set. Priority plays an important part in this respect.

Developer and start and end date of the solution

This records the developer who handles the issue, and the date on which debugging started. The end date of issue correction is also recorded.

Status

The status indicates the phase which an issue is in. The following classification can be used:

- 'reported, new'– tester has reported a new issue;
- 'reported, again' – the tester has reported a repeated issue;
- 'taken on' – the developer is handling the issue;
- 'completed, not transferred' – issue correction completed, but not yet transferred to the test environment;
- 'retest' – issue correction completed, transferred to test environment, can be processed by tester;

- 'retest approval' – correction of issue approved by tester;
- 'retest rejected' – correction of issue rejected by tester;
- 'rejected' – developers will not take on the issue;
- 'withdrawn' – tester withdraws the issue;
- 'deferred' – issue will be processed at a later stage, or after the current release.

The form shown in Figure 5.6 can be used to register issues. In respect of content, it is broadly in line with the above.

Issue report			
Name of application: Version number:	Issue number:	Appendix: Y/N	
Description of the issue, including the test case in which it occurred: Appendices:			
Type of issue	Priority ● Urgent ● High ● Medium ● Low	Test blocked Y/N	Status ● Reported ● Taken up ● Completed, not transferred ● Retest ● Retest approved ● Retest not approved ● Rejected ● Withdrawn ● Deferred
Reported by:	Reported on:	Taken up by:	Taken up on:
Solution plan ready:	Solution realization ready:	Description of the solution:	

Figure 5.6 Template for an issue report

5.8 Test product management after the test process

Outdated testware is unreliable and, therefore, cannot be used for the execution of a new regression test. In order to be able to reuse testware, and the test environment, they need to be updated regularly. This section suggests how to perform this operation. The emphasis is on testware and test environment management between projects.

After a test process has been completed, the different products from the project need to be managed so that they can be used as a starting point for any follow-up projects. This concerns the following:

● The test environment – the test object (the application), as well as the infra-structure (hardware, middleware, DBMS) subjected to the test;

● Testware – test-specific matters such as test strategy, test plans, clusters, test conditions, test cases, navigation scripts, and test data.

This section takes a specific environment for a single system as its basis. As discussed earlier, it is also possible to layout and manage a test environment for several systems, often including the required test data. The principles mentioned here apply to the management of a test environment for a single application, and to the management of an integral test environment.

5.8.1 Preconditions

Organizing test product management after the completion of a test process has a number of preconditions. The most important is that someone has to be appointed as manager of the test environment and testware in between test processes. The second is that management after the completion of the test process is executed systematically, and forms a permanent record of the tasks and responsibilities of the test environment and testware manager. The responsibilities that must be assigned include the following:

● who files the test environment and the testware;

● who manages which test environment components between test processes;

● who manages the test tools;

● who makes the test environment and the testware available when a new test process starts.

In addition, agreements must be made on the services and quality attributes to be supplied by the manager. For example, what is the maximum period between the request for a test environment and testware from a test project, and its completion by the management organization? These agreements can be formalized in a service level agreement.

The manager determines all responsibilities, in consultation with the development, operations, and computing departments, and the test organization. It is important to note that the manager does not always execute the activities person-ally. However, the manager must accept responsibility for the management of the test environment and the testware between two projects, even if other parties or subcontractors are employed to perform key tasks.

5.8.2   Procedure

The procedure below describes the development of the process from the announcement of a new release up to, and including, the filing of the test environ-ment and the testware.

Step 1: announcement of a new test object

The trigger to start a new test process is the development department's announce-ment of a new test object release. The department also indicates to the test organization which modifications, both technical and functional, have been implemented compared to the previous test object version. This enables the test organization to schedule the time at which the required test environment and test-ware has to be made available by the manager.

Step 2: executing a call-out order from the test organization

The test process organization composes a call-out order, within the agreements made with the manager with regard to tasks, responsibilities and services, to make the test environment and testware available. After the test organization has learned when the new release of an application to be tested can be delivered, the call-out order is sent to the manager.

Step 3: making the test environment and testware available

The manager ensures that the components required for composing the call-out order, mentioned in Step 2, are acquired. To this end, the following actions must be initiated:

- acquiring the required infrastructure;
- allocating infrastructure;
- structuring the desired test environment;
- restoring filed testware from a previous release.

Step 4: adjusting and running the test

After the manager has made the testware available, the testers adjust it where appropriate. Adjustments are only made to this testware version, not to other available versions such as local copies. These adjustments can consist of adding and modifying test cases (because of modifications, additional functionality, or other aspects to be tested) as well as removing test cases that have lost their relevance. The latter is important to avoid needlessly increasing the number of test cases, which would reduce manageability. If necessary, changes are also made to the test environment, such as a new database version or hardware component.

Configuration management, results management and content management during the testware test constitutes an important part of the project tasks. After the testware has been adjusted, the test is run and the test results are checked. Advice is then provided with regard to the release of the test object.

Step 5: returning the test environment and testware

After the test results have been approved, the test environment and testware are put on hold and transferred to the manager. To this end, a transfer document is used and the physical test environment and the physical testware drawn up by the test organization are supplied. The responsibility for the management of the test environment and testware is passed back to the manager.

Step 6: filing the test environment and testware

In this step, the test environment and the testware are filed in such a way that the same test environment and testware can be retrieved on request. Therefore, the filed versions of the test environment and testware cannot be modified without first being released by the manager.

5.9 Summary

After completion of the Analysis phase and (if the test is automated) the navigation scripts have been developed, the test can be run. After the test run, the results have to be analyzed. Deviations from the expected results are included in the issue management. Data recorded includes which result has been established and on which date, who is handling the result, and other information needed to identify the issue and update its status. After completion of the test run, the test set needs to be transferred to the standing organization – to this end, a transfer set is composed. The key role of management must also be considered.

6 Test management

6.1 Introduction

Manual testing is a complex task, and automated testing is even more complex. In addition to designing good clusters and automating by means of correctly functioning navigation, many obstacles can arise that are not content-related. This chapter addresses test management issues and provides some tools for dealing with them. We do not intend to give a comprehensive treatment of subjects such as project management and organization theory. However, we do discuss some issues that frequently arise during test processes:

- resistance;
- commitment;
- lack of clarity with regard to responsibilities;
- conflicts outside the test process;
- motivation;
- dependencies.

These are rather common key issues that have occurred in one form or another in many projects. None of them are insurmountable, so long as they are addressed adequately and in a timely manner. Therefore, it is essential that the test management task is covered in some form or other in each test assignment. For small projects, this can be one of the team members, but for a larger team there is often a particular employee who is responsible for this task – the test manager. In practice, the test manager spends a large amount of time on 'environment management' – factors, expectations and obstacles outside the actual test activities.

6.2 Resistance

The introduction of a new working method can induce resistance. This may occur at various levels in the organization, take various shapes, and have various backgrounds. This section examines a number of typical instances of resistance in some detail and provides some suggestions for dealing with them. However, note that there are no standard solutions for dealing with resistance.

Resistance is not the exclusive territory of the test manager or test consultant. Anyone who introduces a new working method can encounter resistance. This also applies to the person who works as a navigator or analyst. It is often useful to consult a manager and/or client, or more experienced colleagues, when resistance is observed. This section provides strategies for recognizing resistance and dealing with it.

Resistance arises when a certain development is deemed undesirable, either for the organization or for an individual or a group within that organization. This assessment can be correct or incorrect – it can also be a consciously reasoned impression of a more or less subconscious feeling. Resistance is often not expressed openly. Frequently the true causes of the resistance may not be apparent, as resistors are reticent about giving reasons openly since they could be judged to be as negative. The forms of expression that the test manager or test consultant should be aware of are usually behavioral, and/or more general. The following are examples of expressions that can be observed:

- 'Let's reconsider';
- 'Fine, but are we ready for it?';
- new objections are raised time and again;
- silence;
- people say 'Yes', but act disapprovingly;
- 'Okay, but in this specific instance ...';
- a problem is denied;
- postponing;
- changing the subject;
- dominant behavior, for instance, jokingly putting down the people who are involved or have advocated systematic testing.

However, the underlying resistance may be as follows:

- 'I don't understand';
- 'I hadn't expected all this';
- 'This will cost me my job';
- 'We cannot make such efforts';
- 'Now "they" find out that we don't test properly here';
- 'I would like to score in this area myself';
- 'I would prefer to take my chance with another party'.

Most of these are examples of resistance that can be solved. TestFrame can be easily fitted into an existing situation. The decision whether or not to develop a test systematically, and to automate it or not, can be made for each cluster. The emphasis should be more on giving information about what TestFrame really means, and, most of all confidence building.

By far the most common cause of resistance is a lack of confidence. Typical elements are:

- testing is still our domain, although there is a new approach – its introduction does not mean that others are suddenly taking the lead;
- systematic testing is not difficult – after a while we will understand it just as well as those who are introducing it;
- we can learn to do it as well as the outsiders who are introducing it;
- we will not become dependent on an external party;
- by introducing systematic testing, the people now involved in testing continue to be involved in it, and they will even take the lead.

6.3   Commitment

This is a key factor in every activity in an organization – it is the willingness of executives and other staff important to the test process to invest in the activity, show interest in it, award it priority, etc. It is often difficult to create commitment for testing, and to retain it in the long term. Testing is sometimes seen as boring, something which does not yield instant benefit, and is less interesting than, for instance, developing new systems.

Commitment can be gained by offering solutions, not new problems. Although this seems obvious, this rule is often overlooked. Some people want to prove themselves as testers, and do so by spouting impressive test theories and concepts, defined in difficult terms. Compiling lengthy lists of every task that has to be completed before the testing can even start definitely puts people off. Try to avoid this situation at all costs! Divide the material to be tested into clusters, indicating how the navigation can be structured, etc. It is especially important to offer concrete solutions rapidly.

Explain, especially during the first contact with an executive who has little testing experience, that systematic testing and test automation involves monetary cost and human effort. The sooner this is acknowledged and accepted, the more likely it is that these costs and efforts can be included in budgeting processes, such as annual plans and project plans.

A system that operates properly promotes a positive image, a fact that many executives do not appreciate. Often, only the negative aspects are noticed since errors in a system do lead to problems and annoyances. However, the opposite effect can be achieved by providing a high quality system – then your own position, and that of your department, improves. The perfect operation of a system leads to a rapid increase in confidence. Analogies outside the IT sector are plentiful. For example, various products have a dominant market position without strongly distinguishing themselves by product characteristics or a favorable price. They achieve this by means of a 'quality image', reliability, and the absence of faults. Consider the benefit that ISO quality assurance gives to many companies.

When pressure on time scales and budgets builds up, as a project progresses, attempts are made to cut the costs of test effort. Staff who are important for both test development and test automation are 'temporarily' reassigned to relieve pressure. Although this often happens, it considerably increases the risks involved in a project. It is very difficult to prevent this in the end, but an experienced test manager will always try to 'return to the problem at hand'. Testing is, by definition, an activity that takes time and money, and there are always options for removing or scaling back some aspects. An organization cannot afford disruption of the business process and the question has to be whether the original objective for testing is still relevant. If a client decides to invest less in testing, this decision has to be recorded formally, with the implications noted for the record.

The most dangerous pitfall for a test manager is to adopt a problem to become, as it were, the owner of a problem that is beyond their control. A test manager has to try to say nothing about the results of tests ('there are no more errors in the system') but rather to undertake, together with the available staff, to execute a particular test effort. If the number of staff, or other resources, is reduced, this automatically implies that fewer testing activities will be carried out. This is not necessarily bad, but the decision and the responsibility for it are the client's, not the test manager's.

One of the simplest measures is to ensure that the executives have a clear insight into what testing involves. This applies to a number of issues:

- test development progress;
- test run development;
- test results and their implications for the risks run by the system;
- obstacles that occur, such as the setbacks mentioned in this chapter.

For a number of key issues, it is wise to inform the executives in a timely manner as to how the test (automation) process evolves, and which key issues and obstacles are expected at which times. A risk analysis, as described in Section 2.3, is a minimum requirement for starting up a test process. Such an approach helps avoid 'surprises', thereby giving a greater feel of control. It also helps to neutralize certain developments – for instance, the political game of laying blame when delays or setbacks occur is easier to play this way.

Test objectives enhance confidence in the correct operation of the system, by finding errors in as timely a manner as possible. If no errors are found this does not necessarily mean that the test has not been carried out properly, or that testing is a redundant activity. However, practice proves that, in most business environments, finding critical errors greatly strengthens the position of the test process. It supports the earlier decision of investing in the test process.

6.4   Lack of clarity with regard to responsibilities

A problem often encountered is lack of clarity in the allocation of responsibilities to the various departments involved, and to the project and its environment. Testing is an activity that requires a great deal of collaboration, and roles and responsibilities need to be clearly defined.

An example is the question, 'Who is responsible for this test?' A project leader, who is under pressure, often points at the users – 'it is their system, they have the expertise'. On the other hand, the users indicate that the developers are responsible – 'they have to supply a system that operates properly'. A test manager cannot afford to let this situation continue. He or she should aim to obtain clarity by any means, and cannot do this alone. This typically requires one or more discussions, and a decision by the executives who have greater responsibility than the test manager.

One rule of thumb is that the developers must adhere to the specifications, and that users have to ensure that these specifications are complete and correct. About half the errors in a system are caused by incorrect or incorrectly understood specifications; the other half by not working in compliance with those specifications technically. Therefore, both parties must contribute to the testing of information systems, each from their own unique perspective.

Another example is the question of who should examine the errors. There is a clear answer to this – the tester cannot go beyond establishing, as clearly as possible, that the outcome is not as desired. Determining the cause and remedying it is not part of the testing. Testers are bound to lose much more time searching than developers, which is disproportionately at the expense of the test efforts. It is better for the tester to try to find the next deviation.

Members blaming each other is very risky for a test team – this can easily start when a project takes more time than expected. In particular, test automation and interpreting test results are activities that often require more time than expected. Delays in the overall project should not be attributed to testing which takes longer than expected. Sometimes, planning pressure leads to an unstable system being supplied to the testers – one that has a large number of errors. Some of those errors can also delay the testing itself because the test environment has not been structured as it should, or because faults occur regularly due to problems in a workstation's memory management which interrupts automated tests. Some time later, everyone forgets about these problems, and the test itself is viewed as the delaying factor.

A 'health test' can be a way around this problem. Try to establish unambiguously if the operation of a system is perfect, and if there are any problems with factors such as memory management using one or more separate clusters. If these tests fail, it makes very little sense to proceed with other tests.

Another measure is to state from the start, for example at project meetings, that this phenomenon often occurs, and that attention should be paid to it. The developers must draw up clear and demonstrable system tests that must be completed successfully before a functional acceptance test is run.

6.5 Conflicts outside the test process

Working relationships are not always harmonious and business like. Particularly in complex projects, many conflicts and unresolved collaboration issues play a role. For the test activity, such a situation, by definition, implies increased risk which should be acknowledged and controlled by the test manager. If such risks exist, this will occupy an important part of the test manager's time, especially when the time for the test run is approaching. It makes sense to allocate the daily control of the analysis and navigation processes to others within the team, giving the test manager sufficient time for environment management.

Tension and conflict are sometimes not immediately noticeable. One indication can be the moment the test manager is confronted with a general vagueness. Pointed questions receive evasive answers, or there is a lot of talk but very little of it is focused. If there is also very little response at meetings or presentations, this evasive behavior points to hidden conflicts and resistance. Some investigation and specific questions can lead to more clarity.

The test manager has to do their utmost to avoid becoming involved in a conflict. Looking for allies is standard behavior in conflicts. However, going along in this way usually weakens the options for exerting the influence required to complete testing successfully. Neither should the test manager try to solve problems as a kind of mediator. In practice, it is difficult to reconcile this with the role of test manager, with regard to both time and position.

Problems in the fulfillment of the mediator role can, for example, also lead to risks for the test process, if only because it demands a disproportionately large amount of time and attention. However, conflict must be regarded as a risk for the testing, as well as for the project as a whole. That is why it is important to inform the project management.

6.6 Motivation

If the number of tests to be developed and automated is very large, and there will be completion times of six months or more, the motivation of the analysts and the navigators can become a problem. This can, of course, also happen in smaller projects but it is less likely. This is a highly undesirable situation for the people involved, as well as for the organization. Therefore, the test manager should view it as a main task to acknowledge such problems as they happen and take the appropriate action.

Motivation problems can sometimes be recognized directly through an employee's remarks, but often there are only indirect signals. A typical alarm signal is, for example, cynicism about work, colleagues, or the work environment. Low productivity, failing to undertake actions, or failing to fulfill promises also frequently occur. Usually, a personal interview is sufficient to solve these problems.

Explicitly expressed motivation problems must still be addressed, because entirely different motives can lie behind them, other than just the monotony experienced during work. Motivation problems must always be treated seriously, but effective action can only be taken after the cause has become clear. If the cause is not established clearly, a great deal of energy can be wasted in varying the work, whilst the person involved turns out to be dissatisfied about an unfulfilled promise of his line manager.

Lack of motivation can never be used as an excuse for doing a poor job. A test manager has to treat motivation problems actively and, especially, visibly but should never get involved in negotiations – e.g. 'I will do a good job again if you see to it that I get a raise'.

The main causes of motivation problems are:

- unsuitable work – for instance, using someone with a non-technical background who lacks the ambition to develop in that direction for navigation work;
- monotony of the work;
- founded (or unfounded) feeling of not being appreciated, or not getting enough attention;
- factors outside the test work.

Using personnel for activities with which they have no affinity has to be avoided as far as possible. If necessary, appropriate consultation should be held beforehand. It must be made clear that, once the employee is allocated the job concerned, the activities must be executed in a loyal fashion, and that test processes can take more time than expected – it is, therefore, not a simple matter to determine the timeframe beforehand.

There are several ways of breaking monotony while testing. As long as a test manager commits actively to this, it is always possible to solve this type of problem. Some options include:

- promote contact with colleagues in the field, by means of coaching and mutual reference visits;
- participation in groups and platforms that are involved in the project;
- varying or enriching the activities – for example, testing other parts of the system, varying navigation and analysis, or taking on activities such as coaching or team leadership;
- seeing if boring and monotonous tasks can be performed more skillfully or automated in some way.

One can also consider leaving the team.

It has become almost standard to take on new, inexperienced colleagues for longer test processes and have them trained by those already in the team. This prevents many motivational problems and disseminates knowledge effectively throughout the organization. Naturally, this measure must be recorded in the test plan.

A test manager also needs to prevent the test team from becoming too isolated in the project. Regular communication with users and developers has a positive effect. It clarifies the purpose of the work as part of the whole. Test managers should avoid monopolizing external relations. An effective distribution of the activities improves the team's motivation, and reduces the manager's own set of tasks.

A founded, or unfounded, sense of insecurity about being appreciated can have a negative effect on motivation. If an employee's performance is good, actions have to focus on making this visible. For example, does employee excellence get sufficient reward? Due to executives' busy agendas, not enough attention is paid to activities that are executed well. As a result, there is often no recognition of excellent performance in an appraisal interview (e.g. an idea that has been successfully implemented or a critical presentation that went well). Remarks by the line manager about the positive things said about the employee are sometimes enough to alleviate the feeling of insecurity.

Attention is related to appreciation. A common problem is the lack of attention from the test manager to what happens in the test process. Again, a busy schedule and the feeling that things are going well are usually the cause. Proper organization of the work helps – for example, instituting team leadership for analysis as well as navigation. Furthermore, interest must be shown on a regular basis. A motivation enhancing measure that works very well is to provide information about what is happening outside the test process. For example, what has been discussed at the project management meeting, and which issues others are working on. This can be done at a plenary test team meeting, as well as in personal conversation with an employee. Moderation is the key in this respect – otherwise, the attention will no longer be effective, or may even have an adverse effect.

6.7 Dependencies

Tests and test automation are more related to, and dependent on, other activities than most of the system's other development activities. For example, in order to arrive at a test environment, many technical and organizational measures need to be taken, most of which are outside the test team's responsibility and authority. Other typical key issues are the availability of sufficient information to serve as a basis for the test, and making an operational version of the system to be tested available to the navigator as early as possible. If, for example, users must be involved in the testing, they need to have sufficient time to complete it.

The test manager must address these issues in the test plan. Thought should be given as to which dependencies are the most critical. They should be described clearly, and agreements made that are in turn recorded clearly. Attention must also be paid to contingency planning – i.e. what needs to be done if a circumstance occurs that has not been planned for?

Two problems that occur frequently deserve special attention in this respect. Firstly, the test environment is an absolute requirement for a successful test process. If there is no test environment, there will be no test. A test environment consists of at least:

- a technical environment;
- a database, protected from developers and users;
- correct software versions that need to be tested, and on which the test software depends.

The second issue is the speed with which errors are corrected. Failing memory management, for example, can cause a system to suddenly stop operating, or to no longer operate properly after a few actions (e.g. becoming much slower, or having a system error).

Planning is one of the areas where the test manager has to process the numerous dependencies involved in the project. The test design (in particular, cluster identification) can take place at an early stage. Developing and tuning several of the clusters can also be started early on. This does not apply to the navigation which can roughly be divided into:

- preparatory activities – such as the navigation design and building up the interface layer, and the specific functions required to be able to work with the system to be tested at a technical level;
- execution – the implementation of the individual action words.

Naturally, the preparatory activities can start at an early stage, but the execution activities cannot. They require, at least, a detailed technical design. In practice, an operative version of the system to be tested is also indispensable. The navigation activities should therefore not be started too late, but not too early either. Once started, sufficient experienced navigation capacity has to be available to be able to automate the tests in the short time available. An experienced navigator can also highlight some of the activities by using several layers in the navigation. The action words are then translated into actions for each screen. The screen actions are subsequently implemented when a suitable version of the system to be tested is available.

During the project, the test manager has to be continually informed about what is happening throughout the project. In particular, an expected delay in development activities can have implications for the whole test project. The other project participants must ensure that promises with regard to making operational software versions available, for example, are fulfilled. Highly practical matters, such as timely ordering of the hardware for the test environment, also belong in this category.

As in any environment where people work together, not all information is reliable, complete, or available on time. Deliberate as well as unintentional interference can occur. Deliberate interference happens, for example, when a subproject leader fails to report a delay because they are hoping to catch up on them before they are noticed. Unintentional interference happens, for instance, when a project leader fails to pass on an important modification in the system design to the test team.

Above all else, the test manager must aim for a healthy, collaborative atmosphere. Even more than in other disciplines, testers must be willing to collaborate. Ensure that any deviations found are not attributed to a single person, and that conversations of test team members with others are always friendly, patient and open, even if they have to uphold an opposing point of view. This requires constant alertness from the test manager.

6.8 Summary

In this chapter, a number of examples of resistance have been discussed – these can be encountered in practice when systematic testing is introduced. They must be taken into account within a test process. Time must be spent eliminating these types of resistance, or at least reducing their effect. Other factors that are important are the degree of commitment, a lack of clarity in responsibilities, conflict situations outside the test process, motivation, and dependencies.

Appendix

TestFrame Virtual Language (TVL) was developed to clarify the examples in the navigation path within TestFrame. TVL is a language used in a virtual test tool – virtual because it is not an existing product, but is solely intended as an example for test scripts. This appendix describes this language so that examples can be read. In addition, it gives an impression of what a test tool's script language can look like, and what its functionality is.

All similarities to existing test tools are purely coincidental, although the main functions of such a test tool have, of course, been specified. This section assumes some knowledge of the various screen elements (objects) in GUI applications.

 ## A.1 Basics

The basis of TVL is a variant of the Basic programming language. Some test tools work with a script language similar to Basic. However, there are also test tools that work with other languages. This section gives simple descriptions of the possible commands used in approaching a Windows interface. Firstly, there is a short introduction to the language itself. The second part discusses the commands for controlling and reading the application.

 ## A.2 Comments

It is a good habit when programming to place comments in the code – these clarify the different elements of the program. Comments are used to explain the reasons for certain choices. A comment is indicated by means of a single quote (') in TVL as shown in Example A.1. All the text following the quote in a script line is interpreted as comment.

```
End Sub 'End of subroutine

'This is a complete comment line
```

Example A.1 Comment

A.3 Subroutines and functions

TVL distinguishes between subroutines and functions. Both are procedures (small, modular pieces of code) but subroutines do not return any values – functions are subroutines that do return a value. A value always has to be attributed to the function, and this value will be returned to the invoking procedure or function. For example, calculating a sine is typically a function. A subroutine is often a sequence of invocations, even if the final result is uninteresting, it was the whole purpose of invoking a function.

The subroutine

To define a subroutine, the key word **Sub** is used followed by the name of the procedure. The subroutine is concluded with **End Sub**. Example A.2 shows the format.

```
Sub StartApplication
        Shell ("c:\windows\calc.exe")
End Sub
```

Example A.2 Subroutine

The function

To define a function, the key word **Function** is used followed by the name of the function, followed by parentheses – any parameters are held in these. The definition ends with **As <type>**. A function always returns a value – when a function is defined, the type of return value has to be entered with the key word **As**. The possible types are described in Section A.4. A return value must be entered at the end of a function. There are two ways of doing this – with the key word **Return**, or by providing a value by means of the function name, as if it is a variable. Ensure that the coding standard is used to display the type of the function immediately in the name. A function is concluded with the key word **End Function**. A typical format is given in Example A.3.

```
Function gi_DifficultCalculation (i_Figure As Integer)
        gi_DifficultCalculation i_Figure * 2
End Function
```

Example A.3 Function

A.4 Variables and constants

Variables play an important role in navigation. In order to be able to explain the use of variables clearly, the different types are examined first.

Data types

The list in Table A.1 shows the various data types.

Table A.1 Data types

Type	Possible values	Example
Boolean	True or False	True
Integer	Full figure	–10
Float	Figure with a period	3.1415926
String	Text	'TestFrame Virtual Language'

Declaration of variables

In TVL, declaring variables is mandatory and the variable type must always be indicated. The declaration can be denoted by one of two key words – Dim (local) and Public (general). Dim indicates that the variable is known at module or function level, and Public indicates that the module is known generally within each module. This is followed by the variable's name – there are no restrictions with regard to length, but special characters (such as periods, commas, quotes, etc.) cannot be used. The variable name is not case sensitive in TVL (in some test tools it is), but it is customary to use a standard format for the name. One such standard is the Hungarian notation which shows the variable's type in its name, so that it is immediately clear which type of variable it is. The type of variable must also be indicated – as with functions, this is indicated using the key word As followed by the type. Three declarations are shown in Example A.4.

```
Public gs_StatusLine As String
Dim b_RefreshStatus As Boolean

Function gi_Example () As Integer
Dim i_Counter As Integer
        … More codes …
End Function
```

Example A.4 Variables and their declaration

Possible conversions between the various data types are not taken into account. They are automatically converted into the appropriate type. For instance, gi-Example = 3.1415 results in the value 3, because gi-Example is declared as an integer.

A standard format is used for the names of variables – more information about this can be found in Section 4.7.1.

Constants

A constant can be thought of as a variable whose value never changes. One can only be defined outside a function, and it is always Public. A constant is indicated by using the key word `Const` – the type is not indicated. After it has been created, no value can be allocated to a constant, and the value cannot be changed. Example A.5 shows this.

```
Const gcb_OK = True
Const gcb_NOT_OK = False
```

Example A.5 Constants

Arrays

An array can be thought of as a list of similar variables. The variables in the list can be accessed using an index. The declaration of an array is indicated the same way as for a variable except that square brackets follow the name, []. The maximum number of list elements the array can hold is stated in the brackets. Example A.6 shows how an array containing ten different elements of the string type is declared.

```
Dim as_Example[10] As String
```

Example A.6 Array declaration

Numbering the elements always begins at 1 and increases in units up to, and including, the maximum number stated in the declaration. Therefore, the valid indices in the above example are 1 to 10 (inclusive). Allocating values to the various array elements works in the same way as for variables, except that an index has to be indicated. In addition to being a number, this index can be a variable. In Example A.7, the array `ai_Example` is filled with the values 10 to 1.

```
Dim ai_Example[10] As Integer
Dim I_Counter As Integer

For I_Counter = 1 To 10
Ai_Example[I_Counter] = 10 – i
Next
```

Example A.7 Example array

Associative arrays are also supported. These work not only with a numeric index but also with a text index which helps easy creating of a record structure. Example A.8 shows how to create a record structure with them.

```
Dim as_Record[3] As String

As_Record["Brand"] =                "Philips"
As_Record["Number"] =               "150"
As_Record["TypeNumber"] =           "8587"
```

Example A.8 Associative array

Flow control

TVL has various ways of determining the course of the script – the concept is called flow control. Table A.2 gives a list of the various flow control structures.

Table A.2 Flow control structures

Keyword	Explanation
If–Then–Else	Tests a condition and changes the flow based on the result of the test
For–Next	Repeats an action a given number of times
While–Wend	Repeats an action as long as a test condition is true (starting condition)
Do–Loop–While	Repeats an action while a test condition is true, or until a test condition becomes true (final condition)
Select–Case	Differentiate to multiple code fragments depending on a specific test

Conditions

Conditions must often be defined for flow control. A condition always produces a Boolean value – i.e. it always produces either a True or a False value. Table A.3 gives a list of operators with which conditions can be composed.

Table A.3 Operators

Condition	Meaning
>	Larger than
<	Smaller than
>=	Larger than or equal to
<=	Smaller than or equal to
<>	Not equal to
And	Logical AND (Boolean operation)
Or	Logical OR (Boolean operation)
Not	Logical NOT (Boolean operation)

If–Then–Else

The most frequently used way of inserting flow control in test scripts is to use the key word If. An If makes a comparison and then executes one part of the function if the comparison results in True – the key word Else executes the False part. The key word If is followed by the condition in which the key words And (logical And) and Or (logical Or) can be used to test a composite condition. A composite condition is easier to read if the various basic conditions are enclosed in parentheses.

The close of the If–Then–Else construction is indicated by the key word **End If** after the statements to be executed. This type of flow control is illustrated in Example A.9.

```
Function gi_ExampleFunction(s_Type As String, i_Number As Integer) As
  Integer

        If s_Type = "Double Screw" Then
                i_Number = i_Number * 2
        End If

        If (s_Type = "Screw") And (i_Number > 10) Then
                Return 10                          'True branch
        Else                                       'False branch
                Return i_Number
        End If
End Function
```

Example A.9 If–Then–Else

For–Next

An important way of executing iterations in TVL is through the For–Next command. Using the key word **For** indicates that an iteration will take place. After the key word, a variable must be given a certain initial value. That initialization is followed by the key word **To**, which is followed by the final value of the variable. The iteration is then repeated and the counting variable incremented by one each time the loop is completed, until the end value is reached. A different counting interval can be indicated as an option using the key word **Step** – this must follow the end value and the size of the interval must be entered after the key word **Step**. Use of the For–Next loop is shown in Example A.10.

```
Function gi_ExampleFunction (i_Number As Integer) As Integer
Dim i_Counter As Integer, i_Total As Integer

        i_Total = 0
        For i_Counter = 1 To i_Number
                i_Total = i_Total + i_Counter
        Next

        For i_Counter = i_Number To 1 Step -1
                i_Total = i_Total + i_Counter
        Next
        Return i_Total
End Function
```

Example A.10 For–Next

While–Wend

In contrast to the For–Next loop, the While–Wend construction does not use a counter, it checks a condition. This is especially useful if a calculation, or some other process, needs to be checked in a loop. The key word that indicates the start of this loop is While and it is followed by a condition – the condition can be either basic or composite. The loop is concluded with the key word Wend (short for 'while end') and all the lines between While and Wend are executed as long as the condition is true. An illustration of its use is given in Example A.11.

```
Function gi_ExampleFunction (i_Number As Integer) As Integer
Dim i_Value As Integer

        i_Value = 2
        While i_Value > 0 And i_Number <> –1
                i_Value = i_CalculateStrangeNumber(i_Number)
                i_Number = i_DetermineNextNumber(i_Number)
        Wend
        Return i_Value
End Function
```

Example A.11 While–Wend

Do–Loop–While

This is essentially the same as the While–Wend loop, except that the Do–Loop is completed at least once, and the conditions are not checked until the end. The loop is initialized by the key word Do and followed by the lines to be executed in the loop. The end of the loop is indicated by the key word Loop While, followed by either a basic or composite condition as shown in Example A.12.

```
Function gi_ExampleFunction (i_Number As Integer) As Integer
Dim i_Value As Integer

        Do
                i_Value = i_CalculateStrangeNumber (i_Number)
                i_Number = i_CalculateNextNumber (i_Number)
        Loop While i_Value > 0 And i_Number <> –1
        Return i_Value
End Function
```

Example A.12 Do–Loop–While

Select–Case

To offer more options, the Select–Case structure can be used instead of the If–Then construction. Using Select–Case, some text or a number is indicated as a control factor and each can execute its own piece of script. This function is initiated using the key word Select Case followed by the value to be used as the control. Each comparison starts with the key word Case followed by the comparison value. If the comparison value is identical to the control value, all the script lines are executed until the next Case. A construction in which all the cases are dealt with is also possible using the key words Case Else. The end of Select–Case is indicated by the key words End Select. This is illustrated in Example A.13.

```
Function gs_ExampleFunction (i_Number As Integer) As String

        Select Case i_Number
                Case 1
                        Return "Found: 1"
                Case 3
                        Return "Found: 3"
                Case Else
                        Return "1 or 3 NOT found!"
        End Select
End Function
```

Example A.13 Select–Case

A.7 Text manipulation

When working with test tools, texts often need to be retrieved from the screen and compared to the expected values. Sometimes it is necessary to manipulate those texts (strings) so that the right pieces of text can indeed be compared. A list of functions that can be used for text string manipulation is given in Table A.4.

Table A.4 Text string manipulation commands

Command	Explanation
Mid	Returns an inner part of a string
Left	Returns the left part of a string
Right	Returns the right part of a string
Len	Determines the length of a given string
&	Combines strings

The Mid function ('middle') determines an denoted portion of the string – this part is then returned as a string. The Mid function has three parameters, the last of which is optional – the original string, the start position, and the number of characters. The start position indicates from which character position in the original string the new string is returned. The function is illustrated in Example A.14.

```
Function gs_ExampleFunction () As String
Dim s_String1 As String, s_String2 As String, s_String3 As String

        s_String1 = Mid("We'll fix it later, if it doesn't work",24,3)'Gives "it"
        s_String2 = Mid("We'll fix it later, if it doesn't work",36)'Gives "work"
        s_String3 = Mid("We'll fix it later, if it doesn't work",30,1)'Gives "s"

Return s_String1 & s_String2 & s_String3                'Gives "it works"

End Function
```

Example A.14 Text manipulation Mid function

A.8 GUI functions in classes

Up to now, only TVL's 'general programming language' has been discussed. The following describes a number of specific test tool script language concepts.

To perform actions through a user interface, there have to be functions that can perform the same actions as the user. These are divided into so-called 'classes'. A class indicates which type of interface element is concerned. All the interface functions belong to one of the basic classes (such as window, edit, and button). They are separated from the interface elements by a '.'.

The interface elements are explained for each class. After that, an overview of possible operations that can be executed on the interface element is given. The most interesting operations are described in more detail.

A.8.1 Window class

The window class is important because the window is the interface element in which all the other objects have their place. The window can be recognized by the fact that all the elements within the window move with it when it is moved on the screen. The window title is used for identification. The various functions are listed in Table A.5.

Table A.5 Window operations

Operation name	Explanation
Window().SetFocus	Moves the window to the foreground
Window().Shown	Shows whether or not the window is visible
Window().Close	Closes the window
Window().GetAttr()	Retrieves a property of a window
Window().Maximize	Maximizes the window
Window().Minimize	Minimizes the window
Window().Restore	Restores the window
Window().Click()	Clicks within the window on the given coordinates
Window().Move()	Moves the window to the given coordinates
Window().GetText()	Gets all the text within the window except the window title

Window().SetFocus is an important function in TVL because it ensures that all the screen elements within this window, that follow this command, can be accessed. The command activates the window and moves it to the foreground. Example A.15 shows how it can be used.

`Window().GetText()` allows text to be retrieved from a window. There are no mandatory arguments but *x* and *y* coordinates can be entered as an option to allow a certain part of the screen text to be read. Example A.16 shows the function in action.

```
Function gs_ExampleFunction () As Integer

        Window("* – Notepad").SetFocus
        Type("This will be typed in Notepad")

        Return OK

End Function
```

Example A.15 Window class `Window().SetFocus`

```
Function gs_ExampleFunction () As String

        Window("* – Notepad").SetFocus
        Return Window("* – Notepad").GetText

End Function
```

Example A.16 Window class `Window().GetText()`

A.8.2   Button class

The button class contains all the screen elements which can be pressed to end a dialog or make a selection. This is a simple class that contains few functions – they are listed in Table A.6. In this class, the button name, or text pertaining to it, have to be entered as an argument. There are three subtypes – push button, radio button, and check button. A push button can be pushed. A radio button forms part of a group of radio buttons and if one of them is selected, all the others are deselected – hence, only one radio button can be selected at a time. A check button can be selected and will remain selected (usually a cross in a box).

Table A.6 Button operations

Operation name	Explanation
`Button().Push`	Pushes the button
`Button().Shown`	Shows whether or not the button is visible
`Button().GetAttr()`	Retrieves a property of a button
`Button().Select()`	Selects or deselects a button

Example A.17 shows how `Button().Push` can be used.

```
Function gi_ExampleFunction () As Integer

        Window("Save As").SetFocus
        Button("OK").Push
        Return OK

End Function
```

Example A.17 Button class Button().Push

A.8.3 Edit class

This class contains all the elements that enable the user to enter text. The element can consist of one or more lines. The functions are shown in Table A.7.

Table A.7 Edit operation

Operation name	Explanation
Edit().SetCursor()	The cursor can be placed in a particular position
Edit().Shown	Shows whether or not the Edit is visible
Edit().GetAttr()	Retrieves a property of an Edit
Edit().SelectText()	Selects part of the text

Edit().SetCursor() enables the cursor to be placed in a particular position in an entry field. The purpose of this function is to ensure that typing starts from this position.

Edit().SelectText() allows a piece of text to be selected in an entry field. It is then possible to copy and paste, or to replace one piece of text with another.

A.8.4 List class

The list class contains elements that display a list of items from which one or more can be selected. Its functions are listed in Table A.8.

Table A.8 List operations

Operation name	Explanation
List.Select()	Selects the given elements from a list
List().Elements	Gives all the elements that are within a given list
List().GetAttr()	Retrieves a property of a list

Using `List().Select()`, one or more selections can be made from a list element – this is the main function within the list class. See Example A.18 to see how it can be used.

```
Function gi_ExampleFunction () As Integer

        Window("Save As").SetFocus
        List("Save as:").Select("Text documents")
        Button("OK").Push
        Return OK

End Function
```

Example A.18 List class `List().select`

A.8.5 Menu class

This class contains all the elements that are presented as menus within a window. The menus can be found just below the title bar of a window. Other menus can be linked to this menu – they are called submenus. Table A.9 lists the main functions in this class.

Table A.9 Menu class operations

Operation name	Explanation
Menu().Select	Selects the given element from a menu
Menu().Elements	Gives all elements that are within a given menu
Menu().GetAttr()	Retrieves a property of a menu

`Menu().Select` is the main function of the menu class, because it can be used to select a menu. After activating the window, the menu is entered. The underlined characters in menu lists are interpreted as normal characters, and submenus are indicated by means of the texts of the menu elements, separated by a ';'. Example A.19 shows its use.

```
Function gi_ExampleFunction () As Integer

        Window("* – Notepad").SetFocus
        Menu("File;End").Select        'Closes the application Notepad
        Button("OK").Push
        Return OK

End Function
```

Example A.19 Menu class `Menu().Select`

A.8.6   General functions

In addition to all the specific functions associated with specific elements, general functions which apply to many screen elements can also be used.

Table A.10 General functions

Operation name	Explanation
Type()	Types the text with the keyboard

Using the **Type()** command, the entered text is typed. As with normal use of the keyboard, the text is entered in the active screen element. Therefore, it is necessary to activate the screen element before a Type command is executed. Special characters, such as the enter key, have to be indicated in square brackets. An enter key press is therefore indicated by [Enter], an f1 key by [f1] and the downward arrow key by [Down]. The shift, alt and control keys are indicated by a preceding s, a and c respectively. Thus, the combination of shift and end key is indicated by [sEnd]. Example A.20 shows the use of the Type command.

```
Function gi_ExampleFunction () As Integer

        Window("Save As").SetFocus
        Edit("Filename:").SetCursor(1,1)
        Type("[Home][sEnd]")              'Selects all existing text with the keyboard
        Type("Example.txt[Enter]")        'Types the filename followed by Enter
        Return OK

End Function
```

Example A.20 General function Type()

References

[Beiz 90] Beizer, B. (1990) *Software Testing Techniques* (second edition), Corrolis Group.

[Beiz 95] Beizer, B. (1995) *Black-Box Testing*, John Wiley.

[Blac 99] Black, R. (1999) *Managing the Testing Process*, Microsoft Press.

[Boeh 79] Boehm, B.W. (1979) *Software Engineering Economics*, Prentice Hall.

[Buwa 99] Buwalda, H. and Kasdorp, M. (1999) 'Getting Automated Testing Under Control', in *Software Testing and Quality Engineering*, pp. 39–44.

[Dust 99] Dustin, E., Rashka J. and Paul J. (1999) *Automated Software Testing*, Addison-Wesley Longman.

[Fews 99] Fewster, M. and Graham, D. (1999) *Software Test Automation*, Addison-Wesley.

[Hetz 88] Hetzel, W.C. (1988) *The Complete Guide to Software Testing* (second edition), John Wiley.

[Jans 00] Janssen, D. (2000) *Joint Testware Development (JTD)*, Conference Paper for Test Congress 2000, London.

[Kane 99] Kaner, C. (1999) 'Improving the Maintainability of Automated Test Suites', in *Software QA*, 4(4).

[KitE 95] Kit, E. (1995) *Software Testing in the Real World*, Addison-Wesley.

[Mari 95] Marick, B. (1995) *The Craft of Software Testing*, Prentice Hall.

[Myer 79] Myers, G.J. (1979) *The Art of Software Testing*, John Wiley.

[Mors 93] Mors, N.P.M. (1993) *Beslissingstablellen*, Lansa Publishing (in Dutch).

[Mors 94] Mors, N.P.M. (1994) *Kwaliteitszorg door Acceptatietesten*, Lansa Publishing (in Dutch).

Index